MW01490074

Lost My Way in the Darkness

Book 1: Jack's Journey

a novel

by Mack D. Ames

Dedicated to my wife, Laurel,
and our sons, C & M.

We treasure our 'forever' boys and humbly
pray they will walk in the Way, Truth, and
Life for all eternity.

Content Warning Labels

Lost My Way in the Darkness is a coming-of-age novel that explores the lives of some teenage boys in everyday and challenging situations, including mature themes that polite society prefers to leave undiscussed, such as sexual orientation, peer-to-peer sexual assault, domestic violence, neglect, and substance use. The characters use foul language at times and period-relevant expressions you may find offensive. The story has a redemptive theme involving the Bible and the gospel of Jesus Christ. Just as some Christians and I disagree on the material in this book, people of non-Christian beliefs may take issue with my portrayals of how the world operates or who determines the standards of right and wrong.

Based on the advice of secular and Christian counselors, I have posted **Content Warnings** before sections or chapters that may be triggering due to the content. I didn't include warnings for swearing because it's not excessive. Finally, this second edition has several changes and updates, but it still fits the genre that author and reviewer Shelley Burbank called *#GrittyInspirational*. www.shelleyburbank.com. Thank you.

Foreword

What do you do when you've married the love of your life, had a child with her, and then you lose her in an accident? That's what happened to Joe Bannister. He and his wife Debbie had a little boy they named Jack. One day, when Jack was eight years old, Debbie was riding her bicycle home from visiting an elderly friend, and a drunk driver killed her in a hit-and-run accident. The driver was later apprehended and held accountable, but Jack and his dad, Joe, were still bereft of their beloved Debbie. What was Joe to do with a young boy to raise?

In due time, he remarried, and his new wife, Stephanie, loved Jack just as much as he did, perhaps even more. Steph saw the pain little Jack carried in his heart for the awful loss of his mother. She observed that Joe and Jack were so alike that it caused friction that became a wedge in their relationship. In many ways, Stephanie became the glue that held the family together through thick and thin, but when she first married Joe, young Jack only saw her as "the Dragon."

Joe and Steph did their best to demonstrate love to Jack, but the boy withdrew from them, bottled his emotions, and began hanging out with unsavory kids in the neighborhood. As Jack's attitude became more hostile and his behavior raised their concerns, Joe decided to leave the city behind and move back to his hometown in the eastern part of the state, hoping and praying that the change of scenery would do them all good. Now, here they were in Newtowne, Maine, hoping against hope that Jack's new friends were better than his old ones.

1: Meeting Jack

Do you know what moving from the city to the backwoods is like? I was born in Portland, Maine, and lived there until I was eleven. The summer before my sixth-grade year, Dad and the Dragon—my stepmom, Stephanie—moved us from there to Dad's hometown more than a hundred miles northeast of Portland, basically, to the middle of nowhere! He didn't bother talking to me about it first. He didn't see if I wanted to move or if I'd miss my friends. Nope. We just picked up and drove off. It's been the suckiest summer since—well, never-you-mind. It just sucked.

I missed my old house. I liked living in the city. We were in the state's biggest city (our *only city,* by most standards); out-of-staters knew it when I said where we lived. We were close enough to Boston to go to Red Sox games at least once every summer! Dad had a good job, and I could get anything I wanted.

Every place local worth going to was within biking range, including school, parks, the grocery store, and the newsstand. We were close to the ocean, so beaches and state parks were nearby. Dad and I went fishing most weekends and camping once a month from spring to fall. But then we stopped when...well, we stopped. Life was good there until it wasn't because...it just wasn't, okay?

My dad, Joe, was on the road a lot during the week for his job. Then, he got a different job and worked closer to home. I'm not sure why. When he remarried after...well, he remarried, and things weren't the same anymore. He and I didn't get along as well as before. Camping stopped completely. He took me fishing once every two months if I was lucky. He didn't have time for me anymore, so I was on my own a lot. Not latchkey alone; just no one to entertain me, play, or hang out with. Then, he didn't like the kids I hung out with, so he decided to move. At least, that's what I overheard. It's been three awful years, and he just made them worse.

Everything I've ever known has changed. Again. Just like three years ago. He probably thought he was doing the right thing, but did he stop to consider how I felt about it? *No.* I've been ripped more than two hours' drive away from everyone I know and dropped into a town where it takes a *car* to get anywhere worth going. *Nothing* is close by.

Dad says it's "good for me" to live in the country like he did growing up. Plus, his wife got a job at a Christian school, and part of her contract *requires me* to attend there! They think that'll be good for me, too. I'm not too fond of the idea, but there's no getting out of it. Even if I make friends in our neighborhood, I won't attend school with them. It's so aggravating!

Our home is in Newtowne—s*tupid name.* There's nothing new here. Dad has already started his job, so it's just Steph and me at the house, unpacking box after box after endless box. I can't find a single reason to stay in this godawful, lame, and lonely place. If only M--... never mind. *Sigh. It always comes back to that.* My heart aches. *It's not fair!*

After opening the last box for my bedroom, I gave up and wandered outside to explore. Some trees behind the house seemed like a good place to look around, so I headed there to escape people; I had no desire to see anybody.

Within a few minutes, I was on winding paths under the trees. It was curious that so many had no branches within four feet of the ground, but I didn't think about it for long. It was too much fun to pretend they were tunnels created somehow just for me. Dad wouldn't be able to find me out here, and neither would that wretched woman he'd married so soon after Mom—

The distraction of tree tunnels wasn't enough to keep me from slumping into a heap under a giant pine and breaking down in tears. *Why? O, God, why?* Thoughts failed as I sobbed and tried to catch my breath.

After several minutes, my heaving chest slowed, and I was calm again. I tried to pray as Mom taught me when I was little, but my frustrations flared as always.

Dear God, Mom loved you! And she said you loved me, too. So, why did you let her die? I don't get it. She said you'll never leave me and always listen, but God? W..where were you when that drunk k..killed my Mom?

The more I tried to pray, the angrier I became, and I reached the end of my rope. *You never answer me! You're not there! If you are, you sure don't seem to care! You know what, God? I'm done with you!*

My thoughts turned vocal. "It almost kills me to say this, but I don't think Mom was right about you. I think you fooled her into thinking you were good, which is sad, 'cuz she's gone now, and she was the only person that ever cared about me, and it's ALL YOUR FAULT! I *HATE* YOU!" Tears streamed down my cheeks, and I didn't feel any better, but I'd finally admitted my feelings. God, if he existed, had done me wrong when he let Mom die that night, and he wasn't going to hold my conscience anymore.

6

Still, I had to be careful how I expressed myself around Dad. He didn't take disrespect toward God lightly, and I was dependent on Dad and Steph. *I can fake it. I've been faking it for three years, anyway.* I didn't care anymore. He can deal with it. I'm done. God doesn't care about me, and I don't care about him.

As if to demonstrate how finished I was with God, I wiped my hands off each other before continuing to explore. A few minutes later, I found myself in a small clearing. I was surprised that some trees had been cut there and a makeshift fort had been assembled. From the shoddy workmanship, it was clearly the work of other kids, but if it meant there were others my age around here who did this, I could join them and improve it. Just then, I heard voices behind me.

"Hey, kid! Who are you? What're you doing in our fort?" Two boys about my height and age approached me menacingly.

"I-I'm Jack." I stammered at first but then asserted myself. "This is your fort? You sure your sisters didn't build this?" I couldn't help mocking them. "Who are you, anyway?"

They glanced at each other and back at me. The first one said, "I'm Blake, and that's Vince, and if you know what's good for you, *Jacko,* you'll clear off."

Blake looked like he never ate enough, but his attitude told me not to underestimate him. On the other hand, Vince was beefy and strong, even if he was only eleven or twelve years old. I wasn't as skinny as Blake or as bulked up as Vince, but I was angry enough to stand my ground either way and living around street kids in Portland had taught me a few lessons about fighting. I wanted to make friends, but I wouldn't say I liked their attitude.

"Make me."

Blake signaled Vince, and the stockier boy charged at me. I sidestepped his move, tripped him, and added a shove for good measure. Blake moved in and took a swing at me, but I blocked it and threw a counterpunch that nailed him in the stomach. He doubled over, gasping for air. By then, Vince was up and ran at me again. I met him with my fists up, and in moments, he was also on the ground, cringing from a blow to his face.

I was ready for more but hoped they'd quit since the odds were against me. Still, it was put up or shut up time for these jerks. "Well? You gonna make me leave, or can I stay?"

"All right. All right," panted Blake. "You can stay." He and Vince sat down on one of the logs. "Where did you learn to fight like that, Jack?"

I didn't feel like revealing that, so I changed the subject. "You guys obviously live around here. Whereabouts?"

They told me which houses were theirs, and Vince said, "So you just moved into that house that was for sale? Where did you live before?"

"Portland."

"Portland! Why'd you move to Newtowne? What grade are you in?" They spoke over each other with their questions.

Until then, I'd been mumbling but decided I might as well talk to them. "Uh, family reasons. Going into sixth. What about you guys?"

8

"Same. We're going to be classmates, huh? That's cool. We've already gotten our fighting out of the way, so we might as well hang out, right?" Blake and Vince laughed. "That's how we became friends." They gestured toward each other. "The first time we met, we had a knockdown, drag-out, and next thing you know, we're best buds."

"Yeah, I could use some friends," I muttered, "but I don't think we'll be in school together."

"Why not?" Blake was suspicious.

"My stepmom is a teacher at City Christian School, and I'm required to go there. Her contract says so."

"Oh, brother, that's rich." Blake rolled his eyes.

"You're telling me. I don't even want to go there." I kicked at the dirt. "It's gonna be so grody!"

We talked a little longer, and then I returned to the house, where I got to think about Blake and Vince. I mentioned them to Dad and Steph. They didn't seem very impressed, but I was grateful to have made friends with neighborhood kids my age. It made life a little easier to cope with, especially since I was dreading the start of school in a few weeks.

The Dragon kept saying I'd like it there. "You'll make friends there, too," she said. "Good ones. They'll be positive influences on you," as if to say that neighborhood ones here were bad like they were in Portland. Stepmothers are *so* lame.

Every day, Dad was gone to work by the time I woke up, so I only saw him at supper most of the time when he was too tired to say much. Besides, he usually took the Dragon's side, so I didn't listen to him, either. It was one more source of frustration and anxiety as I waited for school to begin.

2. Whitman's Corner Store

A couple of days after I met Blake and Vince, I was out in my yard trying to fix a flat tire on my bicycle when they rode in on theirs.

"Hey, Jack, what's up?" Vince asked.

"Flat tire. Not sure how. Stuck here till I can fix it."

"Lemme see that," Blake said. "Your dad has been putting new shingles on the garage or something?"

"Yeah, why?" I replied.

"You've got a nail in your tire, dumbo," Blake laughed. He pointed to it. "That's easy enough to fix if you have a patch kit. Do you?" When I shook my head no, he continued, "Well, I've got one. I'll be right back. While I'm gone, why don't you and Vince pick up all the other nails you can find so we don't all get flats? I don't have that many patch kits, dumbo." He laughed again as he rode off.

I don't know why he called me 'dumbo,' and I hope he doesn't keep doing it. I tried to let it go and started looking for other nails with Vince. I found one. "Got one," I said to Vince.

"Got three!" said Vince. *"Nyah, nyah."* He taunted and laughed. "I'm winning!"

"Oh, no, you don't. I've got two more; we're tied! No, here's another one. Got four!" I squealed.

"All right, girls, enough!" Blake interrupted our game.

10

I clenched my fists and stared at Blake. "Whaddyamean, girls?"

"Oh, quit your bellyaching, Jack. I ride away for five minutes and come back to you two squealing like a couple of girls, that's all. It was just a joke. Jeezum, what are you, three years old? Don't be such a baby!"

My face reddened. "Sorry," I mumbled.

"Aw, forget it," Blake said. "Come on, Vinnie, help me fix this tire."

"Geez, Jacko, your dad sure got careless with the nails. He's lucky he doesn't have one in his car tire. When your bike is fixed, we need to make sure there aren't any more nails around. What a pain in the a---, I mean, neck."

"Language!" Vince hissed at Blake.

"Aw, knock it off, Vin. I caught it in time."

When the tire was fixed, Vince turned to Blake and said, "We've still got time today; should we show him?" Blake nodded, so Vince said, "Say, Jack, have you been to Whitman's yet?"

"Whitman's? What's that? I've been stuck here since we moved, except for going to church with Dad and the Dragon—I mean—my stepmom."

"It's a general store about twenty minutes' ride from here, Jacko," Blake said. "They've got all kinds of stuff there—candy, soda, baseball cards, potato chips, beef jerky, that sorta thing. Think you're up for it?"

"I can do it!" I said, hoping I didn't sound too whiny. "I just gotta tell my stepmom where I'm going to be. I'll be right out."

"Try to get some money from her while you're at it, Jacko," called Blake as I ran into the house.

When Jack was gone, Blake turned to Vince. "Are you thinkin' what I'm thinkin'?"

Vince looked at his friend. "You mean, if he doesn't bring any money, we'll see if he'll still get something from the store? Yeah, of course! But if he brings coin, we'd better be careful with him. He goes to church, you know. He might be a goody two-shoes."

A couple of minutes later, I was back and ready to go. "She gave me a couple of quarters. It ain't much, but she said she's been to that store already, and they've got some cheap stuff. Let's get going."

We got on our bikes and began riding toward the store two or three miles away. Almost immediately, we hopped off to push our bikes up the one hill we'd face going to the store; it wasn't a long hill, but it ran just before my driveway, and there was no way to get a running start. We resumed riding and enjoyed coasting for the next half-mile when we got to the top. It was farmland on either side of the road, with little traffic to disrupt our ride.

Halfway to the store, we crossed the town line into Nolan. Blake explained that kids from this other town attended our Newtowne High School but that Nolan and Newtowne had their own elementary and junior high schools. We rode for about 20 minutes, and then I saw a four-way stop just ahead. On the right was an old, clapboard-sided building with a sign above the door that read, "Whitman's Corner Store." The other boys gestured to a grassy bank on the left, where we tossed our bikes before crossing the road to enter the store. A bell jingled as we walked in, and a man in his mid-forties called out, "Welcome to Whitman's. How can I help you?"

12

"We're just here to get some candy and stuff and show a new kid the place," Blake said.

"All right. Holler if you need anything." The man went back to whatever he was doing. I was fascinated by everything in the store. I saw tools hanging on the first wall and small engine parts in boxes and displays. On another wall, there was a display case of refrigerated meats, cheeses, butter, and novelty ice cream treats, and on a third wall were bread, crackers, peanut butter, jams and jellies, dog and cat food, and all kinds of other dry goods. In the middle of the store, there were short racks of candy, baked goods, peanuts, popcorn, baseball cards, gum, nails, screws, pens, pencils, notebooks, and so many other odds and ends that I couldn't keep track of it all. I wondered if Mr. Whitman could or if that even was the guy's name.

"So, whaddya think, Jack?" Vince asked. "You like the corner store?"

"Yeah, this is cool! I'm going to check out what I can get. Are you guys getting anything?"

Vince nodded and winked. "We never come here without getting at least one or two things. Why ride all this way for nothing?"

I looked around the store. The array of candy was impressive, and it was so cheap, too. Penny candy, five-cent candy; if I counted right, I could take a lot home. But I also wanted some baseball cards and bubble gum, which were more expensive. Fifty cents wouldn't get me baseball cards; I needed a dollar. I sighed. Well, I could get a pack of gum for 35 cents and then spend the rest on penny or 5-cent candy. I made my selections and went to the cash register.

"Did you find what you were looking for?" the man asked.

I nodded. "Kind of. I found everything all right; I didn't have enough for the baseball cards. I'll have to bring more money next time." I paid for the gum and candy and left the store. Moments later, the other boys joined me.

As we got on our bikes to leave, a boy about our age arrived at the intersection from a different direction. Blake shouted at him, "Hey, you! Fat boy! This is our store! Get outta here!"

The other boy looked startled and scared. He turned his bicycle around and rode back in the direction he came from. "That's right, little four-eyed freak!" hollered Blake, "and don't let me catch you here again, or there'll be hell to pay!" As the stranger rode away, Blake and Vince cracked up laughing. "D-did you see his face?" Blake sputtered. "Oh, my God, I-I thought he was going to wet himself! What a riot!"

"I think he might've done just that, Blake!" Vince replied, roaring with laughter. "Isn't that a puddle on the road over there?"

I just looked at them, puzzled. As far as I could tell, the other boy hadn't said anything or done anything wrong, but my new friends had made it clear that Whitman's was their territory. I shrugged. It had nothing to do with me, so I rode my bike home.

The easy, coasting ride to Whitman's meant a harder, forever incline going back. Blake and Vince had been riding this route a lot longer than I had, so their legs were used to it, but I found it exhausting. Still, I didn't want them to think I was a wimp, so I stood up to pedal. Even when my legs screamed "no more," I didn't quit. It took twice as long to get home, and I knew I'd need to improve my speed if I didn't want to get bullied like the kid at Whitman's.

We finally got home and went to the fort to hang out. Blake asked me, "What did you get at the store?"

I showed him. "I wanted to get baseball cards, too, but I didn't have enough, so I just got gum and some penny candy. I'll get baseball cards another time. What did you get?"

Blake said, "Well, I just got a pack of gum. I think Vinnie got more than I did this time. Vinnie?"

The third boy smiled. "Funny about those baseball cards, Jack. I heard you talking about them, so I checked 'em out for you. How's this?" With that, Vince pulled two packs of cards out of his pocket and tossed them to me. "They're all yours, bud."

"I can't take these, Vince! I can't pay you back!" I protested.

"No payback needed, Jack," Vinnie said. "Just enjoy 'em."

"Gee, thanks, Vince." The smile on my face kept growing. "Man, I've been dying to get some good cards all summer."

"Well, open them up, and let's see who you got, Jacko," said Blake. "You got any Red Sox in there?"

3: Price of Friendship

"What do you guys want to do today?" I asked Vince and Blake. It had been a week since our trip to Whitman's, and I was looking for new ways to pass the time. We were in Vince's yard because his dad had told us to stay out of the house. As long as it was summer, he didn't like the kids being inside, except to use the bathroom or to get out of the rain. In the latter case, he'd prefer they go to someone else's house.

"Why don't we go fishing?" Vince said. "We haven't done that in a while. You have a fishing pole, Jack?"

I shook my head. "No, but my dad does. I can use it if he says so."

Blake chimed in, "What are you waiting for, Jacko? Go ask him."

"I can't. He's at work already." I kicked at the dirt in frustration.

"Then go 'borrow' it, *dumbo*," Blake said, "and ask for 'forgiveness' later. Better yet, we'll be done fishing, and you can put it away before he knows it's gone."

My eyes went wide. "That's dishonest, Blake. He'd catch me, and then I'd be in trouble!"

"Oh my friggin' word, Jacko," Blake egged me on. "Don't be such a wuss. Live a little! Right, Vinnie?"

Vince nodded. "Come on, Jack. We can't do everything for you. Do you want to go fishing? Then you gotta bring a pole."

I wasn't quite sure what Vince meant when he said, "We can't do everything for you," but I didn't want to chicken out in front of my friends, so I rode home to get my father's fishing rod. It was in the garage, and while it wasn't expensive, I knew I wasn't supposed to borrow it without permission. At the same time, I tried to rationalize disobeying Dad. He wouldn't want me to upset my friends;

he wouldn't mind this one time, I tried to convince myself. As I reached for the pole—

"Jack, what are you doing?" It was the Dragon. "Has your father given you permission to use that?" she asked.

I recovered from being startled and turned to face her. "Yes," I lied, hoping my face didn't give me away. "He said that as long as I take good care of it, I can go fishing with my friends."

She didn't let me go just yet. "When did he say that?"

"A couple of days ago. Uh, you were in the house, and we were talking out here in the garage." I was amazed at how easy it was to lie once I got going. "As long as I don't do it too often, he's okay with it." I shifted on my feet. "Can I go now?"

Steph looked at me warily. "Well, all right, Jack. Be careful with it."

"Of course." I gritted my teeth and lifted the pole from the garage wall, grabbed the bait box, and rode back to Vince's house.

"What took you so long?" Vince asked.

"The Dragon caught me," I said.

"You got it, though. Must be a good liar," Blake said, laughing. "Let's get going. The stream's just down the road a little way. Even if the fish aren't biting, it's a great place to hang out."

In truth, we didn't need bikes to get there, but as it turned out, it was good I had mine. We had so much fun that I lost track of time. When I realized how late it was, I had to race home to put the pole back so my dad wouldn't notice I'd used it. At supper that night I expected the Dragon to bring it up, but she didn't, so I figured I could get away with it another time.

A couple of weeks later, we decided to go fishing again. This time, I was ready with the fishing gear. "Come on, Blake," I said when he was slow to get moving. "What's taking you so long?"

"Hold your horses, Jacko!" snapped Blake. "What's your rush, anyway? Got a hot date waiting?"

"Ew, gross, no! Girls are gross," I said. "I just wanna get to the stream while the fish are still biting. What's your problem, anyway?"

Blake mumbled something I didn't hear, but Vince knew what it was. He shoved me and said, "Mind your own business, Jack. Let's get going. Blake will catch up when he's ready."

Vince and I walked to the stream to carry a bag lunch, too. "I didn't see any reason for us to hafta come home in the middle of our fun just for a PBJ," Vince said when he handed the sack to me. "There's some apples in there, too. Just somethin' my mom put together for us. She's just happy I'm out of the house for the day."

I wondered if the Dragon would make a lunch for me like that, but I didn't dare ask. She might remember what I'd told her about using Dad's fishing pole and talk to him about it, and then I'd be in trouble—no use bringing grief on my own head.

Still, I sighed as I thought about what it must be like to have a real mom, and just like that, my eyes filled up with tears. I tried to blink them away before Vince could see them, but then I sniffled a couple of times.

"What's wrong with you, Jack? PBJ and apples make you cry?" Vince sounded half-amused and half-irritated. "It's what we have, okay? You don't want it; you don't have to eat."

"No, no, Vince, it's not that," I said quickly.

"Then what is it?" Vince demanded.

"You're gonna think I'm stupid," I complained.

"I already think you're stupid," Vince said. "What's the big secret, Jack?"

By then, we'd reached the stream and settled in to start fishing. I turned to Vince and said, "You wanna know why I moved here from Portland?"

Vince shrugged. "I guess so, sure."

"My mom was killed by a drunk driver three years ago. My dad remarried, and we moved here to escape all the bad memories. It was messing me and him up a lot. When you talked about your mom making lunch for us, it just made me think how much I miss her, that's all." I paused. "See? I told you you'd think I'm stupid," I said as more tears fell down my cheeks.

"Wow, Jack, that sucks," Vince said.

"Tell me about it," I said.

"Tell you about what?" Blake asked. "What's going on between you girls here? Vinnie, did you hurt Jacko's feelings? Jeezum, what a couple of pansies!"

"Shut the frig up, Blake," Vince shot back. "Took you long enough to get here. What were you doing, cleaning your old man's shorts?"

There was a long pause while Blake and Vince glared at each other, and then, finally, Blake laughed. "Cleaning his shorts? What is that supposed to mean? Oh my gosh, what a lame insult, Vinnie! Let's get fishing."

My friends' banter lightened my mood as I approached a large rock at the edge of the stream. I frowned as I got closer to it because it was farther from the bank than it seemed at first. Still, I decided to jump to the boulder; it would be a prime spot for fishing. I did my best to get a running start, but as I leaped into the air, my foot slipped in the mud, and I crashed against the rock. I heard a sickening crack, and my heart sank.

"Oh, no! I broke it!" Sure enough, the handle of my father's fishing pole had snapped in two. "What am I gonna do?"

Blake looked at me. I could tell he wanted to tease me, but for once, he bit his tongue. "Yeah, that's not good, Jack. I'll tell you what, though. My dad has some wood glue in the garage. When we get back today, we can glue that rod back together. When it dries, your old man won't realize what happened to it. It'll be fine. You'll see."

I realized later that he lied as soothingly as he knew how to keep me from falling apart. After all, he wasn't the one who had borrowed the fishing rod without permission. What could my father do to him? Then he changed the subject. "I'm hungry. Vinnie, where's that bag lunch?"

As we ate, we talked about the Red Sox. As usual, our favorite Major League Baseball team slumped at the wrong time. "Why is it that they never make a decent trade at the deadline?" whined Vince. "I mean. They needed starting pitching, and they didn't get anybody."

"What are you talking about, Vinnie?" countered Blake. "Their best starter is returning from surgery in a couple of weeks, and they have three other good pitchers. Why waste trades for more of that? They needed relief pitching, and that's what they got."

"You're both wrong," I said. "The Sox need a starter, a middle reliever, and a first baseman. They got two relievers that can't pitch worth crap, and they gave up too much for both of them. This season has just gone down the tubes for them. It's disgusting. Let's talk about something less discouraging."

"Negative Nancy," Blake said. "Could you be more depressing today? What's gotten into you?"

Vince started to defend me, but I shook my head. We fell silent while we finished eating. When we were done, I said, "Your mom makes good PBJ's. I feel a little better now, but I'll be much better when we get this dumb fishing pole fixed."

"That's my mom," said Vince. "Jack of all trades, master of none. She can make sandwiches, pull cookies out of packages, toss in an apple from a grocery bag, and make strawberry Quik with milk, but she can't cook or bake to save her life. Whatever. I'm sick of this fishing crap. Let's go home, fix this stupid rod, and be done with it."

When we got to Blake's house, his dad was in the yard. "Home so soon? Did you catch anything for once?" There was an unmistakable taunt in his voice.

"Nothing worth keeping, Pop," Blake said. "Say, where's your wood glue?"

"What do you need my wood glue for?" he grumbled.

"Jack, here, broke his pole. We need to glue it back together." Vince spoke up.

21

"Won't do it any good," Blake's father groused. "First cast, it'll come apart."

"What?" I didn't like what I was hearing.

"You heard me, boy," he snapped. "The first time you use it, that rod will break again, just like it is right now. Only thing that's good for now is whippin' ya or burning in the stove. From the look on your face, I'd say it's not yours, either. What'd you do, steal it from your old man?" Mr. Harris stared keenly at me. "So, that's it, huh? Well, it's none o' my business where you got it from. Wood glue's on the second shelf on the left, Blake. Put the boy's rod back together, and when it's dry he can take it home. Be sure to put the glue back where you found it, or there'll be hell to pay."

"Yessir, Pop," Blake said. He took the long way around to the garage, avoiding his father's reach, to get the glue. By the time he returned, his dad was in the house. I wasn't completely sure, but Blake seemed to sigh with relief not to see 'Pop' there. I was comfortable around most adults, but this gruff-spoken man was more than a little scary.

The three of us worked together to put the fishing pole to rights. By the time we were done, I couldn't even see where it had broken. While the glue dried, we played wiffleball in the yard, taking turns pitching and batting, with the third being the umpire. It was the New York Yankees vs. the Boston Red Sox.

As always, a brawl ended the game before a winner was decided. Favoritism was alleged, argued, and it took a growl from Blake's dad to stop the fight. By then, the glue was dry on the fishing rod, so I took the hint that it was time to go home. When I got there, I returned the pole to its place in the garage, knowing my fishing days were done. Still, I'd proven myself to my friends, and I was happy about that.

4: "I've Got You Pegged"

Summer vacation ended earlier for me than for my friends. City Christian School began before Labor Day, while theirs started after the holiday. They mocked me mercilessly about that. I just reminded them that I'd be out earlier in June. That shut them up for a good, oh, five seconds or so. Have I said I was dreading the new school thing?

Then the Dragon went and over-explained the bus ride and all that. "You'll be riding the bus to school, Jack. It stops at the top of the hill to pick you up, and it'll drop you off at the end of the day," Steph explained.

"Why can't I ride with you? I don't wanna ride a stupid bus. I don't know anybody."

"Your day begins before mine does, and I get out before you do. It just won't work. Besides, you'll make friends. You're good at that." She smiled at me. I hated that smile. She was so fake.

"Fine." I stomped off to my room.

"Do you want me to walk up to the bus with you on the first day?" she called after me.

"No! I can go by myself!" I hollered back. "I don't need the Dragon," I mumbled to myself.

"What was that last part?" she said.

"Nothing important," I called back. "I'll be *fine*." The more I thought about it, the more I realized that I really would be fine. *Why was I begging to ride with her, anyway? I don't want more time with her! If I must go to this stupid school, I might as well put as much distance between us as possible.*

The following day, I rose early to get ready for school. Steph had made a lunch and laid out clothes for me. Dad was there, too, a rare day of going to work later than usual. "It's not every day I get to see you in the morning, Jack. You're starting at a new school, and I wanted to be here for you."

Dad gave me a pat on the back as I headed out the door and up the hill to wait for the bus. *A pat on the back, dad? Really? You used to hug me every day! I know I should be thankful that you took the time to see me off on my first day at the new school, but everything you do lately seems forced, and forced affection isn't real affection, in my book.*

There was no mistaking it when my bus arrived. The side of it read in giant letters, "CITY CHRISTIAN SCHOOL." I turned around and looked down the hill, where I saw Dad and Steph standing at the mouth of the driveway, waving to me. I waved back and got on the bus.

A handful of sleepy faces greeted me as I walked along the aisle and looked for a place to sit. Then I saw a slightly familiar boy about my age. He was the first person with a smile, and he motioned to the open seat next to him and said quietly, "You can sit here if you want to." It seemed as good as any other spot, so I sat down. The boy stuck out his right hand and said, "My name's Andy Madison. What's yours?"

24

"Jack. Jack Bannister." I shook hands with him. "Nice to meet you, Andy. You know what? You look familiar. Where have I seen you before?"

"Nice to meet you, too, Jack. I'm not *sure* where we've seen each other, but I *think* it might've been at Whitman's Corner Store a few weeks ago. You were with a couple of other boys."

That's when it hit me. Andy was the kid Blake had threatened when we'd left Whitman's! I still didn't know why Blake had it in for Andy; he seemed like a decent kid.

"Oh, yeah, I remember. Sorry about that. I had no idea what that was all about," I said.

Andy shrugged. "Me neither, but I didn't want to find out. Anyway, what grade are you in?"

"Sixth. You?"

"Me, too! Sorry for being so excited, Jack, but you seem like a nice guy, and I'd like to be friends with you. Can we be friends?" Andy was friendly and shy, all at the same time.

"Sure, Andy. Being here on my first day with a friend will be nice. Thanks." I relaxed as the ride continued and dreaded school a little less. It turned out that Andy and I had a mutual interest in the Boston Red Sox, so we talked about their recent progress in the season.

I liked football, too, but he said he wasn't allowed to watch TV on Sundays, so he didn't follow the NFL. Not watching TV on Sundays was new for me, but Andy said it was a rule his parents had for 'keeping the Lord's Day holy' or something like that. I'll be honest: I liked this kid, but he sounded like a real goody two-shoes.

25

Within a couple of weeks of the start of school, Andy and I were good friends. I discovered that Andy was as kind to everyone else as he was to me on that first day, but that he was also naïve about specific social situations and that some of our classmates took advantage of his good nature by bullying him. He wasn't coordinated enough to play catch or dodgeball well, so he was picked last for teams. I could see how that hurt Andy's feelings and made him withdraw socially.

It was sad because Andy was very smart, gentle, and funny, but people kept judging him because he wore thick glasses, was a little chubby, and didn't play sports. Plus, he'd been at that school since kindergarten, and so had most of our classmates, and it was clear that my new friend had been bullied for years. I'm no saint, but seeing my friend on the receiving end of bad behavior irked me.

Andy helped me with homework and showed kindness that I didn't get from my neighborhood friends. He never used harsh words like Blake or Vince did, and he didn't call me "dumbo" or any other put-down, not even in a laughing way. He didn't call anybody a mean name, even though other kids in the class picked on him. It angered me when other boys and even some of the girls called Andy "fatso," "slowpoke," or "baby." Andy acted like he didn't hear them, but I was pretty sure my new friend did, and I knew that the playground saying of "sticks and stones may break my bones, but words will never hurt me" was a crock of baloney.

Even though we were in sixth grade, we still had recess. I valued that time for expelling the extra energy built up while sitting in classes all morning. Running around outside kept me from acting out in class, but when I saw Andy retreating from the rest of the class during those times, I felt torn. We talked about it one afternoon on the bus ride home.

"Andy, can I talk to you about something bugging me?"

"Sure, Jack, what is it?"

"I've noticed that you go off by yourself most of the time during recess." He began to get defensive, so I quickly continued, "I don't mean that as a criticism, bud. I understand how many of our classmates are. I don't want you to feel I'm trying to ignore you at recess. A problem I've had at school is not using recess to get rid of my extra energy. I have a tough time concentrating in class as the day goes on, so Dad has hammered into my head how important it is to run around as much as possible whenever I get the chance. I'm rambling." I stopped and looked at my new friend, not knowing how he would react.

To my surprise, he was smiling at me. "Why are you smiling, Andy?"

"Thanks for telling me that, Jack. It's easy to understand when friends say what's on their minds. I admit I've taken it personally sometimes when you've gone with the others to play a game, but now that I know why you do that, it won't bother me again! I have plenty of imagination to spend my recess alone, and you don't have to worry that I'm lonely or sad about that, ok? Really. I make up stories in my head, and later I write them down. It's fun for me. Hey, don't look at me like I have three heads!"

We both laughed. I *did* find it weird that he enjoyed writing made-up stories, but maybe my friend would be an author someday. Perhaps he wouldn't. I'm glad he had a hobby he enjoyed, and I told him that.

The conversation made our break times at school easier, especially when we remembered that we had *these times*, the bus rides, for hanging out. As our friendship grew, the bullies in the class learned I would stand up for Andy, and they learned to leave him alone. I wasn't someone they wanted to mess with.

On top of Andy's gestures of friendship, his parents regularly invited me to their home to hang out with him for a few hours on Saturdays or for sleepovers. I couldn't believe it because it made their house so full! I'm an only child, but Andy was the youngest of six, with a brother and four sisters. I admit some envy for how Andy's older brother, David, seemed to watch out for my friend, and I wondered what it would be like to have a brother of my own.

Of course, I also saw that Andy wasn't perfect! He didn't get along with his sisters as well as he did with our classmates. Two of his sisters drove Andy crazy, and they argued over *everything*. Still, his parents were in charge, and discipline followed if arguments weren't resolved.

I saw Andy get in trouble several times. When that happened, Mr. and Mrs. Madison would apologize to me for disrupting our plans while explaining that actions have consequences, and the consequences in those cases meant our time together had to end at that point. Then they'd take me home. I marveled at the love they showed one another and to him. I'd never seen family dynamics like that anywhere else.

I still spent time with Vince and Blake, especially on Sundays, but I had too much homework every day during the week. If I didn't finish my homework on time, our teacher assigned a punishment called 'sentences.' It didn't matter what the 'crime' was, whether late homework, talking out of turn, tardiness, or any other rule we broke, she assigned writing "I will not talk in class, or I will do my homework on time" or whatever it was, twenty-five times.

If we didn't turn those in on time, we had to finish the original sentences and another twenty-five "I will have my sentences done on time" to the homework we were still trying to complete. It was a nightmare. She seemed to give them out more to confident kids in the class than to others. Andy and I got them a lot, and he rarely misbehaved. I know once that he had one hundred sentences due, plus all his homework! His parents were very upset, but not at him. I don't understand why she treated him so poorly.

She also had the annoying habit of checking our lunches before we ate to ensure we didn't have more than one dessert. If we did, she'd take one and throw it in the trash. Many parents were angry about that; we kids were, too! But she kept doing it all year.

One day at the fort, I told Vince and Blake about our teacher, whom I called the "witch," and they laughed. "You mean, with a 'b,' Jack?" Blake snorted, but I said, "I get what you mean, Blake, but no, she's a witch. She has black hair and wears black dresses, and I swear her eyes bug out of her head. I think she even cackles when giving us homework or punishments." I sighed. "School would be lame if it weren't for Andy."

"Who's Andy?" asked Vince.

I realized I'd stepped in it, and I tried to cover my tracks. "Oh, a kid in my class. He's funny. We ride the bus together. We've become friends, and it makes school tolerable. Cool kid." *Dang it. Said too much again!*

"You ride the bus together?" Blake asked. "Where's he from?"

"Next town over," I muttered. "Why do you want to know?"

"You've met a kid from Nolan and become friends with him," Vince said. "Maybe we want to meet him, too. If you say he's a cool kid, we should be friends with him, too, right, Blake? Or is that going to be an issue, Jack?"

"Come on, fellas," I said. "He's a smart, funny kid, and we get along. Does that mean there needs to be an issue?"

Blake held up his hand. "Oh, I know who it is, Vinnie! It's that fat, four-eyed dweeb that tried to visit Whitman's Corner Store the day we took Jack there!"

I shook my head. "No, Blake, you're wrong. It's not the same kid; it isn't who you—."

"Listen, *dumbo*, I know I'm right," Blake said. "You may be able to fool your old man and the *Dragon* with your lyin', but I've got you pegged. You're hanging out with that limp-wristed wuss-boy! What'd you say his name is, Andy? I'll tell you what, *Jacko*: You hang out with your little boyfriend all you want, but if he tries comin' over to our town, he'll get what's coming to him."

Blake spun on his heel and walked away. Vince shrugged at me and followed Blake. I stood there, dumbfounded.

30

5: Friendship of Lasting Value

Columbus Day weekend was approaching, and the weather was unseasonably warm. Peter and Sarah Madison were going to be busy that Saturday, but they gave Andy permission to ride his bike to my house. "He's always riding over here, so why don't you ride to his place for a change?" his mother said. Andy was excited about it, but he was also nervous. He hoped he wouldn't come across the bullies from my neighborhood.

The day arrived, and Andy got ready to go. He'd never ridden this far before, and he wasn't sure how long it would take to get here. He telephoned me to let me know he was leaving. Turning to his older brother, he said, "See ya later, David!"

"Have fun, little brother!" David said to Andy. "I'll see you when you get back." It was rare for David to be at home, but Andy had heard him make a deal with their parents to finish his homework on Saturday so he could have a cookout with his friends on the holiday.

Andy went out to his bike and rode the quarter-mile downhill to the four-corner intersection where Whitmans' was. When he got there, he turned right and continued toward my house. He hadn't gotten very far when his heart sank. Though he didn't know their names yet, he saw Vince and Blake approaching him in the opposite direction.

He pedaled faster and tried to ignore them. As they rode past him toward Whitman's, he thought he heard one of them say, "You'd better ride fast, fat boy."

Andy went as fast as he could, but being on a one-speed meant he couldn't go any quicker than his legs could take him, and the road slanted uphill more than he realized. He began to feel winded, so he had to coast for a while. When he'd caught his breath, he pedaled harder again, only to run out of breath, and so on. Then he looked back and saw they were already returning from the store. They were gaining on him faster than he could get away!

Suddenly, the boys stopped chasing him, and for a moment, he thought he was safe. But one picked up a small tree branch from the ditch and resumed the chase. Andy realized they were riding 3-speed bikes and were going to catch him. He thought the boy with the stick would poke him with it, and he braced himself.

Instead, the boy stuck the branch into the spokes of Andy's rear wheel, causing the bike to stop suddenly. He was thrown over the handlebars onto the gravel and tar, where he skidded along several feet, ripping his jeans and cutting his knees, shins, and hands. His bike twisted, and the chain broke. The wind was knocked out of him, and he lay there, gasping for a breath.

The uninvolved boy said, "What did you do that for? I thought you were going to poke him!"

Andy's attacker just laughed. "Look at him! That'll teach you to come to our town, you sissy! C'mon, Vince. Leave the loser, and let's get going."

When they were gone, and he'd caught his breath, Andy sat up and looked at himself. Nothing seemed broken, except for his bike. He stood up shakily.

Should I go to Jack's house or go home? he thought. He was dizzy, and he realized he wasn't even halfway to my house yet. Given his and his bike's condition, he turned around for home. He had no choice but to push his bike, but even that was hard because the front wheel was bent.

An hour later, Andy arrived at home. He was exhausted and sniffling when he entered the house. David was shocked to see him. "Little bro, what happened to you? Jack's been calling! Are you okay?"

"N-no," Andy whimpered. "J-jack's f-friends b-beat me up. T-they b-broke my bike, a-and..." he dissolved into tears of pain and frustration.

"Oh, hey, little bro, c'mere. Lemme see what's going on with you." His brother's words and touch were gentle. "Okay, Andy, we're going to get you cleaned up in just a minute, but first I gotta call Jack and let him know you're not coming, ok?"

Andy nodded. "Please tell him I'm sorry. I really, really wanted to be the one to ride there this time."

"I will." David picked up the phone and called the Bannisters. "Hi, it's David Madison, Andy's brother. May I speak to Jack, please? Sure, I'll wait. Hey, Jack, Andy won't make it to your house today." There was a pause. "Well, he was on his way there, and he was attacked by what he called 'Jack's friends.'"

Andy noticed that David's voice wasn't gentle anymore. He spoke up to David, "One of 'em called the other, 'Vince.'"

David told Jack, "Andy just said that one of them called the other, 'Vince.' Is that Vince Jackson?" Another pause. "Right. That must mean the other kid is Blake Harris. I've heard of them."

David listened. "Say, Jack, you wouldn't happen to have their phone numbers, would you? Hang on, let me get a pen. Okay, Blake's first... and now Vince's...great. Thanks for those."

"Jack, he's hurt pretty bad. Andy wanted me to tell you he's 'sorry. He really, really wanted to be the one to ride there this time.'"

Andy could tell that Jack was talking again.

"No, I know you'd never do this to Andy. I don't blame you for this, and neither does he. All right, yeah. I appreciate it, Jack. Yeah, I'll tell him. Bye."

David hung up the phone. "Jack says he's sorry his neighborhood friends are such jerks, and he hopes you feel better soon. Now, let's get you cleaned up, little brother."

About twenty minutes later, David had Andy cleaned and treated in fresh clothes. He gave him something to eat and told him to relax on the couch. "I have a couple of phone calls to make," he said. Something in his face told Andy to be glad he wasn't the one receiving a call from his older brother today. He listened in, though, and David became his hero again.

"Hello, may I speak to Blake Harris, please? Blake, my name is David, and I'm a friend of Jack Bannister's. Word has it that you attacked another friend of Jack's today on his way to Jack's house—yeah, that kid on the bike. Roughed him up pretty bad, coulda put him in the hospital."

Andy was shocked to hear his brother switch so quickly from calm and polite to harshly threatening. "So, I hear you think you're a tough guy, Blake, so let me put it to you straight: That kid is my little brother. If you ever lay another finger on him again, my buddies and I will teach you a lesson you'll never forget. You got that? Good."

He hung up and dialed Vince's number. The conversation with Vince was pretty much the same. When Vince tried to deflect blame, David said, "You know what, Vince? If you thought Blake was outta line, you should've stopped to help Andy, but you didn't. That makes you just as guilty as Blake, so *can* it."

When David finished his phone calls, he turned to Andy again. "I don't think those punks will bother you again, Andy. Some of my friends go to high school with Vince's older brother, and he won't be happy that Vince is caught up with the Harris kid in stuff like this. He'll make sure Vince stays in line."

"Anyway, whaddya say, champ? Are you up for a game of Monopoly? Wait, I have an idea."

He went back to the phone and dialed it one more time. "Hi, Mrs. Bannister, this is David Madison again. Could you bring Jack over to our house, by any chance? You can? Great! Thanks." He hung up and looked at me. "Let's see if we can salvage some of this Saturday, okay?"

When Steph told me that David had called to invite me to the Madisons, I was happy to go, but the day was already off to a weird start, and my nerves were on edge because of what Blake and Vince had done. I hoped I could relax and enjoy my time with Andy and David, but why would Andy want me around when my other friends were so awful to him? I crossed my fingers for the best but prepared for the worst, not knowing what to expect after our day's bad start. Steph dropped me off and said to call when it was time for pick up. David welcomed me into the house, where Monopoly was on the dining room table. Andy greeted me warmly, and we began the game.

I was glad to be at Andy's house but sad that my neighborhood friends ruined my other plans. I didn't know what to do about Blake and Vince. I liked hanging out with them, but they'd done a number on Andy. I didn't particularly appreciate being caught in between friends this way. It angered me to see the cuts and scrapes on Andy's arms, hands, and legs, although I was amazed that his glasses didn't get broken. They seemed to get broken in gym class or on the playground. Andy chuckled when I pointed that out. I was also jealous of how David cared for his little brother, but I tried not to show my envy too openly. I didn't want to come across as emotionally needy.

When Andy got up to use the bathroom, David surprised me by asking, "Hey, Jack, are you okay?"

"Why wouldn't I be?" I answered a little shortly.

"Well, you seem a little upset, that's all. I'm all ears if you need me," David replied calmly.

I wondered how David saw through my attitude so easily; maybe he was safe to talk to. "Uh, David? Can I ask you something?"

"Sure, bud, what's up?" David gave me his undivided attention.

"I, uh, I don't know what to do about Blake, Vince, and Andy," I confessed. "I mean, Andy's such a good friend to me, but the other guys and I are friends, too, and I'm not happy with what they did to Andy, but I'm still friends with them, and I don't know what to do. I'm confused." I paused. "What should I do?"

David smiled at me. "Andy knows you are his friend, Jack, and he also understands that Vince and Blake are your friends. You're not going to lose Andy as a friend over this."

"I-I'm not?" I was surprised.

"No, you're not, Jack," Andy said, returning to the room. "Your friendship means too much to me to throw it aside like that. You weren't the one that attacked me today, and just because you're friends with the ones that did doesn't make you the same as them. I don't think they're good influences on you, but you are still my friend, and I am still yours."

It was Andy's turn to be surprised as I jumped up and gave him a half-hug. "Thank you, Andy! Thanks for being my friend. I don't deserve friends like you."

Andy smiled as he returned the half-hug and patted me on the back. "Thanks for being my friend, too, Jack. None of us deserves good, but we can thank God for good friends." The hug ended as he spoke, and we sat down to finish our game. I disagreed with Andy that God was the one to thank, but I kept my mouth shut.

"Thanks for the advice, David," I said.

David shrugged. "I'm not sure I gave much advice, Jack, but you're welcome. I will add my $.02 to what Andy said a minute ago. Those two boys aren't good to be around, Jack, and they're going to cause you trouble someday. I've met other members of their families, and, well, you ought to find better people to hang out with is all I can say."

"I'll be all right, David. Thanks." I appreciated what they'd said but didn't want more advice than necessary. Thankfully, they let the matter drop, and we got on with our fun afternoon. I understood and appreciated their concern for me, but I wasn't asking them to fix my whole life, and they seemed to get that.

Later the next week, the guys and I met up in the fort. Vince and Blake suggested we go to Whitman's again, while I wanted to go for a hike. They knew I was upset over what they'd done to Andy, but none of us wanted to talk about it. As a result, the tension kept us quietly at odds. We had trouble agreeing on what to do.

As fall turned into winter, followed by spring, we couldn't settle on anything, and I saw Blake and Vince less often. We'd occasionally go sledding or ice skating, but if I wanted to hang out in the fort or make a snow fort, they thought that was stupid. And if they wanted to throw snowballs at the chicken barn across the road and break the windows, I wasn't interested in the petty vandalism. The months passed, and we excused our failure to hang out on school taking up most of our time.

Also, I was spending a lot more time at Andy's house. His parents invited me over frequently, and Andy and I went sledding or built snow forts during the winter months. Sometimes, I helped him and his dad with chores, like cutting and stacking firewood. It sounds weird to find that fun, but it was good to have something to do and a good friend to be with. Mrs. Madison always fed me, and she was easy to talk to. I'd never found an adult so easy to open my heart to, and it was clear that she cared about me, because she'd ask how I was doing in math or English class, or how things were going with the Drago—I mean—my stepmom and my dad, and things like that.

Sometimes, Dad and Steph would invite Andy over on a Saturday, and we'd go out to eat. That was fun, too. I never took him to the fort, though, 'cause that was for the neighborhood gang only. He didn't mind. He understood the importance of keeping my friend groups separated.

The school year dragged on, as it often does when you don't like where you attend, but I had Andy's back. He tutored me in math, English, and history. With that partnership in place, he survived socially, and I got enough homework done to pass sixth grade. We were both glad to see the school year come to an end.

As I looked back, sixth grade turned out as I thought it would. The religious school was annoying, but I was glad I'd become friends with Andy. His family had been very welcoming and understanding toward me all year long. Oddly enough, his parents were teachers, but they weren't like the jerks we had at our school. Our classroom teacher was the worst. Wow, was she mean! Clearly, she had her favorites in the class, and everybody else'd better watch out.

For example, I knew Andy was a Christian, so I observed in amazement when our supposedly 'Christian' teacher tried to convert Andy to Christianity all the time! One rule of teaching at that school was attending the church that operated the school. Since Andy went to a different church, our teacher thought it meant that Andy couldn't possibly be a Christian! I even heard him tell her that his kindergarten teacher at City Christian had 'led him to the Lord,' but our teacher wouldn't listen to him. She was convinced he couldn't possibly be a Christian because he went to a different church than hers.

We learned in her class that bigotry means "obstinate or unreasonable attachment to a belief or opinion in prejudice against a person or people on the basis of their membership of a particular group." If that didn't define our teacher's attitude toward Andy, then I couldn't think of anything else that would, and she was completely blind to her bigotry!

Andy had been going to that school since kindergarten, and he told me that not all his teachers had been like that, but this one was a real doozy. I agreed. *Dizzy Doozy* was my nickname for her when I was talking with Andy, but when I really got upset about something she did, I referred to her as *itch Witch. I never called her that around Andy, though; he would've chewed me out! She never helped us with math when we didn't understand the assignments, and it seemed to me that it was because *she* didn't understand the math, either.

I'm pretty sure that Andy was just as aggravated by her as I was because he kept saying all year that the only thing that made school tolerable in 6th grade was having me there with him. It made me feel pretty good, and I tried hard to behave myself so I'd be there for my friend. Still, I had a rebellious streak and found trouble quickly. I got suspended twice, once for fighting and another time for "allegedly" stealing petty cash from the office. It wasn't much money, so they didn't involve the police, but I was skating on thin ice with the school administration by the time the year ended. I couldn't wait to break free and enjoy vacation with my friends—all of them.

6: A Safe Place for Me

Even though we hadn't been able to agree on what to do together for several months, I found myself missing Vince and Blake. Maybe it was my rebellious streak acting up, or perhaps I just liked their rough-and-tumble natures, but either way, I was looking forward to spending more time with them when vacation began that summer. I wanted to see Andy some, too, and my dad suggested I become self-employed mowing neighbors' lawns. I liked his idea since it would give me money to spend on trips to the corner store and save for more significant purchases later.

I found out that Andy would be working with his dad all summer, which bummed me out, but Mr. Madison told me that Andy wouldn't be busy *all* the time and that I was welcome to go over and help with the haying if I wanted. I'd never tried it before, but it sounded interesting. He even offered to pay me based on my ability to move hay bales. That got my attention!

Dad agreed it was a reasonable offer, so I told Andy to let me know when they'd be haying, and I'd help. I think having a friend in the field made him happy.

School let out for us the second week of June. The public schools Blake and Vince attended and Mr. Madison taught at didn't get out for another week. By the end of the month, good haying weather was upon us, and Mr. Madison had his first field mowed, raked, and ready to bale. He told Andy to call me and see if I could help pick it up.

"David and his friends are my regular crew, son, but they're busy today, so if you and Jack can do the work, that'd be a big help. You're both still young, but there are only about 170 bales, and I think one or two wagonloads will suffice," his dad said, according to Andy.

I was thrilled to have my first chance at this work and rode over on my bike right away. Per Andy's instructions, I wore jeans, not shorts, and a T-shirt. He had recommended a long-sleeve shirt, but it was too hot for that, I reasoned. I regretted it later, but we live and learn, don't we?

"Where do you need me, Mr. Madison?" I asked when I got there.

"Well, Jack, for now, you and Andy can stay here at the house. I'm going to start baling in a few minutes. Andy has a pair of gloves for you. Help Andy hook up the other tractor to the wagon, and he'll bring it to the field. While I'm baling, come to the field and make sure the bales coming out of the baler don't get in my way for the next pass around the field. You'll catch on to what I mean. As I get a couple of windrows done, you two can start stacking the bales—Andy will show you how to do that. When the baling's done, we'll pick up the hay together. All right?"

I nodded, and Mr. Madison headed off to the tractor and baler to get the work started. "Heya, Andy!" I called to my friend. "I'm supposed to help you hook up a tractor to a wagon?"

"Hi, Jack!" Andy said excitedly. "I'm so glad you could come over today. Here." Andy handed me a pair of brown cotton gardening gloves. "These will protect your hands from blistering on the twine when you handle the bales." He chuckled. "I know you're a tough guy and can handle this work without 'em, but trust me today, okay?" he raised an eyebrow and grinned.

42

"Wear 'em. And yeah, I'll get the other tractor and back it up to the wagon. I'll need you to put the pin through the wagon tongue into the hitch. It's easy. Let's go."

As Andy sauntered toward the barn, I looked at him with newfound respect. *If the bullies at school could only see him now! If Blake and Vince could only see him now! This kid they think is so weak can run circles around them out here. My gosh, they have no. friggin'. idea. I wasn't used to seeing 11-year-olds handle farm equipment independently, but that's what Andy did. I'm worried about impressing the kids in my neighborhood, and here's Andy, driving tractors, hooking them up to other equipment, moving hay bales— he's no wuss!* A smile crept across my face, and I realized I was dawdling. "Hey, wait up!" I called and sprinted to catch up to my friend.

Andy pointed to the two tractors inside when we got to the barn. "I'll be driving the orange one, the Allis-Chalmers, today, but we need to move the red one, the Farmall 200, first. It's not running just now, so we'll have to push it, okay? I'll put it into neutral, and then we'll start pushing."

"Where are we pushing it to?" I asked.

"Straight out the back of the barn," said Andy. "It's a bit sloped out there, so as soon as we get some momentum going, I'll hop up and steer it out of the way. We need to be able to pull the load of hay through the barn when the wagon's full."

"What's wrong with the Farmall?"

"Needs a new battery. Dad just hasn't had time to get one this week," replied Andy.

When we'd gotten the red tractor out of the way, he got on the other one and started it up. He drove it out of the barn and to the wagons out front. He backed up to the tongue of the wagon, which I lifted and held in place until the tractor hitch lined up with the end of the tongue. Then I took the pin from the tractor and put it through the hole in the tongue and hitch. I then attached the cotter pin at the bottom of the hitch pin to secure it.

"All right," said Andy. "Last chance for a bathroom or water break! Any takers? No? Then, let's get to the field. Dad will be waiting."

A few minutes later, we arrived in the field. Mr. Madison had started baling, but something had stopped him. We walked over to see what was going on.

"I need more twine, Andy. You know where it is. Both of you go and bring a bale of it to me. Quick as you can."

We turned for the house and I asked Andy, "Do we drive back?"

Andy shook his head. "It would be easier to carry the twine on the trailer, but it's faster to go on foot. Be careful with running through the hayfield, because the ground is very uneven, and the last thing my dad needs now is for us to twist our ankles."

I understood. We jogged to the farm as quickly as possible. Andy showed me where the baling twine was. "It's weird that the twine is called a 'bale' like the hay is called a 'bale,' isn't it?" I spoke.

"Yeah," said Andy. "I don't know why that is. We've just always called it that. Come on, let's hurry back."

When we returned to the field, Andy's dad only took a few minutes to thread the twine into the baler and get it running again. In the meantime, Andy showed me how to stack the bales already made, and then we hung out while his dad resumed his work.

"You put two side by side, then two in the opposite direction on top of them, criss-crossing them as high as you can go. Then, if something delays pickup and they're left in the field, and it rains, only the top bales get ruined," Andy said.

There weren't many to stack yet, but I marveled at his knowledge. "You're a fountain of farm information, Andy!" I grinned as I complimented him. "I never knew this about you before."

My friend smiled back. "It's not something that comes up in everyday conversation but thank you for the compliment. So now let me ask you, Jack, what do you think? Is haying for you?"

"Hmm. I like being outside, and I like hard work. Haying is both of those." I smiled. "I like being with you. And your family," I added. "I feel, um, safe here."

"I'm glad. I appreciate your help today and having you here. I like it when you're here. You're a good friend, Jack." Andy smiled at me. "Dad's waving for you. I'll stay here." *Why did he mention feeling 'safe' here?*

The afternoon wore on, and we finished our work. With Mr. Madison's help, we picked up all the bales in one load. Andy drove the tractor, I loaded the bales, and his dad stacked them on the wagon. We counted 166, just a handful fewer than he'd expected to get from that field. We didn't unload them in the barn, though, because a customer had called to say he'd buy them off the wagon the next day—a move which would save him fifty cents per bale. Andy was relieved because he wasn't a fan of barn work, which he said was hot and stuffy and set off his allergies.

Mr. Madison said I was a good worker, earning ten dollars for my efforts. "I may not be this generous every time, Jack, but you proved yourself worth that as a first-timer. Keep up the same pace or better, and you might replace some of my regular crew." He grinned and gave me a friendly wink. "Sarah has a pot of spaghetti on the stove for us. You boys hungry?"

After supper, Andy's dad gave me a ride home with my bike in the trunk. Mr. Madison spoke to Dad and Steph when we arrived at my house. "Jack was very helpful. I appreciate your letting him come today. I'm sure he and Andy get along well, so it made my son's day more tolerable." He smiled and shook Dad's hand.

"We appreciate that you were willing to have him all day, Mr. Madison," Steph said.

"It's Peter," he said, "and Jack is welcome any time. Sarah fed him supper, by the way. He built up quite the appetite in the hayfield!" With that, he took his leave.

When he got home, Andy was waiting to talk with him. "Dad? Can I ask you something?" he asked.

"Sure, Andy. What is it?" They didn't have father-son conversations often that didn't involve discipline, so when Andy initiated something like this, Peter Madison tried to be patient with his youngest son.

"Why do you take so much interest in Jack?" Andy said. "I'm not jealous or anything," he added quickly. "I'm just curious why you and Mom have invited him over as much as you have."

Peter Madison sat down in his rocking chair and picked up his Bible. Andy squirmed slightly but tried not to show it. "Andy, I'd like you to read James chapter one, verse 27, out loud."

Andy took the book from his father, opened it to the reference, and read, *"Religion that God our Father accepts as pure and faultless is this: to look after orphans and widows in their distress and to keep oneself from being polluted by the world."* He looked up at his father with question marks in his eyes.

"Son, your friend is not an orphan, but his mother died three years ago. That has caused Jack a lot of heartache and distress. Doctors and specialists say that children can heal from emotional pain better than anyone else, but it is important to help children with their healing first. Your mother and I are trying to help Jack without pointing out that's what we're doing. We're also trying to help Joe and Stephanie. They love him, but they haven't had much time to get to know themselves as a couple the way they should. It's a complicated relationship for all three of them."

"Oh, okay. That makes more sense now. Uh..." Andy hesitated.

"Is there something else, son?"

"Well, today, when we were talking while you put the twine into the baler, I asked him if he thought haying was for him. One of the things he said is that he feels 'safe' here. I spent a lot of time this afternoon wondering why he'd say that."

His dad thought about that for a moment. "I'm not sure what Jack meant by finding this to be a 'safe' place for him, Andy. He could mean it's spiritually, emotionally, or physically safe, but I suspect he means emotionally. When he's here, he doesn't have to win your friendship. He doesn't have to impress you or us. We care about him, and he knows it."

Andy nodded, and Peter continued, "Your friendship with Jack has helped him greatly, so we have tried to help even more. Joe Bannister has said that you've positively influenced Jack and that his time in our home has been good for him, too. We can't replace his family, and we don't want to, Andy, but we've taken an interest in this young man because it's right to love those who have lost so much. Does this answer your question?"

"Yessir, it does." He jumped up and hugged his father. "Thanks, Dad. I love you!"

His father hugged him back. "I love you, too, son. Now, let's get a few more chores done before it's time for bed."

"Okay, Dad." Andy followed his dad outside to prepare the equipment for the next day of haying.

After Mr. Madison left I found out why Andy had suggested the long-sleeve shirt for haying. I took a shower, and man, did all those scratches hurt when they got wet! I decided then and there that I'd do what Andy did—wear a t-shirt with an unbuttoned long sleeve shirt over it to protect my forearms. I also realized that my muscles were beginning to hurt, but that made me smile, because I was proud of doing hard work. After drying off and putting on clean clothes, I went to the kitchen to sit with Dad and

Steph. They served up dishes of ice cream for the three of us and asked me about my day.

"How was haying, Jack?" asked Dad.

"It was fun," I said. "And you know how some of the kids at school and Blake and Vince have bullied Andy 'cause they thought he was a wuss and stuff? They shoulda seen him today!"

"What was he doing today?" Steph said.

"He was driving tractors, hooking them up to equipment, moving hay, acting like a boss! He'd run circles around those kids out there. It was really cool!" I was beaming as I recalled my friend's acumen for farm work.

Dad and Steph shared a smile. I could tell they were happy that I had found a good friend in Andy, and that I was welcomed by the Madison family. And speaking of family, they had news to share with me. Dad spoke first.

"That's great, bud. I'm glad you had a good time, and that you could see a side of your friend you hadn't seen before. I'm proud of you! Mr. Madison had good things to say about you. You did well, son." He paused, giving me a moment to bask in the positive reinforcement.

"Thanks, Dad. I appreciate that." I wasn't used to such effusive praise from my father, but I was pleased to receive it. Still, it seemed that Dad had more to say. "Is there something else?"

"As a matter of fact, there is, Jack. Steph and I have news to share with you, and I think this is a good time for it. You're going to be a big brother!"

The moment that Dad began saying that he and his wife had news to share with me, I felt mini panic coming over me. The last time Dad had to tell me 'news' was the night Mom died. The good emotions from seconds earlier evaporated. Then I heard, "...be a big brother!" Immediately, the panic subsided.

"I-I'm g-going to be a brother?!" I exclaimed. "When? How? Never mind how..." I blushed. "When?"

My folks laughed. "In about seven months."

"Wow! Oh, uh, congratulations!" I jumped up and grabbed each of them in a hug. Steph and I were both surprised, but I knew this was worth hugging the Dragon for. After all, if I couldn't ever be a younger brother, I could be someone's big bro, like David was for Andy. I couldn't wait to tell my friends!

7: Hot Day, Hot Tempers

The next morning, I woke up early and looked for Vince and Blake. The weather forecast predicted the 90s and humidity, so I thought swimming would be a good plan for the day, but if they wanted to go to Whitman's first, we should do it before it got hot. I rode to Vince's house, but he wasn't home. The same was true for Blake. I rode home and walked out to the fort in the woods. They weren't there, either; the work we'd done to fix up the fort had been broken down. I stayed to repair what I could.

While working, I heard Vince talking to Blake as they walked toward the fort. "I can't believe that guy called you, too. My brother Eddie was ready to kill me when he found out about it!"

"Ready to kill you? Why wasn't he ready to kill what's his name, the caller guy?"

Vince sighed. "Pay attention this time, Blake! I know it's a little confusing for you, but since you won't let this drop, I'll explain it one more time. The caller doesn't go to school with Eddie, but Eddie has a good friend who hangs out with him. Ed's *friend* heard about us hurting Andy from Andy's *brother—who is the caller guy*—which Eddie said made *him* look bad because *I* was involved, so *he* was ticked off and ready to kill *me*! And I wasn't even the one who put the stick in his spokes and knocked him off his bike—*you* were!"

"Way to throw me under the bus, asshole."

"*Language!*" said Vince.

"Shove it, Vince."

"You know what, Blake? You're just upset because you got caught for once. You did something stupid, someone got hurt, and you got caught. *Grow up*, Blake."

Vince turned away as they arrived at the fort and saw me watching them so he didn't see Blake scowling and balling up his fists.

"Hey, Vince," Blake growled.

"Wha–?" As Vince turned, he received a punch in the face from Blake, which made him stagger back. He fell against a tree. "Ow, you jerk! What'd you do that for?" Before he could regain his feet, Blake charged, pinned him, and began hitting him anywhere he could land a fist.

Vince tried to defend himself, but he was at a clear disadvantage. I sprinted from the fort's other side and tried to pull Blake off Vince. "Blake! Stop!" I yelled. I pushed and pulled until Blake finally released Vince, who gasped for breath.

When Vince had caught his breath he said, "What got into you, Blake? I didn't throw you under the bus. You got what you had coming to you. That's just a fact. You hurt Jack's friend Andy and got caught. *I* didn't hurt Andy, but *I* got caught for not stopping you and helping Andy after he got hurt. We both got what we deserved. Geez, Blake, what the hell??"

Vince turned and went into the fort and sat on one of the stump stools we'd made the previous fall. Blake looked at me. "I suppose you gave the guy our phone numbers?"

"Of course I did. You hurt my friend." I stood my ground but felt nervous butterflies in my stomach. I didn't want to fight Blake. "If you leave Andy alone, then you won't get pounded into the ground by David and his gang. I know them. They're decent guys but won't hesitate to crush you if you hurt Andy. They're very protective of him."

"Thanks for nothing, Jack," Blake muttered. "All I do is try to tease a kid a couple of times, and you treat me like I'm trying to kill your boyfriend."

"He's not my boyfriend, Blake. He's just my friend." I sighed. "Geez, guys, didn't this happen months ago? Why are you talking about it this morning?"

"'Cuz Blake brought it up this morning," Vince said through the wall. "He's still upset about it."

"Oh, brother, Blake. Let me give you something else to think about, ok? I've been looking for you guys all morning."

"Oh yeah? Why?" Blake was still grouchy, but curious.

"Well, first, do you wanna go to Whitman's today? I did some work at Andy's farm yesterday and got paid for it, and I'd like to treat you guys to some candy or something. Plus, I wanted to tell you my family's news." My excitement was returning.

"You want to treat us? Why?" Vince and Blake spoke at the same time.

"You guys have been friends with me, and I want to share something with you, that's all. Just to be nice, I guess. You've gotten things for me at Whitman's, right? So, now it's my turn. Anyway, my real news is that I found out last night that I'm gonna be a big brother in a few months!"

"Oh, hey, congrats, Jack," Vince said.

"Yeah, congratulations, Jacko," Blake added. "When do you wanna go to the store?"

"I figured we should go now, and then go swimming at the stream later when it gets hot. Sound good to you?" I looked at them. They nodded. "All right, then. Shake and make up, and let's go!"

Dusting themselves off from their disagreement, we got up and headed back to our respective homes to get our bikes. I stopped in the house to let Steph know where we were going.

"Enjoy yourself, Jack," she said, smiling at me. "What're you going to buy for yourself?"

"I'm gonna get some more baseball cards, for one thing," I said. "And I'm gonna get each of them a candy bar." When I saw the look on her face, I added, "They've been my friends since we moved here, and they've gotten things for me at the store, and I want to thank them for that. I think that's something Andy would do."

53

Steph nodded thoughtfully. "I think you're right. That's very kind of you, Jack. Be careful on the road!" *I should tell the Madisons what a good influence Andy has been on Jack.* As soon as Jack was gone, she picked up the receiver and dialed their number.

"Hello, Sarah? This is Stephanie Bannister. Oh, I'm very well, thank you, and you? That's good. Yes, Jack is fine. I think he's a little sore from haying yesterday, but he sure slept well last night! Ha ha, yes, thank you. Well, I just wanted to let you and Peter know how much your son is positively influencing Jack. He just left here to go to Whitman's with his neighborhood friends, and he intends to buy something for each of them, to thank them for befriending him, in part because he thinks it's something Andy would do, he said. I wanted to caution him about his friends but bit my tongue. Now was not the time to rain on his parade. We've just begun to build a bridge between us, and I didn't want to burn it. Oh, I know they're not perfect boys, Sarah, but God is working on them, isn't he? Joe and I do so much appreciate you and Peter and all you do for Jack and us.

"While I have you on the phone, Sarah, I want to share our happy news with you. Joe and I are expecting!" She paused while the other woman spoke. "Oh, thank you! You're so sweet. We're very happy, and Jack is excited to be a big brother. To be honest, I think he's seen how your David is towards Andy, and he wants to be like that for his own sibling." There was another pause as Sarah Madison spoke.

"You are so correct, Sarah. It just goes to show how God uses each of us to minister to one another. Even David is influencing Jack. Mmhmm. Well, I ought to be going, so I'll talk to you later. No, we're keeping the news to just a handful of people for now but given how much you and Peter have meant to us this year, Joe and I wanted you to know. All right, you take care, too. Bye now." She hung up the phone and sat down. *Oh Lord, thank you for the Madison family. Bless them for helping Jack.*

By the time my friends and I got to Whitman's Corner Store, it was approaching noon, and the sun was beating down. We skidded to a stop in the dirt, dumped our bikes against the grassy bank, and sat under a tree for a few moments, listening to the crickets chirping. Waves of heat radiated from the pavement, and the air barely stirred. At last, I gasped, "I need a drink! Let's go inside." We rose from the ground and walked across the road. The humidity was almost worse than the heat, and we had to unstick our clothes from our bodies as we walked. A thermometer outside the store read 96 degrees, and it was in the shade.

Once inside the store, we looked around for something to drink. Mr. Whitman spoke first, "What do you need, boys?"

"Do you sell anything to drink, mister?" I asked.

"I've got sodas in the cooler over there," he pointed to another part of the store. "Forty-five cents apiece."

"You got a hose outside?" asked Blake. He wasn't interested in paying for his drink.

"Yes," Mr. Whitman said. "It's around the corner of the building, but it's been sitting in the sun all day. The water will be quite hot by now."

Blake shrugged his shoulders. "I'll check it out. Come with me, Jack, Vince." He left the store, and we followed him around to the right of the store, where the hose lay coiled up like a snake basking in the heat. Blake picked up the nozzle and gave it a squeeze; the water was almost boiling! He dropped it in surprise.

"Motherfu...dger!" he yelled.

I blanched at the word coming from Blake's mouth. It wasn't that I was a prude, but I knew it wasn't one to use in everyday conversation. I also knew that Blake had just barely kept from finishing it for real. Vinnie just whacked Blake on the arm and hissed, *Dude! Language!*"

"That friggin' thing is scorching hot!" complained Blake, shaking his hand. "The nozzle, too! Dang, that hurt."

"Geez, Louise, you big baby," Vince said. "When did you become such an idiot? Let me do it." He reached down with his hand inside his shirt as a glove and picked up the nozzle. He turned the spray away from them and squirted it until the water came out cold. "Now it's safe to take a drink," he said, leaning down and quenching his thirst. "Jack? You want some?

When I nodded, Vince handed me the nozzle, which had also cooled down. "You don't need to use your shirt for this anymore."

When each of the us had finished drinking to his heart's content, we returned to the store. "Thanks for the water, Mr. Whitman," I said.

"You're welcome. What else can I get you? Something you're going to pay for?" he said with a smile.

"Baseball cards!" I smiled back. I was surprised to see Mr. Whitman frown for a moment, but I forgot the frown when I saw the supply of cards. "Blake and Vinnie, choose a candy bar for yourselves, my treat." I turned back to the cards and began looking through the stack to find what I wanted. When I'd chosen two packs, I went to the cooler and selected a bottle of ginger ale. Then I joined my friends at the cash register. "What'd you guys choose?" I asked them.

"Blake picked a Milky Way and I chose a Three Musketeers bar," Vince said. "Thanks for these, Jack."

"You're very welcome, Vince. My pleasure!" I don't know why I was so happy to spend my money on them, but it did make me happy. I think Andy would be proud of me, and the thought of making Andy proud made me happy.

I paid for everything and headed outside to join the guys under the tree, where, to my surprise, they were already eating something. "What else did you guys get? I didn't see you buy anything?"

"We got a few pieces of penny candy. You want some?" Blake said.

"Sure! What do you have?"

Blake showed me a few pieces, and I selected one. I unwrapped a caramel creme and popped it into my mouth. "Oh, that's so good," I sighed happily. Thanks, guys!"

"What did you get, Jacko?" Blake asked.

"Well, besides your candy bars," I said, "I got two packs of baseball cards—guaranteed Red Sox in each—and a bottle of ginger ale. Did you get anything besides the penny candy?"

"I didn't," Blake answered, "but I think Vinnie might have. Vinnie?"

"I'll tell you later. Let's get going. I'm ready to go home and change for swimming!" Vince looked a little tense, but I didn't feel like getting into a big discussion again, so I just agreed to leave.

An hour later, we were at the stream. About a thousand feet from our old fishing spot the stream opened wider, making it the perfect place to swim on a hot day like this one, if swimmers didn't mind the feel of fish on their legs. It was deep enough to jump in, but not for diving, and it was clear, clean water. Trees shaded the fishing area, but this spot was in the sun, so the water was warm, and while it had no sandy beach, the tall grass growing along the banks provided soft undergrowth when getting out of the water. We also hid our snacks in the tall grass, which acted as a cooler, preventing our chocolate from melting and my ginger ale from becoming too warm to drink.

It was the first time that I had thought about my father's broken fishing pole since the incident the previous year, and it threatened to spoil my beautiful day. *Am I feeling guilty?* I hadn't felt like this in years, and I tried to shake it. Then Vince appeared and handed me a pack of baseball cards. "Wha–?"

"They're for you, Jack. Take 'em." Vince insisted.

"Vince, why? That's the second time you've given me baseball cards. You don't have to do that, you know." I was surprised and taken aback by the gesture. I was also beginning to feel a little suspicious.

"I know, but you like them, so I guess I just want you to have more of them." Vince shrugged.

"When did you get them?" I asked, curious.

"Today, at Whitman's."

"You did? I didn't see you buy them," I replied. I decided to make them spell it out, but I fervently hoped it wasn't how it sounded.

Blake joined us as I said that. His tone dripped with mockery. "That's 'cuz he didn't buy them, dumbo. He lifted 'em."

Crap. I stopped looking through the new pack as my eyes went wide. "Lifted? You mean, you stole them?"

Vinnie's face reddened as he looked down. "Of course, *dumbo*," Blake said. "We never buy anything at Whitman's." He was bragging now.

"You don't?" I was shocked. "Y-you mean the penny c-candy today was stolen, too? And the baseball cards last year? Vinnie?" I demanded.

Vince finally looked up at me. "Yes, Jack. I shoplifted the baseball cards. It's what Blake and I do when we're there." He sighed and rolled his eyes in exasperation. "Look, it's not like it's expensive sh–I mean, stuff. We're not hurting anyone. You spent more money on stuff today than the cost of what we lifted. Whitman is still making money, so what's the big deal?"

I had to think about that, so I shrugged. *What was the big deal? Maybe Vince was right. Maybe it made no difference. I ought to ask Andy, or Mr. Madison, about it. I bet they'd know.* "I dunno, guys. I've just never known anyone personally that's a thief, I guess. Kinda shocking, to tell you the truth."

"Listen, *Jacko*," Blake said, "we're not beating anyone up. We're not stealing big stuff; we're just doing little stuff for fun. It *isn't* a big deal. Just forget about it, all right? What are we doing tomorrow?"

"I've got haying tomorrow. Wanna give it a try?" I was half-hoping they'd say no, so I wasn't disappointed when they turned me down.

"Hahahaha!" Blake doubled over. "Haying? You mean, moving bales and sh--, I mean, crap? Why would I want to do that? OOhhhhh...to help Andy. You just like seeing your boyfriend all sweaty."

Blake began a sing-song taunt. "Jacko and Andy sittin' in a tree, k-i-s-s, i-n-g. Oof!" He got knocked onto the ground with a faceplant into the dirt. When he rolled over, Vince was on top of him. "What's wrong with you, Vinnie? You wanna be the one kissing Jacko?"

Vince stood up. "You know what, Blake? You can be a real jerk sometimes. You really don't want friends, do you? You just want a miserable life by yourself. You think you're sooo hilarious, making all these dumb jokes, but you're not. 'Cuz your jokes aren't funny. They're just mean words, Blake. You sound just like your old man."

At that, Blake scrambled to his feet. "You take that back!" he screamed at Vince. "I am NOT just like my old man!" he trembled with rage.

"You are when you talk like that, Blake. I suggest that if you don't wanna be just like him, you stop taunting Jack and me like that, 'cuz one day you're gonna wake up without friends, and then where will you be?" Vince stood his ground. In his view, Blake had been asking for this all day, and he wasn't going to back down this time. He was sick of his 'friend' being a jerk all the time.

Then he turned to me. "You know what Jack? It's been a long day. I think we're done. You should go see how the Dragon's doing in this heat and humidity. I'll get Fake

Blake to calm down before he goes home, all right? Have fun at Andy's tomorrow."

After Jack left, Vince looked at Blake again. "You know what you need? You need to chill the f*** out."

"Vinnie!" gasped Blake. "*Language!*"

"Oh, shut your f****ing pie hole, Blake. Jack's not here anymore." With that, Vinnie gave Blake a shove. In a desperate move to keep from falling, he grabbed Vinnie's arm. That threw both boys off balance, and they landed in the stream, laughing, cussing, and blaming each other, as always.

8: Caught & Released

With all my deceit and sneaking around, I knew that my "luck" would run out at some point. Hanging around Blake and Vince was fun, but I was catching on to their games and realizing that shoplifting at Whitman's Corner Store wasn't the only place they stole from. Plus, even though they'd both turned 12 that summer, I knew they had started smoking cigarettes, and due to their influence on me, it was only a matter of time before I'd begin, too. In fact, I'd already started planning when I'd have my first smoke.

The last thing I wanted was to be back in school, but even I recognized that I had too much freedom during the summers. And when I was away from Andy so much, I lost my way. I had been to the Madison home many times in June and July for haying and hanging out, but they weren't the people I was around as readily as breathing like Vinnie and Blake were. I had some skeletons that were going to be found out soon enough.

One morning in late July, I sat at the kitchen table, eating a bowl of frosted flakes while Steph folded laundry. She was beginning to show a little belly from the growing child inside her, making me think of all the things I might do with a younger brother or sister, even though I would be more than ten years older than the new kid. I considered everything I had wanted my dad to do with me, which triggered my memory of the broken fishing pole. I pondered what I could do about the situation, and it hit me—my haying money! I could replace Dad's fishing pole if I saved enough of my haying and lawn mowing money over the next few weeks. He'd never know the difference!

I was so excited by the idea that I burst out, "Steph, I have an idea for Dad's birthday in September! I want to buy him a new fishing pole! I've been saving some of my haying and lawn job money. If I save the rest of it from now to the end of August, I should have enough to get him a new pole. When I have enough, will you help me get one for him?"

"I'd be glad to do that, Jack," Steph replied. "But why does he need a new one?"

Oops. I was flustered for a moment. Then I said, "I used his a few times and realized it's time to get him a more modern one, that's all. I've been looking at some catalogs and would like to do this for him. Please don't tell him."

"Okay," she said.

Phew. She bought my idea. Just a few more weeks, and I'm home free. I finished breakfast and went on with my day.

That night at supper, my father had a surprise for me that turned my idea on its head. "Jack, I've been thinking a lot about how hard you've been working at the Madisons' and mowing neighbors' lawns this summer, and I have to say, I'm very proud of you." I beamed at the rare praise from Dad.

"You took my challenge seriously, and while you've taken time to enjoy your summer, you've also funded your expenses while saving money for the future. That's showing true maturity and responsibility, son. You've grown up a lot since we moved here. I'm so pleased with how well you've done that, Steph, and I agreed that I should take the rest of this week off so that you and I can spend quality time together. Her sister is visiting from New Hampshire tomorrow, so you and I are going on a camping trip. How's that sound?"

I couldn't believe my ears. He and I hadn't gone camping since before mom died. It was one of our favorite father-son activities. I got very excited about it for a moment, but then I realized a big problem: camping meant fishing, and Dad's fishing pole was useless!

"Jack? Are you okay?" I realized I hadn't answered Dad yet.

"Sorry, Dad, I was lost in thought about the last time we went," I lied smoothly. It was only a partial lie, I told myself. *Then why do I feel so guilty about it? Shut up, God! Leave me alone.* I suppressed my thoughts. Dad was still looking at me. I put my happiest fake smile on for him. "It sounds great, Dad! Thank you! May I be excused to go start packing?"

"Sure, son. Steph washed some clothes and folded them for you. They're on your bed. Pick out what you want. We'll be gone for three nights, and while the days are still warm, it'll be a bit cool in the evenings. Keep that in mind with your choices. And Jack?" Dad paused to ensure I was paying attention, "I really don't care if you change your underwear every day, but make sure you have enough dry socks. We'll be doing some fishing and hiking, and wet socks will mess up your feet quick."

I scrambled out of my seat, cleared my tableware, and went to my room to pack. My mind raced as I decided how to handle the fishing pole debacle. Ultimately, I went to bed with no plan in place. I slept poorly, waking up almost every hour. At 3:00 a.m., I got up and went to the bathroom. When I returned to my room, I noticed a piece of paper sticking out of my school backpack, which had been on the floor by my closet all summer.

I pulled the paper out and grinned. It was a note Andy had passed to me during the Dizzy Doozy's math class several months earlier: *"Hang in there, Jack!"* it read. *"Take a bath in math, and spell well to stay out of hell-o, how are you? :-)"* It had made me relax and take a deep breath that day, and it did the same at 3:00 in the morning.

What would Andy do in this situation? Well, duh, Jacko, he'd tell his dad the truth and take the consequences. I sighed as I realized what I needed to do, but with a plan finally in place, I fell asleep and slept soundly until my dad woke me up a few hours later.

"Are you going to be ready to go in about half an hour, Jack?" my father asked. My answer was a groggy nod as I sat up and stretched. Dad had nearly left the room when I called him back.

"Dad, I need to talk to you." I tried to keep my voice steady, but it wavered slightly.

"What is it, son? Is something wrong?" He sat down at the end of the bed, a concerned look in his eyes. "Jack? What is it?" My voice caught in my throat. Dad suspected that what I had to say was making me lose my courage. "Son, if you have something difficult to say, say it. I'm your dad. I can hear whatever it is."

"Dad, I've...I've been dishonest with you. A-A lot."

"About what, son?" His face had grown serious, but not angry.

"You know how you said that I could use your fishing rod last year with your permission? I used it without asking first. Steph caught me, and I l-lied to her and said that you'd given me permission. I did it a few times, figuring that if I got it back on the rack in the garage before you noticed that it was gone, then no harm done. But then I was fishing with my friends, and I fell while I was carrying your pole and it b-broke." I couldn't stop the words spilling out, but tears were coursing down my cheeks, too. I could see the disappointment in my father's eyes, and I felt so ashamed.

"And then we used wood glue to put the pole back together, and when it dried I put it back on the rack, but my friend's dad said that it didn't matter that we put it back together, 'cuz the first cast would break it again, so I haven't used it since, and I knew that the next time you and I go fishing you'd find out, so I decided to use the money I was earning the rest of this summer to buy you a new one for your birthday, but then you sprang this camping trip on me last night and you wanted to go fishing, too, so you were going to find out today about the broken fishing pole and I was so worried it kept me up most of the night and I'm so sorry for lying and sneaking around and being such an awful son!" I was bawling like a baby by the time I finished confessing my sins to him and threw myself into Dad's arms.

Dad squeezed me tight. "Oh, my dear boy, there's been much darkness in your heart for so long. Come now, okay? That's enough crying. There, there, now." He patted my back soothingly, and I sat back, wiping my face. Dad pulled a tissue from the box next to the bed and handed it to me. "Here. Blow your nose. Feel better?"

"Why aren't you yelling at me? I thought you'd be angry," I said.

"Honestly, son, a year ago, I might've been. But the Lord has been working on me this past year through Steph and Peter Madison, among others."

I looked at Dad like he had three heads. "That's right, Jack. You're not the only one befriended by Andy and his family. God has used them to help all three of us in one way or another. I'm not a perfect man now, nor will I ever be, but Mr. Madison has been helping me see that I need to rely on God more and on myself less. I've been learning a lot about God's grace."

"So, you're not angry?" I asked again.

"No, Jack, I'm not angry. I *am disappointed* that you chose to lie, sneak around, and try to get away with what you knew was wrong. These are attitudes that will take over your life if you don't ask Jesus to take them from you. However, I also have a secret to reveal to you about the fishing pole."

66

"What's that?"

"I already knew about it."

I went pale. "How long have you known? Why didn't you say something?"

"I've known for about five months. I was thinking of taking it with me on a business trip last spring when I was going to have some free time, and when I took it off the rack one morning, it didn't feel right. I looked closely at the handle and could see where it had been glued, so I figured out what must have happened. I asked Steph if she knew whether you'd used it, and she admitted you had, though you'd told her I'd given you permission. She clearly didn't want to get you in trouble, Son. You should consider that the next time you feel aggravated with her.

Anyway, I spoke with Andy's dad to get his advice about how to address this situation and then decided to wait for you to admit to it. When I told him that I was taking this camping and fishing trip with you, he agreed that you'd probably come clean and tell me what happened."

I didn't know what to say, but I tried anyway. "You knew all this time?" All he did was nod. *How did Dad keep from blowing his top? This is so not like him!*

"By the way, Andy's coming, too. We're picking him up on the way. Also, I've replaced the handle on that pole, so it's good to use for now."

"Andy's coming with us? Really?" My sorrow was gone like a switch, and my excitement returned in spades. Then it faded a little. "Dad, I need to take care of a couple things before we go. First, do you forgive me for lying and sneaking around and breaking your fishing pole?"

"Yes, Jack, I forgive you," he said. "What else do you need to do?"

"I need to ask Steph to forgive me. I lied to her, too."

"She's in the kitchen. I think she'll be happy to hear from you."

I ran to the kitchen and said, "Steph? Can I talk to you, please?"

"Sure, Jack, honey. What is it?"

"I lied to you last year when I said that Dad had permitted me to use his fishing pole, and I'm sorry for that. Will you forgive me?"

"Jack, sweetheart, yes, I forgive you. Jesus has forgiven me of my sin, and the Bible says I must forgive others who sin against me. I knew you were lying the day you did it, so I have been praying for you to admit to it ever since. If you've been talking to your father about this today, then you know I did not break my word to you—I didn't tell him about our conversation until he figured out that the pole was broken for himself." She stopped for a moment, but then she spoke again.

"I want you to know that you can trust me, Jack. If you tell me something that you want kept secret, if it doesn't involve hurting yourself or others, I will keep it secret. I think I have passed that test, haven't I?" Steph looked me in the eye, and I nodded. "Not bad for a dragon, huh?" she added with a twinkle in her eye.

I gasped. *How did she know?*

Then she drew me in for a hug. "Have fun camping with your dad and Andy," and she kissed me on the cheek. "Love you, dear boy," she whispered.

No, I thought. *Not bad for a dragon at all.*

9: Camp BannisterMadison

I began packing the car with my gear while my dad made a phone call. I also got my father's gear, the cooler, tent, sleeping bags, and other equipment Dad had set out earlier for the trip and put them in the trunk. I kept my pillow with me because I figured I might doze off in the car, even if Andy was with us. All the excitement and anticipation aside, I felt the effects of sleeping only a few hours the night before. When I went to see if I had everything in the car, I was puzzled because my dad's fishing pole and bait box were there.

At that moment, Dad emerged from the house. "Grab those and put them in the car, please, Jack. Quick obedience, son."

I picked them up and did as I was told without saying a word; I was too shocked to do anything else. After saying goodbye to Steph, we got into the car and began the short drive to Andy's house. Dad glanced at me and said, "When I saw that my fishing pole was busted, I repaired it properly. It will work just fine this week. From the shocked look on your face a few moments ago, I'm guessing you never checked it again after gluing it back together, did you?

I shook my head, and he continued, "You're not going to use this pole this week, Jack. That's one of the consequences of your disobedience. However, I will help you and Andy make your own fishing poles, like my dad taught me when I was your age. They won't be as fancy as this one, but you still may catch a fish or two with them." I nodded my agreement, and within a few minutes we arrived at the Madison farm, where Andy was waiting on the porch with his father.

As soon as dad shut off the car, I hopped out and jogged over to greet them. "Good morning, Mr. Madison. Hi, Andy."

"Good morning, Jack. How are you this fine morning?" Peter Madison asked, waving to my dad at the same time. "Morning, Joe. Thanks for inviting Andy. He's quite excited. Tent camping is new to him, but I'm sure he'll be fine."

"We're glad to have him along, Peter," Joe said, shaking the man's hand. "Jack and I camped a few times when he was much younger but not in the last two or three years, so it'll be good for him to have a friend along while we re-learn it all. Plus, it's time for us to return the favor; you and Sarah have been so good to us—especially to Jack. We really can't thank you enough."

"Oh! That reminds me," said Peter. "Sarah made these for your trip." He turned to the porch and picked up a paper sack. As he handed it to Joe, he explained, "They're chocolate chip cookies. Made fresh this morning. Just some sugary energy for you and the boys," he said with a smile. "Have fun, boys, and mind Mr. Bannister!"

"We will! See you in a few days!" We waved good-bye to Mr. Madison as we piled into the car. "Have everything you need, Andy?" my dad asked, looking at him in the rearview mirror. The boy nodded eagerly. "Okay, then, here we go!" He backed out of the driveway and headed for our destination.

The car ride was going smoothly for us. We had stopped for gas at a general store along the way, and Dad had bought a can of Pringles to share. While we munched on the chips, I started talking to my friend.

"So, you've never been camping before at all?" I was surprised that this was all new to Andy.

"Never been tent camping. We've taken a popup camper on a long trip once, but this isn't something my family's ever done." Andy was excited and a little apprehensive about the experience. "David goes fishing at the stream down the road, and I've gone with him, but we've never caught anything worth keeping. I can't imagine my mom or my dad sleeping in a tent!" Andy giggled at the thought of it.

"Well, if we're going to the place I'm thinking of, we won't be sleeping on the ground, but we won't be on beds, either. The place has lean-tos," I said.

"What are those?" said Andy.

"A lean-to is a small building with three walls and a slanted roof," Joe Bannister said. "Jack's right about where we're going. We will sleep in a lean-to, so we won't be on hard ground. As a younger man, I could sleep on the ground, but I prefer having a smoother surface now," he laughed. "I'm not going to kid you, Andy. It will still be uncomfortable, but I think we'll be tired enough each night that we won't mind it." He laughed again.

After riding in the car for more than three hours, we boys didn't mind hiking 30 minutes to our camping spot. It was more of a walk than a hike, but since we all carried backpacks, sleeping bags, pillows, and other equipment, it felt like much more work than Andy had expected. Still, it was a nice break from sitting, and he said he was glad to be with us on this adventure.

We set up our sleeping gear and gathered kindling and other firewood before daylight faded. Then Dad lit a kerosene lantern and hung it from a corner of the lean-to so we could see. Andy and I took turns digging a hole for a latrine, which Dad finished when we had done all we could. When the camp was fully set up, we washed up with water from a nearby stream and then sat down for supper. For our first meal, we ate cold chicken that my stepmom had packed and finished with some of Mrs. Madison's chocolate chip cookies. It was a simple meal but filling, and by 8:30, all of us were asleep.

In the middle of the Maine woods, away from civilization, my dad, Joe, was up, dressed, and ready to get the day going long before Andy and I knew the day had begun.

"Wake up, boys! Time for breakfast!" He had a fire in a pit of stones, with a grill over the fire. On the grill, he had a skillet with bacon and eggs. The smell alone should have woken us boys, Andy realized, but then a gain, we'd been mighty tired the night before. We couldn't wait to dig in now that we were awake.

"Jack, get the plastic plates from the tote there," my father directed. "Andy, you'll find the plasticware in the pocket on the side. You boys can drink water; I will have some coffee." When we all had helped get set to eat and Dad had served us, he said, "Andy, would you say grace, please?"

"Uh, yes sir. Let's pray. *'Heavenly Father, thank you for today. Thank you for your beautiful creation, and for the generosity of the Bannisters to bring me on this trip with them. Thank you for keeping us safe on the road and giving* us a good night's sleep. We pray that you would be with Mrs. Bannister and the child that she's carrying, and that you'd bless her visit with her sister. Now, please bless this food to our bodies. Forgive us of our sins. In Jesus' Name, Amen.'"

"Amen." Dad echoed. "Please, dig in. I forgot salt, but if you slide your eggs into the bacon grease on your plate, you'll get some saltiness from the bacon onto your eggs."

"Mhmm, this is delicious, Dad!" I exclaimed around my second bite. "Thanks for making breakfast!"

"Yes, thank you, Mr. Bannister!" Andy said. "This is very yummy." He smiled contentedly as he finished eating. "What are we going to do today?"

"After we clean up from breakfast and you two change your clothes, we go fishing!" Joe announced. "I'm going to show you how to make your own fishing pole, and then we'll find some bait and do some fishing. How's that sound?"

"Great!" we shouted together. "Let's get started." Andy and I went to the stream to fill a bucket with water, and then returned to the campsite to wash the dishes. First, we heated some of the water in a kettle over the fire, and then we used some dish soap from home to wash the skillet, the plates and plasticware, and other items used for making breakfast. When we were done, we dried the smaller items with a hand towel, but left the skillet to dry on the grill over the smoldering ashes. Then we dumped the used water on the fire to douse the flames so we could leave the campsite.

We went into the lean-to and changed our clothes, putting on new socks and shirts, and applying fresh coats of deodorant—Steph and Sarah had hammered that need into our respective heads before the trip began. "You won't be able to shower or bathe this week, so use deodorant every day, or twice a day, if needed!" was the basic message both of us got. Then we applied bug spray to keep the mosquitos and black flies away and went out to find my dad.

"All right, boys. There are three things you need to make your own fishing poles. (1) a stick, (2) some fishing line, and (3) a hook. Because I planned for us to do this, I've brought along the fishing line and a hook for each of you, but you'll have to find your own sticks. Before you do, let me show you how this works. I'll make a small pole as an example, minus the hook."

Dad picked up a stick that measured about two feet in length. "What you do is take the fishing line—I'm using regular string in this example—and you tie the line near the base of the stick, about where you'd be holding it for fishing. Just make sure to tie it with a strong knot, like this." He showed us a knot. "Then you wind the line around the stick as you move the line to the other end of it. When you get it to the other end of the stick, you tie another knot a couple of inches from the end of the stick, like the one you started with, see? After that, with some of the line hanging down to reach the water, you attach your hook to it, bait it, and see what you can catch."

"Cool, Dad! Where did you learn how to do that?" I asked.

"My Dad taught me," he answered.

"Mr. Bannister? Why not just tie one knot at the end of the stick?" said Andy.

"Good question, Andy. I wondered the same thing many years ago. It's because if you catch a big enough fish, the fish will probably break the end of your stick, and you'll lose your hook. By tying it where I showed you, a big fish might break your stick still, but you'll have a better chance of pulling it in and not losing your hook. You guys ready to find your sticks? Then off you go. See you in a few minutes. Remember, you can use what's already on the ground, but don't break off branches from trees."

We fanned out to look for sticks that would serve well for fishing poles. About fifteen minutes later, both of us returned with two or three options each. We showed my dad, who tested the strength of each stick, and then told us to select our favorites to make rods from. Having done that, he cut lengths of fishing line for us, and we tied one end of our lines to the handle end of the sticks. He made sure the knots were tight before we wound the line around the sticks until the line was almost to the opposite end of the "pole," where we tied it again. Finally, he helped us tie a hook to the end of our lines.

"What do you think, boys? Can you fish with these?" he looked at us.

"I think I can, Mr. Bannister," Andy said. "How about you, Jack?"

I pondered it for a moment before breaking into a grin. "I'm sure I can, Dad! Thanks! This was fun."

"You're welcome. We need to dig for worms or grubs for bait, and then we'll be ready to try these out. I've got a couple of empty coffee cans here to use for holding the bait, one for you and one for me. Let's go see what we can find." With that, he led us into the trees again to find bait. He quickly located a downed tree, which he rolled over, and we snatched grubs and worms that scurried around underneath. We also grabbed some dirt to keep in the coffee cans so the bait would have some natural habitat until being used to catch fish. In a few minutes, we had all we needed for the day's excursion, so we headed back to the lean-to.

"Go down to the stream and wash off your hands. Take your canteens with you and fill them with clean water. You'll need to have something to drink while we're away from camp today. And before we go, be sure to use the latrine. You won't have the luxury of toilet paper when we're not here." Dad headed there himself as we obeyed his instructions.

When we returned, he was out and packing up the last of the snacks we'd need. He had already put everything else from camp in animal-proof containers. "Grab your daypacks, canteens, and fishing poles, and let's be off," Dad said when we'd each taken care of business. "There are fish waiting to be caught by us!"

Wilderness fishing was different from lazy stream fishing, but just as fun, Andy discovered. He held back, at first, observing Dad and me do it. When he had seen enough to be comfortable trying it, he got started. We were all happy for him as he landed his first catch.

"That's it, Andy! That's how you do it. Good job!" I was just as excited as my father to see how quickly Andy learned how to handle the fishing pole. Both of us boys were surprised that even our handmade fishing rods were good enough to catch fish. I had caught two keepers, and

Andy had just landed his first. Dad and I didn't need to ask Andy how he felt; his grin stretched from ear to ear.

"How do I get the hook out of his mouth, Mr. Bannister?" Andy asked.

"Do you want me to do it for you, or do you want to do it for yourself, Andy?" Dad replied.

"I'd like to try it, please," Andy said. He shook off his shyness and came to join us.

"Good lad," Dad said, proud of Andy's attitude. "Reach into your fish's mouth and get a solid grip on him so he can't wriggle away from you. Here, bring him away from the water so he doesn't fall back into the water if he slips off the hook. Good. Now, reach with your other hand and maneuver the hook out of his mouth. Yup, like that. You got it! Good job, Andy! Put your fish in the cooler with the others, put another worm on your hook, and cast again!" My dad smiled at him. "You've really taken to this."

"Thanks for your help, Mr. Bannister. And for your patience, both of you. I like to learn by watching; it helps me build my confidence," Andy said shyly. His face reddened slightly, but he was smiling happily, too. "This is so much fun!"

"You're welcome, bud!" I was happy to see him happy. "It's been fun helping you learn how to do this. Maybe you and I could go fishing back home sometime?"

"I'd like that, Jack. That'd be great!" Andy bobbed his head up and down with enthusiasm. "I'd like to see if I can catch another one now. We're waaaay behind your dad's total!" He laughed. Dad had caught at least a half dozen fish of keeper length, knowing we had to have that many for our supper.

"Boys, we can fish for another half hour, but then we'll have to clean our catch before we head back to the campsite, all right? We want time to cook our fish and eat before it gets too late."

"Okay," we said in unison, and baited our hooks for more fishing.

By the time we were done, we boys had caught another fish, giving me three, Andy two, and Dad seven. Dad had already begun cleaning his fish and showed us how it was done. We decided it was safer for him to do that work, but we helped by bringing fresh water for him to use, and by getting rid of the waste when he finished each fish.

In the end, we had twelve fish for supper and were hungry enough to eat all of it. We hiked back to camp and started a fire. It took quite a while for it to become hot enough for cooking. While Dad tended the fire, we boys searched for more firewood, changed our clothes, and dunked our fishing clothes in the stream and hung them up to dry.

Once again, Dad cooked a little bacon in the pan to season the fish, although not much was needed. The trout and rice he brought from home were delicious. When we finished eating and cleaning up, he brought out the makings for s'mores. "Anyone want dessert?" he said with a grin.

"Awesome!" we yelled.

"Go find sticks for roasting marshmallows, then," he said.

"How about the ones we didn't use for fishing, Dad?" I asked. "Do we still have those?"

"Good point, Jack. We do still have them. We'll use those. Get your crackers and chocolate pieces ready, and then you can begin roasting marshmallows."

"How many can we have, Dad?"

"I think three should be plenty for each of us, don't you?"

Andy agreed. "I'm not sure I'll eat more than one, to be honest. I'm rather full of all that delicious fish! I don't want to overeat."

Joe nodded and noted Andy's self-control. *I'll have to remember to tell Peter and Sarah; they've been worried about Andy's eating habits and lack of exercise. He's been a real trooper on this trip.* "Let's enjoy these treats before bed, boys! We have a hike tomorrow!"

"Mr. Bannister?" Andy spoke up. "Can we read the Bible and pray before bed tonight?"

"Uh, sure, Andy. Do you have yours with you?"

"Yes, sir, I do."

"Then I'll leave it to you to decide what to read, all right?"

"Okay. I'll get it ready while you and Jack finish your s'mores, okay?" Andy went to his sleeping bag to get his Bible.

While he was gone, I turned to my father and said, "Why are you letting him ruin a perfectly good evening with that stuff, Dad?"

"How are Bible reading and prayer going to 'ruin' the evening, son?" Dad said.

"Oh, come on, Dad. You know I don't like that religious stuff," I complained.

79

"It's very important to your friend, Jack. Listen to him. Maybe it will make more sense coming from him."

The lean-to wasn't far from the campfire, and Andy heard the conversation. He was naïve about much of life but not about Jack's dislike of the Bible. He was sad for his friend because he knew that the pain in Jack's heart could be healed by the same God that Jack rejected. Andy prayed for him all the time, and so did the whole Madison family. Still, only God could soften the boy's heart, and Andy didn't know if that would ever happen.

When Andy returned to the campfire, he brought his Bible and flashlight and sat beside me. "Did ya miss me?" he joked and elbowed me. I looked up and smiled. From the look on Andy's face, I wondered if he'd heard my complaining.

"I've been reading at home from the book of Matthew, and tonight's reading is from chapter 11, verses 28-30, where it says:

"Come to me, all you who are weary and burdened, and I will give you rest. Take my yoke upon you and learn from me, for I am gentle and humble in heart, and you will find rest for your souls. For my yoke is easy and my burden is light."

"Andy, why does Jesus say his 'yoke is easy'?" I interjected. "What if I don't want to be 'yoked' to anybody?"

"Jack, do you remember that yoke of oxen we saw on the school field trip last year? My dad said farmers use a yoke to keep oxen in step with each other so that they're going in the same direction instead of willy-nilly, all over the place. In a similar way, Jesus keeps us in step with his love, but his yoke isn't heavy and painful. And being connected to him gives us his love, peace, grace, and everything else. Instead of being burdened by our troubles in this life, we can give them to God, and he will give us rest from what drags us down. And we're going to be yoked to God or to the world, so why not be connected to God?

I interrupted impatiently. "How do you know all this sh-stuff, Andy? You sound like the preacher at church!" I'm sure my voice betrayed the mix of awe and mockery that was in my heart, not to mention the word that nearly slipped out. If he noticed it, though, he gave no indication of it.

"Our youth group had a Bible study series on this recently, so it's fresh in my mind. I took a lot of notes. You know me, Jack; can't do anything without taking notes!" Andy smiled at me. "Honestly, bud, the last thing I want to do is preach at you. I was just trying to answer your questions."

Ah, so he *had* noticed my tone. "I'm sorry, Andy. I know you weren't shoving anything on me. I apologize."

"Apology accepted, Jack. Any other questions? Mysteries of the universe I can reveal to you tonight? Which came first, the chicken or the egg? When the Red Sox will finally win the World Series again?"

The mood lightened, and we all shared a good chuckle, especially about his last suggestion. Then Dad brought us back to earth.

"Thank you for sharing that, Andy," he said. "Would you be willing to pray now, too?"

Andy nodded. *"Father in heaven, thank you for being with us today. We pray for Mrs. B and the baby in her womb, and for my family. Help us to sleep well and have a good hike tomorrow. In Jesus' Name, Amen."*

"Amen. Thank you." Dad stood up. "Off to bed, boys. Good night."

10: Camp HarrisJackson

Content Warning

At about the time that Joe was leaving the Madisons' with Jack and Andy, Blake and Vince arrived on foot at the Bannister home, not realizing that their friend was gone for the rest of the week. When they saw a New Hampshire car in the driveway and didn't see any sign of Jack, Vince suggested they knock on the door and find out where he was. Blake made it clear he wasn't going to be the one to do it, so Vince knocked and waited. Stephanie Bannister answered the door moments later.

"What can I do for you boys today?" she asked them. "Are you looking for Jack?"

"Yes, ma'am," Vince said, trying to remember his manners. "Is he around?"

"I'm sorry, but he's gone for the rest of the week. He and his father have gone camping. They should be back sometime Saturday."

"Gone all week?" Vince was stunned. "Wow. I had no idea he was planning to be gone."

"Oh, he wasn't planning on it," Steph said. "His father surprised him with it last night at supper. He didn't have time to let you know if that's what you're thinking. So, like I said, he'll be home on Saturday afternoon, okay?"

82

"Okay," Vince said. "Thanks." He turned and walked down the steps to where Blake was waiting. "Did you hear that?" he asked as they left the yard.

"What?"

"He went camping until Saturday."

"Nice of him to tell us," Blake snarked.

"His stepmom said he didn't know about it until after supper last night. His dad surprised him with it." He snapped his fingers. "You know what? I bet they're gonna go fishing, too, and his dad's gonna catch him for that broken pole! Oohhhh, Jack's gonna catch heck for that!" Vince started cackling with laughter. "Wish I could be a fly on the wall to see that!"

Blake grunted. "Yeah, but I wanted to hit Whitman's again, and he's been the perfect cover there. Old man Whitty hasn't caught us since Jack's been here. So, what are we gonna do while he's gone? I gotta stay away from Pop this week. He's got that look in his eyes again, and I can't take him when he's like this, Vinnie."

Vince nodded knowingly. Blake's dad was not a nice man, and sometimes he was a completely rotten apple. Vince's own home life was nothing to brag about, but it was better than Blake's. "You know what we should do, Blake?"

"No, I don't, idiot. That's why I asked you for ideas, Vinnie." He punched his friend in the arm. "What do I need to do, put it on a billboard?"

"All right, cool down, Blake. I have an idea. Let's do our own camping trip!" Vince said.

"That's your big idea, Vinnie? Gimme a break." Blake wasn't impressed.

"No, listen to me, Blake. You've got a sleeping bag, and so do I. I have a two-man tent I got for Christmas we can use. We go to Whitman's and get some food, even buying some of it if necessary. All we need to do is find a place to put the tent! We camp out, it keeps you away from your Pop, and it's something different from what we've done all summer. Whaddya say, bud?" Vince urged Blake. He wasn't the dominant one very often in suggesting ideas; Blake usually ran the show, but Vinnie really wanted his way this time, so he reached out and touched his friend's arm. "Come on, Blake, please?"

Blake was startled by Vince's touch, and he jumped a little. "Oh, sorry, Vinnie, I kinda spaced out there for a second. Yeah, sure, that sounds like a great idea! I'll grab my sleeping bag and pillow and meet you at the fort in half an hour. Say, why don't we set up camp there? Is that big enough for the tent?"

"Good idea! Yeah, I think that'll work. All right. I'll get my camp stuff and meet you there. I think I've got enough food for today, so we can go to Whitman's tomorrow. Sound good to you? Okay, see you in about 45 minutes. I know you can be ready sooner, but getting all my gear together will take me a little longer." Vince and Blake parted ways. Vince was excited to set up their camping site, especially because he'd never used his new tent.

In the end, it took Vinnie about an hour to get his stuff together and out to the fort. He was puzzled that Blake wasn't there, but he got to work setting up his tent. He got it put up and rolled out his sleeping bag inside, realizing that a two-man tent really didn't have much spare space. It's a good thing we're not full-sized men yet, he chuckled to himself. That would really be a tight squeeze.

He had also brought a tarpaulin he'd found in the garage. It had been used to cover the house roof when it was being re-shingled a few years ago, so he knew it didn't have holes in it. He thought that he should drape it from one side of the fort to the other to protect them from the rain, or to give them shade from too much sun. *How weird is it that I'm kind of playing house? You're not playing house, idiot. You're camping. This is what people do when they're camping. Stop overthinking everything, Vinnie. For goodness' sake, Blake will start calling you a fruitcake. Speaking of Blake, where is he?*

Just as Vince began to worry about his friend, Blake showed up. He had his sleeping bag and pillow, but he also had a black eye and a bloody nose, and he was limping slightly.

"OH MY GOD! WHAT HAPPENED?" Vince was shocked at the sight of Blake's face. He hadn't seen him look like this since…"WHAT DID *HE* DO?" He was so angry he didn't realize he was shouting.

Blake collapsed against Vince, crying. "H-he w-was d-drinking," he sniffled, "and when I… w-went in the house to g-get my stuff," he sniffled and panted, "h-he grab-grabbed me and t-told me that I-I wasn't going anyw-anywhere." Blake sniffled, trying to catch his breath.

Vince held him upright, gently holding his arm around Blake's back to soothe his friend, who continued, "I got away from h-him and got my stuff, b-but when I got outside, h-he was w-waiting for me in the garage. H-he h-hit me in the face w-with my baseball bat, Vinnie! H-he told me that 'no son of h-his was gonna be a qu**r and allowed to live.' And h-he told me to f*** off. Before I c-could leave, he h-hit me on my b-behind w-with the b-bat... ." Blake dissolved into sobs as he told of the pain inflicted by his old man.

Vince was horrified that the drunk jerk hole would speak like that to his son or that he'd raise his hand against his boy in that way. Vince had been paddled a time or two at home, but never with a bat, and certainly never at the hands of someone in a blind, drunken rage.

His friend was mean to Vince sometimes, but he knew that Blake wasn't appropriately loved at home. Vince gently led Blake into the tent to lie down on the sleeping bag, while he set up Blake's gear. Then he started a fire in the rock-lined pit they'd made earlier in the summer. He didn't have a lot of food with him for their first night, but he was sure Blake needed to eat something, and he had some water in a Thermos. He also had half a bottle of Jack Daniels he'd stolen from the house. A little of that might help Blake calm down and sleep better, or he might not want it, given how his dad was such a drunk. He shrugged his shoulders; he could offer it to Blake and let his friend makes his own choices.

Blake drank most of the JD, and then crawled into his sleeping bag and went to sleep. Vinnie stayed up until the fire went out, and then he snuggled into his bedroll. He wondered if Jack was having a better start to his camping trip than they were, but then he realized that if he hadn't suggested this trip, then Blake wouldn't have had a place to go when his dad went crazy today.

It was Vince's turn to cry, but only a little. He was sad for Blake. He rolled over in his sleeping bag until he was closer to his friend, who finally looked peaceful after such a horrible day. As he dozed off, he almost thought that Blake reached out and hugged him?

The sun rose early the next morning over the tarp-covered structure where Blake was the first to stir from his whiskey-induced slumber. It took him a few moments to remember where he was, and once he recalled that, he wondered why he was sleeping so close to the person next to him. *Was it that cold last night? Why am I hugging him? HIM?!* With that realization, Blake rolled over twice in the opposite direction, slamming into the side of the tent, which woke up Vince.

"What's going on?" Vince mumbled groggily. "Is someone trying to get into the tent? Go away! Go away, bear!" he called, sleepily. "Blake? Are you okay? How's your face?"

"W-hat? Oh. That." Blake finally remembered yesterday. "It hurts a little, but I'm fine. Really. No one's trying to get in Vinnie. I just rolled over and hit the side of the tent. Sorry." He wasn't sure what else to say.

What else can I say? "I woke up with my arms around you and I didn't want you to think I'm weird?" Nope. *Not gonna say that.*

Vinnie suddenly started laughing. "It's a good thing Jack wasn't here last night."

Blake's stomach tightened. "Why not?"

"You're always talking about him having a boyfriend, but you were the one with an arm around me last night, Blake." Vince couldn't stop giggling. "Not that you were being weird," he added hastily when he saw the look on Blake's face. "You were tired, in pain, and just needed a friend," Vince said seriously. "I'm glad I could be here for you. Really."

Blake hoped he could trust Vinnie to keep his mouth shut about it. He didn't need anyone else in his life making jokes about who he liked or didn't like, and he especially didn't want Jack to know about last night's breakdown. "Listen, Vinnie, I hope what happened yesterday stays between us. About my dad and me, I mean. It don't need to be anybody else's business, ok?"

The look in his friend's eye told Vince that Blake meant business about that. They'd known each other long enough for Vince to know better than to argue with him about it. He nodded. "Okay, Blake, but-"

"No buts, Vince. I don't need Jack or your parents or anybody else shoving their nose where it don't belong, got it?"

"Got it, Blake."

"Good. Now, what's for breakfast? I'm starving." Blake's comment about breakfast was met with awkward silence. "Vinnie?" he prompted.

"Um, er, well? I didn't exactly prepare breakfast food, to be honest with you. I was so busy getting the camping gear itself, I went light on the food." Vince cringed as he said it, expecting Blake to blow up at him.

"Light on the food? Aw, man, I'm so fu-friggin' hungry!" Blake whined. "What do you have?

"Uh, I have the makings for s'mores!"

"S'mores sound good. Let's get a fire going." Blake's face lit up. "You just did yourself proud, Vinnie! I love s'mores."

Vince worked on starting a fire while Blake looked for a suitable spot to relieve himself. *For all the time we've spent out here, we've never bothered to make a good latrine. We oughtta fix that.* "Hey Vin, did you bring a shovel?"

"Yeah, why, Blake?"

"We need to make a proper latrine out here, man. We've been using this spot as a fort for what, two years? And we haven't had anything to go in! We always have to go running home to drop a dookey. I'm not saying I wanna get in the habit of taking a crap in the woods, but it'd be nice not to worry about choosing the wrong leaf, if you know what I mean. I bet we could figure this out, couldn't we?"

"No doubt, Blake, but do we hafta talk about it while I'm making s'mores?" Vince started laughing. "I mean, what a visual, dude! Melty chocolate and marshmallows. Wet bird poo or something? Mmmm, yum!"

"You're a sick dude, you know that, Vince Jackson? One sick, hilarious dude."

They laughed as they roasted their marshmallows and made their sugary breakfast treats. Vince was happy to see Blake happy, even though his friend's face was still looking rough from the beating his father gave him yesterday. He tried not to let his anger at Blake's dad show on his face. Vince pushed that from his mind. "Blake? What do you want to do today, bud?"

"Why don't we go to Whitman's?" Blake suggested.

Vince hesitated to agree. "Uh, you sure?"

"Of course I'm sure... oh, yeah, my face... and my... I don't feel like riding my bike..." his voice trailed off. "You got any ideas?"

"I was thinking we could go fishing. We don't have to think about Jacko the Whacko not having a fishing pole or whining about his dad's rod." It was rare for Vince to pick on Jack, but he was feeling irritated by everyone that had caused trouble in his friendship with Blake, and that included Jack.

"Jacko the Whacko?" Blake laughed. "That's a new one. And a good one! I might have to use that one, Vin. You crack-o me up, bud," he chuckled at his own joke. "I like your idea, too. Hey, you never know. We might even catch a fish or two we could eat for supper tonight. Can you imagine that? Cooking fish over our own fire out here? Man, that'd be great!"

Out of nowhere, tears sprang into Vince's eyes. "What's going on, Vin?" Blake was shocked.

"I, I dunno, Blake. I guess I'm just so glad that you're happy. You've been through so much crap, and yet you're happy and excited, and it just made me happy, and for some reason—who knows why—I'm just a sentimental mother-f***ing screw up, I guess..."

His voice trailed off as Blake interjected, *"VINCE! LANGUAGE!"* and they both fell to the ground, doubled over in laughter.

"Frick you, Blake!"

"No, frick you, Vince!"

"I don't think I've laughed," Blake wheezed and gasped, holding his stomach, "that hard in years!"

"Me, neither" squeaked Vince, checking his shorts. "I thought I wet myself!" He sucked in a breath and giggled. "But I just sat on something damp!" The two teens lay on the ground, trying to catch their breath from laughing, and cracking up again, until both sighed with exhaustion.

At last, Blake sat up. "Well, come on, Vinnie, if we don't get started soon, we might as well scrap the whole plan. Let's get fishing rods in hand and get to work."

11: Peter Cautions Andy

A few days later, I was home again, hanging out with Vince and Blake at the fort. "How was your camping trip, Jack?" Vince asked. "Just you and your dad, huh?"

"It was great! It was Dad and me and my friend Andy. Don't roll your eyes, Blake. He was really a lot of fun to hang out with. What did you guys do?"

"We camped here at the fort. Went fishing, a little swimming. It was too cold for that; it almost froze our privates off. Had s'mores. Generally, it was cool. I'm glad you had a good time with your old man and your friend, Jack," Vince said. "Since we didn't know you would be gone, we made do."

"Speaking of fishing, Jacko," Blake snickered, "how did your dad react to his broken rod?"

I shrugged. "He knew about it already."

"He what??" Blake gasped. "So, what happened?"

"He discovered the break a few months ago and waited to see if I'd confess to it. When he announced the camping trip, I got so nervous about it, I did just that."

"Oh, I bet he was ticked! He musta grabbed his belt and gone a good round on ya then, huh, Jack!" Blake said sympathetically.

"Actually, he wasn't mad at all," I said, looking at Blake. "Yeah, I was surprised, too. All that sneaking around and worrying about his reaction, and he didn't blow up? Not expecting that. He wasn't mad, he said; just disappointed. I was so shocked by his response that I apologized and asked him to forgive me."

"And did he?" Vince asked.

I nodded. "Dad has never talked to me like that before that I can remember. He's different than he used to be."

"Different how? Whaddya mean by that?" Vince said.

"Well, he used to get really worked up about stuff like that, and if he talked to me about something I did wrong, all I wanted to do was crawl into a hole in the ground and bury myself there. He always made me feel like crap. But this time, I dunno. I guess I felt 'clean' after we talked. It was over and done with, and we moved on to the next thing. And on the trip, he taught me how to make a fishing pole with regular fishing line and just a stick from the woods. We used them, and they actually worked! We made s'mores, and went on a hike, and Andy read from his Bible and prayed, and stuff, and it was cool."

"Wait, wait, wait," Blake said. "Andy reads the Bible and prays? Like, to God? And you found that cool?" he rolled his eyes so hard I thought they'd turn all the way around in his head.

"What's wrong with that?"

"The Bible's for sissies, Jacko!" Blake retorted. "I didn't take you for a sissy!"

"Blake," Vince said in a warning voice.

"Don't you start, Vinnie," Blake warned back. "Not another word."

"You know something, Blake?" I said in resignation. "I'm beginning to wonder why I hang out with you."

"You and me both, Jacko."

Content Warning

In the town of Nolan, Peter Madison greeted Andy when he returned from his trip with the Bannisters. "How was camping, son? Phew!" he said, waving his hand in front of his face. "If your aroma is anything to go by, I'd say it must've been an active time! Before you tell me about it, why don't you take a shower and put your dirty clothes in the washer? Then your mother and I want to hear all about it." Andy's father chuckled as he sent his son into the house.

Grinning, Andy went inside. He hadn't bathed or showered while on the trip, but since Joe and Jack hadn't either, he didn't realize that they all stank. *It stands to reason that we do, though. All that tramping through the woods, sweating, hiking, fishing...no wonder Dad had that reaction!* He got to the bathroom, stripped down, and stepped into the shower. As the hot water poured over his body, he was amazed how much grime he scrubbed away with the soap and shampoo.

When he was clean and dry, and his dirty laundry had walked to the washer on its own—it seemed like it could have!—Andy went to the dining room to find his parents. The room was large enough to have a table that seated the whole family, plus held a couch and two other chairs. His dad was in a rocking chair and his mom was on the couch. He joined her there, reaching over to hug her.

"Oh, you're nice and clean, Andy!" she said. "Your father told me how stinky you were when you got home, and I'm so glad you showered before hugging me!" she snickered. "Really, son, I'm glad you're home. Please tell us about your trip!" she squeezed him in a tight side hug and kissed his head.

"It was a great trip. Thanks for letting me go," Andy began. "Mr. Bannister was really kind and patient with me when I got nervous about something, and he taught me so much about being out in creation. I learned about hiking, fishing, conservation, and things like that. He didn't rush me into activities I wasn't ready to do, and that won me over to trying everything he and Jack seemed eager to do. They've clearly done this stuff before, even though Jack told me it's been ages since they went camping together. I think he really appreciated his dad on this trip, too."

Peter and Sarah Madison smiled widely as Andy talked about the trip. They'd worried a little about how he'd do in the great outdoors since it wasn't something he took to naturally when he was at home. They were also glad that their son's friend and his father had been so encouraging and helpful to Andy when he hesitated to participate in doing what was so natural for themselves.

They had heard from Joe Bannister by phone a few hours earlier; he'd called during a bathroom stop just so they'd know the trip was coming to an end and what time they could expect Andy to be home. Joe wanted them to know how everything had gone and to be aware of some elements that he found particularly impressive but didn't want to bring up in front of the boys.

"I'm glad it was so interesting, and I'm proud of you for trying new things, Andy," his father said. "What else stood out for you?"

"Well, I was impressed by how Jack showed real respect to his father. I've never seen him do that. He's always been a little disrespectful to him when I've been around them, but on this trip, Jack was different, at least some of the time. His dad treated him differently, too. He used to be kind of short-tempered with Jack, but he was very patient with him. That stood out for me. It seems that God's been working on Mr. Bannister. He said so, and I could see it."

Sarah looked at her son keenly. "Andy Madison, that is very insightful. Where did you come up with that?" Her lighthearted tone was gone, replaced with a thoughtful look and serious sound in her voice.

Andy shrugged. "I dunno, Mom. It's just what I've been seeing and hearing. I mean, that's what's going on, isn't it? Am I saying it wrong?"

"No, son, you're not saying it wrong," Sarah said quickly. "It's just that I'm not used to hearing such serious comments from someone your age, especially when I know that you're right. But go on. Was there anything else?"

"Well," Andy hesitated. "The evening after we went fishing, I asked Mr. Bannister if I could read from my Bible."

"And did you?" Peter asked him.

"Yes, Dad. I from Matthew 11. Jack asked about being yoked, so I explained it using the example of the ox yoke we saw on a school trip last year, and what you've told me before about how Jesus yokes us with him to learn to walk in step with his ways. Then his dad asked me to pray, so I did that, too. We did the same thing after the hike the next day, except that Jack had a lot more questions about my reading that time.

"It was from James 1 about being slow to get angry because our anger doesn't accomplish what God wants, and not just hearing God's Word but acting on it.

"We had a long discussion about this, and I think we could have talked all night, but his dad said the conversation would have to continue another time because he needed to sleep so he could drive home today. It was so hard to stop, 'cause Jack was really into it, and this morning he was back to acting like he doesn't care. So, yeah, these were the real highlights of the trip for me. The camping, sleeping under the stars, fishing with my own handmade fishing pole, cleaning and eating my catch, hiking—all that was great—but talking about God's love, mercy, and grace with my best friend and his dad was the best part of the trip." Andy sat back on the couch and sighed happily.

"I'm so happy for you, Andy," his mother said, patting his knee.

"So am I, son," said Peter. "The Lord blessed you in so many ways, and it sounds like you were a good steward of the time with them. Let's pray for your friend now."

"*Father, thank you for the camping trip Andy had with the Bannisters. Thank you for their kindness and generosity toward him, and for the times of Bible reading and discussion they had together. We pray that Jack would keep listening to you and trust you. In Jesus' Name, Amen.*"

"Amen!" Sarah and Andy echoed.

As they stood up from their seats, Andy's father put his hand on the boy's shoulder. When Andy looked up at him, Peter said, "I'm glad your trip went well, son. We know from Isaiah 55 that the Word accomplishes God's purposes, so we trust Him to do that now. However, Andy, a word of caution for you: Jack is being influenced very heavily by his neighborhood peers, and because he sees them more often than he sees you, he may start resisting your friendship if you preach at him. He is going to need your friendship, Andy. Be sure to stay his friend. He knows where God is. All right?"

"All right, Dad. Thanks for that. It's good to be reminded that the seed planting is something I can do, but making it grow is up to God."

"Good lad. Now, there's firewood to move into the basement before supper, so put your gear away and meet me outside in ten minutes. There's something else we need to talk about after supper, but it can wait until then."

"Yes, Dad." Andy did as he was told, though he sorely wanted to just hang out till supper time. It had already been a long day, and happy as he was, he was also sleepy. Still, chores had to be done, and obedience was expected. He wondered briefly what the other issue was that they had to talk about, but soon forgot as they got to work stacking firewood.

After supper, once the plates had been cleared from the dinner table, Sarah said, "Andy, your father and I need to talk to you about something." Her voice was pleasant, so Andy wasn't worried about being in trouble, but he still wondered what could be going on.

"Okay. I'll be right there," he answered. Once again, they sat in the dining room in the comfortable seats. This time, though, he sat in a chair facing each of his parents. "What's going on?"

"Well, Andy," Peter began, "your mother and I know that last school year was very hard on you in many ways. For example, we are aware of how difficult your teacher was to deal with, and that you were not treated well by her nor by several of your classmates. We realize that your friendship with Jack really helped you a lot, and that some of your other classmates are good friends, too, but we haven't been very pleased with your overall experience there for quite some time."

"You knew she was terrible? I thought you had no clue about that!" Andy was astonished that they'd noticed.

"Well, yes, Andy," said Sarah. "Don't you remember me telling you to hide your extra dessert item before she checked your lunch so she wouldn't take it from you? I wrote notes telling her that she had no business taking things that I gave you, but she wouldn't listen. The school administration wouldn't listen, either, so that's why I told you to do that. It's all I could come up with as a solution."

The light bulb went on for Andy. "Wow, Mom, I had no idea!" The more he thought about it, the angrier it made him. "You mean that you and Dad talked to the principal about her, and even he wouldn't help?"

"The biblical approach, Andy, is to go to the person with whom you have the problem, and if no resolution is reached, then go again with a third party—someone uninvolved. We tried both of those solutions, but we got nowhere," his father said. "You've had some good teachers, but we have reached a point where we don't like how that school operates. As a result of that, and because we want you to have a better option for middle school, we are helping to open another Christian school this fall, and your mother will be one of the teachers there."

Sarah took up the narrative. "Now, Andy. We know you have friends where you are now, and we don't want you to feel pressured, but–"

He cut her off. "I want to go to the new school!"

"What about Jack and your other friends?"

"I'll find other ways to see them. I want to go to the new school! Please?"

Sarah looked at her husband. He nodded. "All right, then. We weren't sure you'd want to make the change, Andy. It's a big switch. It means you won't have that seventh-grade teacher you were looking forward to at City Christian."

Andy's shoulders drooped. "Yeah, I know. But I'll be in a better environment, and you'll be there!" his excitement returned. "Oh, wait. Is this going to be more expensive for our family?" He knew how the tuition for Christian school made the bills tough to pay sometimes.

Peter answered the question. "No, son. In fact, since your mother will be teaching there, your tuition will be free, so this will reduce our expenses." He smiled. "But we weren't going to tell you that unless you decided to attend there, because we didn't want it to influence your decision."

"Wow, what a week this has been. Camping, fishing, and now finding out about starting at a new school! What's it going to be called? Is anyone I know going to it?"

"It's going to be called 'County Christian School.' Some of your church friends will be there," his mother said. "And until the start of school, you will be helping to get the building ready. There's a lot of cleaning and painting to do. For now, though, you can read or watch a little TV before you go to bed. We have church in the morning. Love you, son."

"Love you, too. Good night."

12: I Prove Myself to the Gang

We were at the fort, and Blake had decided it was time for me to put up or shut up in the neighborhood gang. He and Vince had been doing the heavy lifting to maintain the reputation of our gang, he reasoned, while I had ridden their coattails since I'd arrived on scene. In fact, I couldn't seem to decide if I was with them or with Andy, "the punk" from the town of Nolan. The free ride was over. At least, that's how Blake explained it to me.

"You know what, Jack?"

"No, what, Blake?"

"It's time for you to step up and decide if you're really with us or with Andy."

"What do you mean by that?"

"I mean that it's time for you to show Vinnie and me that we count in your life or not. Are we really your friends, or are we just safety blankets you come hang onto when Andy's not available?"

"That's ridiculous, Blake! Of course you guys are my friends! You're the first friends I made when I moved here. If it weren't for my stepmom's job, I'd be in school with you

100

guys, and I wouldn't even know Andy. Geez, what's gotten into you?"

"All right, Jack, if you're really part of this gang of friends, then I'm going to challenge you to prove it. Step up and complete the challenge, and there'll be no more talk of you being some candy-assed pussy willow. Fail, and you're out of the gang. Deal?"

"Deal! What's the challenge?"

"Vinnie will fill you in on that. We gotta meet him at Whitman's. Let's go."

Twenty minutes later, Blake and I arrived at the grassy bank across from the corner store. With a nod from Blake, Vince pulled me onto the grass under the maple tree and spoke to me in a low voice.

"We go in and you come out with a pack of baseball cards and a chocolate bar."

"I don't have any money, Vinnie."

"That's your challenge. Don't get caught."

As we entered the store, Mr. Whitman greeted us as always. This time, however, he clearly glared at Blake and Vince, while speaking kindly to me. "Good morning. Beautiful day. School must be starting soon?" When I nodded, Mr. Whitman motioned for me to come closer. "Those two are no-good shoplifters, kid," he muttered. "I just know it. Can't ever catch 'em, but someday I will. You shouldn't hang out with them. You're better off with that Madison kid."

I squirmed to get away from the shopkeeper. I didn't want to hear about Andy; I had to figure out how to sneak out with the cards and candy bar, and I didn't need someone bringing up the do-gooder just now! Oh, there's my chance; Blake and Vinnie created a distraction.

My friends had started an argument at the cash register over which flavor of Hubba Bubba bubblegum was the best, so I managed to put a pack of cards in one pocket and a candy bar in the other before slipping out the door. When I got to my bike, I got on and moved away from sight of the store and waited for my friends. They came out a couple of minutes later, hopped on their bicycles, and rode toward home. I followed them, and when we had gone far enough to be out of earshot of Whitman's, they stopped and turned to me.

"Well?" said Vinnie. "What did you get?"

I pulled out the baseball cards and chocolate bar.

Blake snatched them from me. "The candy bar's mine, and the cards are yours, Vinnie."

"What? I'm the one that lifted 'em," I protested.

"That's right, Jacko," Blake said. "And we're the ones that witnessed you breaking the law."

"You're in our pockets now, kid," Vinnie laughed.

I didn't like the sound of Vinnie's laugh. Did he really mean what he said about being 'in their pockets'? "Oh, like I haven't seen you come out of there with stolen goods," I asserted.

"But have you ever *seen* us steal things, Jack?" Vinnie challenged me. "No, you haven't. We *saw* you do it. You just keep that in mind the next time you start feeling all 'religious' and 'repentant,' all right?"

"Back off, Vin," Blake interjected. "Jack did a good job. He passed the test! Jack, we're just giving you a hard time, buddy. We wanted to see if you could be slick enough to get away with it, too, and you did. So, next time, no big friggin' deal, right? Good. Of course, if you wanna keep paying the man sometimes to keep him from suspecting you, go right ahead, but don't be afraid to take something every now and then, just for practice."

"All right, Blake. I'm just not used to Vinnie being the jerk, you know? Usually you play bad cop and he does the good cop routine, y'know? You two have switched it up on me today, and it's making my head spin. C'mon, let's get home. What are we gonna do this afternoon?"

"Well, fellas, I've got a treat for both of you. Pop's out of town today, and he left a couple of his magazines we can look at and a tape we can watch. It's your rare chance to come to mine. Whaddya say?"

Blake seemed almost giddy with anticipation. Vince and I knew that going to the Harris home never happened when his dad was there, so we both agreed to go. I thought the tape was the latest Superman movie or something, but that's where I got an education, along with the magazines. They weren't *Newsweek* or *Sports Illustrated*, either.

We got to Blake's house and went inside. I'd never been there, and I guess I wasn't sure what I expected, but it was clean and tidy. It was Blake and his old man living there, and maybe someone else, I'm not sure, but I knew that if just my dad and I lived alone, we wouldn't keep the house anywhere near that clean.

Blake told us to leave our shoes by the door—his dad's rule to keep the floors clean—so we did. We went to the living room, withnd chairs were covered in plastic. Blake explained that his dad didn't want anyone spilling anything on the furniture, so they remained covered all the time.

He went to the TV cabinet and looked through the VHS tapes there. "Here it is! I think you'll like this one, guys." He put the tape into the VCR and pressed play. "It'll take a few moments for the video to start, so while the TV warms up and it gets going, if anyone needs the facilities, they're down the hall, first door on the right."

I got up and headed to the bathroom. When I had finished and washed my hands, I heard Vince and Blake laughing, so I hurried back to see what I had missed. "Did I miss anything important?"

"Not yet," Vince reported. "We were just remembering the last time we watched this, and a couple of jokes we made. The storyline of this film is pretty boring, but you'll probably find the action fun to watch." When he said that, he winked. I had no idea why.

A few minutes later, I caught on. I'd never seen anything like it before, but I couldn't take my eyes off the screen. Part of me knew I 'shouldn't' be watching it, but I was seeing things I'd only imagined to that point in my life. I recently noticed girls, but this video showed everything possible, and my hormones responded. I was torn between a burning desire to watch more and the embarrassment of seeing these things for the first time, knowing my friends had watched it before and that my parents *wouldn't* approve.

Content Warning

Then Blake looked up and saw the time. "Oh, crap, it's getting later than I realized. I gotta rewind the tape before Pop gets home so he doesn't know I've been watching it. You two get outta here and I'll meet you at the fort, ok? Hurry up! Move!" His voice was serious and urgent.

We scrambled to our feet, hurried to the door, slipped on our shoes, and headed out. We hid in the trees between his house and mine for a few minutes to see if his dad would come home. Sure enough, about ten minutes later, Mr. Harris drove into the yard. He got out of the car and went into the house. In less than a minute we heard him hollering at Blake, and then we heard a loud smack. "That's it, time to go," muttered Vince. He turned and yanked me away from our hiding place.

As we made our way to the fort, Vince kept growling under his breath. "One of these days, Mr. Harris is gonna pay for what he does to Blake. Somebody is gonna stand up to that bully. He don't deserve that kid. Somebody is gonna give ol' man Harris the kind o' whuppin' he gives his boy, and then he'll know his place!"

I'd never noticed Blake with bruises or anything, so I wasn't sure what Vince was talking about, but I had a weird feeling that this afternoon that was going to change. While Vince and I waited for Blake, we set up the tarp over the fort walls again, securing it in place with ropes we'd brought out for other uses. We moved our stump stools under the tarp and did our best to make the site comfortable. About 40 minutes later, Blake showed up, and I finally realized what a lowlife his old man was.

Blake's face was red and swollen from where his dad had hit him. One eye was shut, with a cut above it along the eyebrow. He wasn't crying, though, which kind of surprised me; I'd be crying if I'd been hurt like that. In fact, it made me sad, because he looked defeated. He walked up to Vince and collapsed against his longtime friend, who caught him in a hug. I stood by and watched helplessly. These two had a bond I knew nothing about, and no matter what I did, I'd never be in their gang, but I also knew I'd never stop trying to prove my worth to them. I joined their hug in silence.

Then I broke away and raced home. When I got there, I asked Steph for a bag of ice and a tea towel to wrap it in. When she asked me what it was for, I told her that one of the guys had fallen and needed ice for a bruise. Thankfully, she agreed to help me without further questions. I was back at the fort within a few minutes and gave the ice to Blake. He looked at me with gratitude with his one good eye and patted me on the back. "Thankth, bud," he mumbled.

"You got it, Blake. I'm in your pocket, remember?" I smiled at him. "I gotta do for you."

13: One Decent Dragon

Content Warning

While waiting for Blake to show up, Vince and I talked about what to do for supper. It was clear that the Jacksons were aware of the situation between Blake and his dad, though why they didn't step in and do something about it puzzled me. I suppose people didn't want to be involved, or maybe they had their own problems. At any rate, Vinnie knew he could at least score some food, maybe PBJs from his mom and a package of cookies and a bag of chips, so after Blake arrived and had settled in, Vin went off to get the food.

All the excitement of the day was gone for me, replaced with uneasy anxiety for my friend and the abuse he got from his dad. I realized how lucky I was to have the father I did, even if our relationship was kind of cold at times. At least he didn't hit me, and he made a point of telling me that he loved me. I began to wonder if Blake had ever heard that from his dad.

"A penny for your thoughts, Jack," he mumbled. "You've been silent since Vin left. You afraid to talk to me?"

I was startled, not realizing how quiet I'd been. "Oh! Sorry, Blake. Noo," I hesitated.

"Well, what is it, then?" After all that had happened today, his patience was a little thin.

"Blake? Has it always been like this for you?"

"You mean, has Pop always used me as his punching bag?" I nodded, and he said, "No. It didn't start until Ma left. When she wasn't around for him to hit anymore, he started hitting me." His voice trailed off, and I could tell there was more to it, but I wasn't sure if I should push the matter.

Then Blake looked me in the eye. "Jack, I'm gonna tell you something only Vinnie knows, and if you ever tell another soul, I'll kill you."

I could tell he meant the last three words, so I held up my fingers like a Boy Scout and said, "Lips sealed, Blake."

He kept his eyes locked on me as he spoke, as if looking anywhere else would make him seem like a liar, but his words and body language showed he was telling the truth. Plus, after what I'd seen today, there was no way I'd doubt him on this.

"Pop doesn't just hit me, Jack. He puts his hands...w-where they don't....no, I'm okay, let me say it! It's gross! It's wrong! It's all wrong, but he's too strong for me, Jack, and there's nowhere for me to go if I run away or if someone calls protective services! It's not all the time, but when he's really drunk and upset, I try to stay outta his way."

He stopped speaking suddenly, and the composure he'd rallied to get through what he wanted to say crumbled. The tough, I-will-do-what-I-want-and-f*ck-what-the-world-thinks-kid I'd come to know was sobbing in my lap. I gently put an arm around his shoulders and sat with him until Vince returned.

"He told you, didn't he?" Vince said quietly as he walked into the fort.

"Yeah. I think he was tired of trying to come up with cover stories." I moved my arm and saw that Blake had dozed off.

"Well, I brought more than food." With that, Vin went outside the fort and pulled in a wagon piled high with camping supplies. "I thought we should be more comfortable." Glancing at Blake and me he added, "I'll get the tent set up for Blake, and then you can help me with the other stuff."

Within ten minutes, we had led a half-sleeping Blake to a spot in the tent and settled him in. Then we went out to tend to the rest of our gear. Vin got a fire going in the pit, while I set up some beach chairs he brought, and put together a makeshift table using our stump stools and planks we didn't use when building the fort. I tied them together with excess rope from the tarp tie-down project and stepped back to admire the finished product. *Pretty crappy table, but it'll do for three preteens in a fort in the woods,* I smiled to myself.

"So, Vin, what did you find for food?"

"Jack, my boy, not only did my old lady make PBJs for us tonight, but she also made some for our breakfast, if we can stand to have such a delicacy two meals in a row!" he chuckled. "On top of the sandwiches, I got a can of Pringles, a box of Twinkies, and once again....drum roll please...."

Blake's muffled voice called from the tent, "The making of s'mores?"

"Bingo! Circle gets the square! The making of s'mores," Vince said. "How're ya feeling, Blake? Care to join us? Mom even gave us a jug of Kool-Aid."

"I'll be right out." His voice sounded sleepy still, but it was good for him to get up and eat. When he stepped out of the tent, he rubbed his good eye and looked at us. "Guess I kinda fell apart today, huh?" His face tinted red with embarrassment.

"Blake?" I said, and he looked up at me, "every one of us has days we 'kinda fall apart.' If we can't handle that with each other, then why are we friends?" Once again, he looked me in the eye. He took the measure of me this time and nodded his agreement.

"Right you are, Jack. Friends it is. For real this time."

"Gosh, would you two get a room or something?" Vince said. "The PBJs are getting warm. Let's eat, already!"

"Stop bi-uh-witching, Vinnie," Blake said.

"Language!" said Vin.

"Oh, screw you, Vinnie," said Blake.

"Screw yourself, Blake."

"No way. Screw Jack!"

"No thanks, fellas! Ehhh... maybe we should skip the screwing and just eat?" I redirected the personal insults to the precious food once again.

We all had a good laugh and dug in. "I have to say it again, Vinnie. Your mom makes great peanut butter and jelly sandwiches. Somehow, she gets the balance of both ingredients so one doesn't overpower the other, and the bread doesn't get soaked through with jelly juice," I said.

"Jelly juice? That's gross!" Blake replied. "I'm gonna puke!" He made a gagging sound in jest.

"Geez, I was just trying to compliment Mrs. Jackson's sandwich-making," I grumbled. The other boys cracked up laughing at me. We finished off the PBJs and reached for the Twinkies.

We'd been laughing, but I could still feel the weight of tension in the air. I considered whether I actually wanted his answer before I looked at Blake again. "Blake, why did you decide to trust me?"

My friend sighed deeply. "Jack, I'm so tired of being worn out by my old man, I don't know how much more I can take. I'm twelve years old, for goodness' sake, and *I'm sick of living*. That's fucked up!" He put his right index up in protest to Vince and said sharply, "Don't say it, Vinnie. Language, I know. But it's true here, okay?" Then Blake took a deep breath and let it out slowly. "I watch porn to prove to myself that I'm attracted to girls, you know? Pop seems to think I like his attention, but I don't. He accuses me of being 'weird,' but *he's the one that's wrong*. I don't wanna grow up to be like him! I can't live with him anymore, but I don't have anywhere else to go!"

He was nearly shouting again and realized his voice could carry further at night, so he quieted down. "Do you think your friend Andy would have any advice for me, Jack? If I apologized to him, do you think he'd be willing to pray for me?" Blake's eyes pleaded as much as his voice.

I was stunned. This changed everything. *Blake wanted to talk to Andy? He wanted Andy to pray for him? What in the world?*

"Jack?" he broke into my thoughts.

"Uh, yeah, Blake, yes. I'm sure Andy would love to talk to you and pray for you."

"Good. Get him here tomorrow." It wasn't a request.

All this time, Vince had been silent, left out of the conversation. It made his mind swirl. *What's Blake doing? What is he talking about, not wanting to live anymore? He can't be serious about that! Oh, wait. I know what's going on. He's gonna trick Jack into bringing that wuss Andy over here so we can teach him a lesson and force Jack to prove once and for all he's with us and not with the wuss. The best part about it,* as far as Vince could see, *is that Jack will reject Andy, but Blake and I won't really accept Jack, either. That will show him! That's an amazing acting job Blake's been putting on. And now Jack is gonna find out that no one comes between Blake and Vin.* He almost laughed at the humiliation Andy and Jack were going to experience and had to fake choking on his Kool-Aid to cover it up.

"Tomorrow?" I said to Blake. "Tomorrow's Sunday. He'll be at church almost all day."

Blake just looked at me. His face somehow was both empty and begging.

"All right. I'll go call now and see if he can come over for the afternoon and stay for a sleepover. That work?"

Blake nodded so I ran to make the phone call.

When I got to the house, I realized I hadn't told Dad and Steph where I'd be, and it took many apologies, pleas for forgiveness, and promises to do better to get what I wanted. Of course, telling them that one of my neighborhood friends wanted to have Andy pray for him and explain the Bible to him helped me, too, even if it stretched the truth.

In fact, I wasn't sure what Blake's motives were. I didn't know if he was putting me on about the abuse just to humiliate me into rejecting Andy, or if all that horrible abuse was real and he truly wanted Andy to pray for him. It's true that I valued my friends and would do almost anything for them—I'd shoplifted earlier today to prove myself to Blake and Vince, for goodness' sake—but part of me was wary of others' motives. I tried to be prepared for unpleasant surprises.

When I called Andy's house, I talked with Mr. Madison. I told him the reason for my request as truthfully as I dared and was relieved when he agreed to it. "I'll bring him over after lunch, Jack. That'll be about two o'clock. I'll make sure he has a pillow, sleeping bag, his Bible, and we'll send along some of Mrs. Madison's baked goods to keep you boys well fed. Good night, Jack."

Before I left my house, I grabbed my own sleeping bag and pillow, and I asked Steph for a snack to share with my friends.

She pulled a bag of bagels from the bread drawer and put them into a cooler with half a stick of margarine

112

and a bag of ice she had made from our ice trays. "This will keep overnight, but not all day. You can get more ice when you pick up Andy tomorrow afternoon, son."

"Thanks, Mo—" I stopped and looked at her. "Thanks." I didn't know what else to say.

"Jack?" She was speaking again. "Is one of those boys in trouble of some kind?" Her voice wasn't accusing; it was compassionate.

I bit my lip. "He got hurt. I... I promised I wouldn't say more, okay? He doesn't need a doctor or anything. I hope. We'll just hang out at the fort for a couple of days, k?"

"Okay, honey. You know you can talk to me if you need to, right?" She reached out and pulled me into a tight hug. "I love you, Jack Bannister. Just as much as if ..." and she let it go. I got the message.

For the first time, I hugged her back. A little. Dragons aren't always bad.

14: "God Doesn't Care"

Vince was glad to see the back of Jack until he saw Blake's face. Nothing had changed on it. There was no evil gleam, no sinister twinkle in his eye, nothing of his usual indicators to clue in Vince that all of this had been a ruse to fool Jack. Vince knew that Pop Harris was cruel and unusual in his punishments at times, including the occasional inappropriate behavior, but Vince had been inappropriately touched, too, and he hadn't made a scene about it. *You just dust yourself off and move on. Nobody's gonna believe you, anyway. They're gonna say you wanted it, and that you asked for it, so you just don't give anyone control over you anymore or you find someone who can protect you, like Blake has protected me.*

"Blake, what's gotten into you?"

"What do you mean, Vince?"

"I dunno. I guess I expected this to be some kind of trick you were playing on Bannister and Madison, and you were going to fill me in as soon as he was gone. I mean, don't you want to humiliate his arrogant butt and his wuss friend, too?"

"You know something, Vince? Yeah, I've wanted to do that for a long time. I've wanted to find some way to get Andy MadHatter and Jacko BanTheStare in the same place, at the same time, and tell them that Blake-F**king-Harris says that they can take their perfect-f**king-families and shove them right the hell up their perfect-f**king-backsides!"

Vince didn't know if he was more amused or shocked by Blake's outburst. His jaw went slack.

"But when it comes right down to it, Vinnie, Jacko the Whacko proved himself to us today without batting an eye, and still wouldn't throw the other kid under the bus. Do you really think we can force him to reject Andy over us? You and I—correct that—*I* busted up Andy Madison last year, and Jack stood by me. Hell, if that's not friendship and loyalty, then I don't know what it is.

"And here, Vin, is the ultimate kicker. Andy *forgave him* for what *we* did. Andy stayed friends with *him* even though *he* stayed friends with the kid that beat him up! Who-the-f*** does that? And *why*? My existence is so damned f***ed up right now, Vinnie, I need some answers.

114

It seems to me that this Andy kid might have some. I know you're freaked out by this, Vin, but honest to God, I don't know how much longer I can take this crap. I ain't kidding, Vinnie. Either I get some answers, or this is the end of the road for me."

It didn't happen much, but Vince was completely at a loss for words. *This was the opposite of what I'd expected. There was no way, no way! Blake wants to talk to the religious kid? Dang, I have some of those nut jobs in my own family. I know exactly what he's gonna say, but I'll hold my tongue for now.* He shook his head. What a surprise. Not how he saw this day playing out at all.

The last thing Jack grabbed on his way out of the house on Saturday night was his watch. He almost never wore it anymore, but he knew he ought to have it with him at the fort to know when to meet Andy Sunday afternoon. When he got back there, Vince looked miserable, which was actually pretty rare for him. Blake, on the other hand, was eager for Jack's arrival.

"So? Is he coming?"

"Yup, but not till tomorrow afternoon. He'll be here around 2."

"What did he say when you talked to him?" sneered Vince. "I bet he was scared to come here."

"I didn't talk to him, to be honest. He'd already gone to bed. He has an early bedtime on Saturdays so he can be wide awake for church and Sunday school." Jack heard the taunt in Vince's voice and wondered if his cynical suspicions were correct. "I talked to his dad, who was more than willing to let Andy come here tomorrow and spend the night."

"Ha ha ha ha... letting his kid walk into the lion's den!" scoffed Vince. "Some dad he is."

"Aw, shut it, Vince," Blake turned on him. "I told you, that's not what's going on with this. I really want to hear what Andy has to say. I might find him personally annoying and stuck up, but something in his life seems to be going better than mine, and I wanna find out what that is and why. I'd rather have you here, but if you can't keep your trap shut and deal with it, then go home!"

"S-sorry, Blake. I d-didn't mean anything by it." Vince was shocked by the intensity rolling off his lifelong friend. "I'll behave," he added meekly.

"Good, Vin. I need you. I need both of you," Blake said, looking at Jack, too. Shifting the attention away from himself he said, "What's in the cooler?"

"Oh, my Mo—, I mean, stepmom sent some food for breakfast tomorrow and some ice," I said, noting that it was the second time tonight I'd slipped up in what I called her.

"Dude! You called her your 'Mom'!" Vince blurted out. "What's up with that?"

Blake nodded. "I gotta agree with Vinnie on this, Jack. What's going on there? You've been calling her 'the Dragon' since we met."

I sighed. "I don't know, guys. Maybe it's that she's pregnant with my little brother or sister and it would be weird for me to call her something different than they will. Or maybe she's just growing on me. She certainly takes care of me as best as she can. No, really, she tries, anyway," I added at the end when they started protesting my positive commentary on Steph. I guess I've complained about her so much that it's hard for them to see her in a positive way.

"Maybe Blake isn't the only one seeing family relationships in a different light lately," I said. "He's facing crap like never before, while I'm seeing less crap in my family than I have in several years. Not that God won't mess that up at some point. He doesn't seem to be on my side."

"Wait, wait, wait," said Blake. "You mean you don't believe like Andy does? I thought you liked all his Bible talk and prayer sh—I mean, stuff—on the camping trip. Care to explain this, Jack?"

"Okay, yeah. On the camping trip, it was cool to listen to Andy talk about the Bible and stuff. It was cool because he's my age, our age, and knows so much about it, and can make it understandable, but it doesn't change the fact that my real mom trusted in God and still died because a drunk driver hit her. What was God doing when that happened? Didn't he care about her then? Did he care about me or my dad? Why would God do that to us? Dad loved God, and God took his wife away. My mom taught me to trust in God, and where did it get me? She told me I could trust God because he would never let me down, but then he took the most precious person in my life away from me! How could I trust him after that? So, yeah, listening to Andy was cool, and he has some great answers from the Bible, but I just don't see how God *actually* cares about me."

"So why do you think I should listen to Andy?"

"I dunno, Blake. Maybe it'll make sense to you."

15: Don't Trust Him!

Before they left for church Sunday morning, Peter told Andy about Jack's phone call the previous night. "It was after you'd gone to bed, and since I thought you would say yes to the opportunity, I said you could go. It means you'll miss the evening service at church tonight, but this is a rare chance to share God's love with some kids that don't usually go looking for it, and I think the Lord is at work here. We'll talk more before you go."

When the Madisons got home from church, they set about preparing lunch. Sarah and Peter went to their room to talk about Andy's sleepover. Peter spoke first. "I told the pastor what's going on and he agreed to pray for Andy at home this afternoon and at church this evening."

"I'm glad," his wife said. "I'm also wondering if we could have a backup plan in place?"

"What do you have in mind, Sarah?"

"Do you think David would be willing to go to the Bannisters this afternoon and do some chores around their house for them, just to be close by in case he's needed?" Seeing the look on Peter's face, she quickly clarified, "I don't mean that he'll be needed to break up a fight, Peter. I'm thinking that Andy might want his help explaining parts of the Bible. Besides that, there's something that I've found out about David and the Harris boy that you may not be aware of."

Peter Madison was suddenly alarmed. "What's that?"

"After the Harris boy attacked Andy last year, David got ahold of his phone number and called him. He apparently threatened to 'teach Harris a lesson he'd never forget' if Harris ever touched Andy again. I don't think Andy's in any physical danger going to Jack's today, but if David were on hand and some reconciliations were taking

118

place, might it not be a great opportunity for David to be reconciled to young Harris, too?"

Her husband smiled at her wisdom and drew her in for a kiss. "You are a true Proverbs 31 wife, my dear! I wasn't aware of David's protective actions regarding Andy, although I can't say I'm surprised by them. He's been his little brother's fierce guardian since day one. Still, an opportunity for reconciliation and forgiveness is not to be overlooked. And just in case this turns out to be a ruse to humiliate Andy in some way, it would be good for David to be nearby for moral support. I'll call Joe Bannister and see if this would work for them."

A few minutes later, Peter gave his wife a thumbs up. She went to David's room and talked with him. He agreed to their plan with relief; he'd been concerned about sending his little brother into 'the lions' den', as he called it, without assistance close by. And he was happy to help the Bannisters put in some firewood for the coming winter.

After lunch, when Andy's gear was ready to go and Sarah had provided some biscuits and cookies for the campers, his parents sat down in the dining room with him and David. Their dad said, "Andy, I'm glad you have this time to see Jack and his friends. We will be praying for you at home this afternoon because this will be a time of spiritual warfare. The Enemy will be trying hard to prevent Jack and the others from hearing the gospel, and only prayer can succeed in that battle. If you feel that you are pressing too hard, then stop and let the Holy Spirit do his work. It's not up to you to convert them; it's up to you to speak and do the Word of God. Remember James 1: Be a doer and not just a hearer."

"Now, it's possible that you're being invited over to be humiliated by Jack's friends, and that they're going to try to force him to reject friendship with you. We have no idea what their true intentions are, son. But God knows, and 'greater is he that is in you than he that is in the world.' Whatever *their* purpose, God's purpose is that you glorify him and enjoy him forever, Andy. We pray that you will do that today with Jack and his friends."

"Yes, Dad."

"All right, then. Your brother is going to drive you there. He'll be helping Mr. Bannister with some chores for several hours. If you need him, just send Jack to get him. Have a good time, son." With that, Andy hugged his parents and left.

The boys at the fort had had a long Saturday, and eventually they called it a night and headed to their bedrolls. Jack let the other two have the tent, and he stayed on the ground nearby. They used their makeshift table as a door to the fort for protection against creeping things, and all three were sound asleep shortly thereafter.

Thanks to the tree cover and the tarp, the sun rose without disturbing their slumber, and it was well after 8:00 before any of them stirred. Once they were up, though, they noticed their hunger. Following a brief discussion of their food situation, Vince suggested they keep the extra PBJs he had brought for lunch, and try grilling the bagels over a fire, instead. The others liked the idea, so he got a fire started while they tidied up the camp, reset the table, and took care of other morning business.

Suddenly Jack smacked himself in the face. "I'm such an idiot! No comments from the peanut gallery! I'll be right back." He dashed out of the fort and down the path about twenty-five feet. He stopped and reached up to a tree branch and lifted down a bulky sack. He jogged back to the fort and set down his goods.

"What is it?" said Blake, full of curiosity, "and why are you an idiot, besides the reasons we can name?"

"My dad told me to bring some stuff to use out here, but on my way back last night, I hung it up in that tree to keep it out of our way until this morning, and totally forgot about it. The only reason I remembered was that I was thinking it'd be nice to have my camping kit to use here, 'cause it includes plates, cups, plasticware, cookware, and stuff like that. It'll make our campout easier to manage."

"Yeah, makes sense," Vince broke in. "Not an idiot if you remember it. Just an I.D. ten T if you don't."

"I.D. ten T?" I said, not realizing what I was falling for.

"You know," he said. "I-D-IO-T." He was grinning wider than I'd seen in a long time. Gosh, I was slow sometimes.

We did the best we could to toast our bagels, and then spread the margarine on them. It was nice to have something other than peanut butter sandwiches or s'mores for a campout meal. We weren't doing too poorly for three 12-year-old boys on our own in the woods, but it was a good thing we were close to home, or our nutrition would suffer.

In addition to my camp kit, I also had a pack of cards, Uno, and Yahtzee games with me, and my transistor radio, so we could listen to the Red Sox games. That would give us some stuff to do while we were out in the fort. If Blake felt up to it, maybe we could go to Whitman's in a few days, but then again, we'd all lifted stuff from there yesterday, so going there again so soon might not be such a good idea. No, we were going to have to find ways to lie low at the fort and hope we didn't go out of our minds with boredom.

Somehow, we passed the morning and early afternoon more easily than I had anticipated, and it was suddenly time for me to go to the house to meet up with Andy. I collected the cooler, along with the trash we'd accumulated, and asked if there were any requests for supplies.

"Do you have a small tent that you and Andy can use tonight? If so, you ought to bring that. If not, then maybe something you can use for a tent-like situation that we can set up for you two," said Blake. "I just think he'll be more comfortable with that than sleeping out in the open, based on what you've said about him."

"Good point, Blake," I said. "I'm glad you thought of that. Okay, guys, I'll be back in a little while. Miss me." I smiled at them and left. *Miss me or not, it's good for us to have some time apart. We love hanging out, but always being together can get a bit much at times, for me and for them.*

When I got to the house, Andy was already there. To my surprise, David was, too, and it didn't look like he was leaving anytime soon. *What's going on? I thought I made it clear that only Andy was invited.* Not wanting to jump to conclusions, though, I greeted both warmly. My dad was talking with David, and I asked dad about a small tent.

He went and got it for me and explained briefly about setting it up. Then he led me to where the Madison brothers were waiting. "Jack, David's going to be here for a while. He agreed to help me put in some firewood for the winter. Normally, I'd have you help me, but you're helping a friend, and he was willing to do it, so that's why he's here. You didn't ask, but I saw the question on your face, son." He smiled at me. "Now, why don't you and Andy take your gear and go join your friends?"

Following Vince's example, I used the red wagon of my childhood to haul our gear to the fort. On the way, I explained about the fort to Andy. He was eager to see it, but even more anxious to meet my other friends. "Jack, I don't know if I'm being set up for humiliation in this, or if this is a real call for help, but I'm trusting God to be my guide. He has never failed me yet, Jack, and I don't expect him to fail me today. Whatever happens out here with your friends, to God be the glory."

Andy's words sliced through my heart like a Japanese katana. *He was trusting in God? God never failed him?? Doesn't he know that this Guy can't be trusted?* My heart began pounding, my hands, sweating, and I suddenly feared for my friend's safety, but it was too late.

We were at the fort.

16: "Not A Good Person"

To my surprise, Blake immediately introduced himself to Andy. "Andy? I'm Blake, Blake Harris." He held out his hand to my friend.

"Nice to meet you, Blake. Andy Madison." Andy took his hand and shook it. "So, you must be Vince?" he said to my other friend. He offered his hand to Vinnie.

"Hi, Andy. Vince Jackson." They shook hands, too. "Why don't you come in and have a seat in our humble abode?" He smiled disarmingly.

"Thanks, Vince. Before I do, I bring 'housewarming gifts.'" Andy grinned as he presented food from his mother.

The food broke the tension, and before long we were all talking and eating like we'd known each other forever. Finally, Blake spoke up to say what was needed to get the ball rolling.

"Andy, I owe you so many apologies, I don't know where to begin. I have been such a jerk and bully to you. The worst of it was attacking you last year on your bike. I am really sorry for that. I understand if you don't want to be my friend or accept my apology, but I've needed to get this off my chest for a long time. I'm sorry." Blake's voice was hoarse with emotion by the time he finished.

We were looking at Blake while he talked and didn't notice Andy until he was in front of our friend. Then he replied, "Blake, stand up and look me in the eye, please." There was authority in Andy's voice I wasn't used to hearing when we were at school, and I wondered if crap was about to get real.

Blake looked up warily at Andy as he got to his feet. "What?"

"I forgive you." Once again, Andy reached out to shake my friend's hand, as Vince and I sat there slack-jawed by what had just happened.

"You what?" Blake didn't believe his ears.

"I forgive you, Blake. Truth is, I forgave you a long time ago," Andy said. "Thank you for your apology, though. It means an awful lot to hear that from you. I'd like to be friends with you if you really mean it. And if you really mean it, are you gonna leave me hanging out here?" he said, waving his hand around.

Blake suddenly realized he hadn't shaken Andy's hand yet to seal the deal. To my surprise, he slapped it away and pulled Andy in for a hug. "I can't believe you forgive me for all that crap, Andy. Just like that, too! Why?" As he finished what he had to say, he ended the hug to look at my Christian friend. "Why would you forgive me before I asked for it?"

"Yeah," said Vince, getting in on the conversation at last. "Blake's been a total jerk wad to you forever, Andy. Why would you let him off the hook like that so easily? I mean, that's total bullcrap, if you ask me. I don't think you're really a Christian. I've got Christians in my family, and they don't act like this. I think you're a total fake!"

Andy shrugged off Vince's anger. "To answer your question about forgiveness, Blake, God has forgiven me of all the wrong I've done in my life, so I forgive you. That's the simplest way to explain it. As for all the other questions you guys may have, I'm happy to do my best to answer them. I'm no big shot Bible teacher. I'm a kid just like you, but I've been raised in a home where I was taught this stuff. Vince, you made a good point that a lot of Christians disagree about how to practice what they believe, so I'm not surprised that you know of differences."

I took that as my chance to butt in, too. "Guys, you wanted Andy to come over today, so I invited him. Honestly, I didn't know if you were secretly planning to humiliate him and me somehow by trying to manipulate me into rejecting my friendship with him—oh, don't act so innocent, Vinnie.

I know how you can be—or if you legit wanted to know how Andy could help you, Blake. Now, it seems from how it's gone so far that your invitation was sincere, so I hope we can have a good discussion this afternoon, and play some games and enjoy some friend time, too. Does that sound like a good plan?"

Everyone seemed on board with that, even though I could tell that Vin was still unhappy about it. However, he had promised to behave, so Blake and I were going to hold him to it. We all grabbed some more cookies and Twinkies and settled in for our question-and-answer session with Andy.

"Before we go further, guys," Andy said, "I need to pray. You can keep your eyes open if you prefer, but I'm going to close mine so I can focus on the fact that I'm talking to God. *'Dear God, thank you for today and this chance to spend time with Jack, Blake, and Vince. Thank you that Blake and I could make peace with each other a few minutes ago. Bless our time together. In Your Name, Amen.'*"

He looked up. "Okay, Blake, I heard that you have some questions for me?"

"Did Jack tell you anything about me?" When Andy shook his head, Blake said, "Well, I don't feel comfortable talking about all of it just now, but I'm really wondering where my life is going, Andy. Ma took off a few years ago, and it's just been Pop and me since then. He's not a good person, so my home life is trash. He puts me through hell every day. I'm about to turn 13 and basically the only reason I keep on living is because of these two guys," he gestured to Vinnie and me.

He laughed bitterly, saying, "Someone has to keep them from running off the rails, so I stick around. I just don't see any other reason to keep living. There's no one else in this world that considers me worth anything. I'm just a rotten, good-for-nothing piece of crap. I don't know how much more I can take."

I looked at Andy, fearing that Blake's verbal vomit was going to scare him off. I doubted that my friend from the farm had ever heard anything so awful about anyone before. What could he possibly offer to help Blake?

"The first thing that comes to mind, Blake, is one of the last things you said. You know, about being a 'rotten, good-for-nothing piece of crap.' Why do you say that? I'm pretty sure Vince and Jack don't see you that way, and I sure don't."

Blake scoffed at Andy. "You don't know me at all. How can you say you don't see me that way, especially after the way I've treated you?"

"The Bible says that we are made in God's image, so we are supposed to treat one another with dignity and respect. This means that as a human being, Blake, I can't view you as a 'rotten, good-for-nothing, piece of crap.' Since I'm a Christian, I *have to* see you as valuable, and I do. Your life is important to me. It's just as important to me as Jack's is. Look me in the eye and tell me I'm lying if you think I am."

Blake just shook his head in disbelief.

"I'll ask you again, my new friend: Why do you call yourself a piece of crap?" Andy's voice was barely above a whisper.

His former bully looked at the ground. "My pop treats me like garbage," he mumbled. "He makes my life a living hell every day. He gets drunk and then he hits me, a-and then h-he t-touches m-me... and he says I like it and that I asked for it..." Suddenly, Blake lurched from his chair and puked all over the ground in front of us.

Andy was the first to reach him, grabbing a bandana from his pocket to wipe the residue from Blake's lips. He stayed with my friend while all the food he'd had today left his mouth and hit the ground. Vince and I were frozen with shock at the scene playing out before us, but I knew I was going to have to move soon, because the smell was going to trigger my gag reflex if I didn't get away from it.

Andy knew that about me. He turned, "Move outside of the fort," he urged us. "Get the shovel and bucket and be ready for cleanup duty when I tell you. Vince? Can you do the shoveling? Good." His attention returned to Blake, whose heaves were slowing down. "Are you okay, Blake? All done? Here, have a swig of water to wash out your mouth. You can brush your teeth in a few minutes. All right. Wipe your mouth with this. Let's move you to a seat over here, my friend."

I watched in amazement as Andy directed Blake to a seat on the other side of the fort and eased him into it. Then he turned to us and supervised the cleanup. Vince shoveled the topsoil layer into the bucket, and I carried it to the latrine to dump it, holding my breath the whole way. When I needed a breath, I'd set the bucket down, run 10 feet away, get fresh air into my lungs, and return to the task at hand.

Somehow, Vinnie and I finished the work of cleaning the mess from the campsite without getting any on us and without triggering my very sensitive gag reflex. Then Andy used the water from the melted ice in the cooler to rinse the bucket and shovel. I noted the awe in Vinnie's eyes for my Christian friend's resourcefulness.

When the cleanup was done, we went back to check on Blake. He had changed his clothes and was lying down in his tent. Andy knelt outside his tent and spoke quietly to him. I couldn't hear what he was saying, but at the end I heard, 'Amen.'

Andy came over to see me. "How're you doing there, Jack? I think now would be a good time to bring in the giant-killer. What do you think?"

"The giant killer? Huh?" I was confused.

He smiled at me. "You know, the one from the Bible that killed Goliath?"

"Ohhhhhh, *that* giant-killer! *Andy and his obscure Bible references!* "Sure. I'll go get him." *This ought to go over like a lead balloon.* "Guys, I gotta go back to the house for something. I'll be back in a few." As I jogged back to my place, all I could do was wonder what Andy had in mind. *Why does he want David now? What can he add to the situation? I sure hope Andy knows what he's doing, 'cuz I don't think this is a good idea.*

When I arrived at the house, Dad and David weren't out in the yard where I'd left them, so I went inside. They were having a glass of lemonade at the kitchen table, talking about sports. "Hey, Jack, how's it going out there? Everything okay?" Dad asked me.

"Yeah, it's fine, I guess. Andy asked me to come get David. He called him the giant-killer."

David snorted with laughter. "The giant killer? Am I that mean?"

129

"No! Like, the one that killed Goliath?" I laughed, too.

"Oh! Ha ha. I get it; he didn't want to say my name in front of the other boys. Huh. Funny. Good idea. Sure, I'll go with you. Any idea why he wants me to go out there?"

I shrugged. "No, but I will tell you that he's getting along fine with Blake and Vinnie. Blake apologized for hurting him last year, and Andy told Blake that he forgave him."

David nodded thoughtfully. "Mmhmm. That sounds like my little brother. He's got a good head on his shoulders, at least some of the time. He ain't perfect, but when he's listening to God, he's doing all right. Mr. Bannister, if you're set here, I'll go see if I can do any good at the fort."

"Certainly, David. Thank you for your help with the firewood. Jack will have his turn in a few weeks, but this is a great start to our winter supply." Dad shook hands with David and the older teen followed me outside.

"Before we go to the fort, Jack, your dad suggested I grab an armful of firewood."

"Why did he say that?"

"He wants to make sure you have enough for tonight. We left some outside the cellar doors. He said you can take from it as you need it for your campouts."

"Wow. I'm not used to him thinking of things like that for me and my friends. Tell you what, David, you grab a few sticks, and I'll take some, too. No sense in you carrying it all."

17: Who Does That?

While Jack was gone, Vince looked at Andy expectantly. "What's all this about a 'giant killer'? Are you and Jack ganging up on me?"

Andy smiled. "No, Vince. There's someone I want you to meet, and Jack has gone to get him. He can answer some of the questions you guys have better than I can, and I think he has something he needs to say to you two, especially. I can see confusion on your face, Vin, but I'm not gonna give it away. You remember how Blake apologized for his treatment of me when we first met? I think the person you're gonna meet may do the same to you."

Then Andy turned to check on Blake and took him a cup of water. Blake sat up and sipped from the cup. "What a mess my life has become, Andy," he mumbled. "Is there any hope for me?"

Andy sat down next to his new friend. "Yeah, Blake, there is hope for you," he whispered. As he considered the reputation Blake Harris had built for himself over his young life, he added, "And asking for help doesn't mean you're weak."

Blake looked at him. "How did you know I'd be worried about that?" he chuckled wryly. "Can you read minds, Andy Madison?" A smile grew on his face.

Andy smiled back as he shook his head. "Nope! I just thought about you and the reputation you've made for yourself as this rough, don't-mess-with-me kid, and I figured that asking for help didn't match that view of yourself." His smile faded a little. "I realize you thought of me as some weakling for a long time, Blake Harris, even though you didn't know me. All you saw was a shy, chubby, kid that wore thick eyeglasses and didn't stick up for himself. Oh, yeah, I know how I come across to other kids. I shocked Jack the first time he came over for haying. He really didn't expect me to be so confident driving the tractors, running equipment, moving the bales, and all that. It took all day to pick his jaw up off the ground!" Andy finished with a laugh. "I'm not sure he knows that *I* knew that. But part of where I get my confidence is from having friends that really support me and have my back. If I know that they'll help me when I fall, then it's a lot easier to ask for help. We're here for you, Blake, and you're asking for help. We're not going anywhere."

Blake smiled at Andy. "Thanks for being here, Andy. I'm glad you're here, and I'm glad we're friends now."

"Me, too."

About ten minutes later, Vince called out, "Jack's back, and he's got some older kid with him!"

Blake and Andy stood up and joined Vince in the cleared dining area. When Jack and David arrived, they put the firewood aside, brushed off the debris from their arms, and joined the others. Andy handled the introductions.

"Guys, this is the 'killer of giants,' my brother David."

"Whoa, you invited *him*?!" Vince was immediately on his guard. Blake looked alarmed, too. "What's going on?"

"David, this is Vince Jackson, and that's Blake Harris," Andy gestured to the two concerned boys.

David reached out his hand to Vince first. "Vince, pleased to meet you." Vince reached out tentatively, took David's hand, and shook it. "Hi." Then David did the same with Blake with the same result.

"Why don't we all take a seat around the campfire that Jack's been tending to during our awkward intros so we can talk?" David suggested. "Nice fort you have here, boys. I'm impressed."

As they settled into their seats, David continued, "Okay, fellas. From what I've heard, there's a lot going on with you guys lately, and Andy asked me to help answer questions because he's not always sure that he'll know what to say. The truth is that my little brother usually knows better than I what to say, but I'm glad to be here for him. I don't think it's a secret how much I love Andy and care about his well-being." When he made that final comment, Blake and Vince chuckled nervously.

David pressed on. "On *that* note, I gotta start with an apology to you two, Vince and Blake. The Bible says that we're supposed to be quick to listen, slow to speak and slow to become angry, because our anger doesn't get the results God wants. Last year, when I called and threatened you because of what you did to Andy on his bike, I was angry. It may have been okay for me to be upset, but it was wrong of me to threaten you. I'm sorry. Will you forgive me?

Blake stared at David closely. When he finally spoke, his words came out slowly. "I'm not sure if *you're* playing *me*, but yeah, David. I forgive you. Will you forgive me for treating your brother so badly?"

David replied, "Yes, Blake!"

At that, Vince spoke up. "I, uh, I honestly didn't think that Andy was for real when he came here today, and then he and Blake made up. Frankly, there are 'Christians' in my family and they don't act anything like you guys, so I thought I knew what Andy was going to say and how he was

133

going to act. I pretty much accused him of bullcrapping us a while ago, but now you come here, and apologize to *us* for how *you* reacted when *we* hurt *your brother*? Then *you* ask *us* to forgive *you* for being protective? Who does that? Yeah, I'll forgive you."

The 17-year-old nodded. "Thank you, Vince. Do you mind if I answer that last question—about why I ask for you to forgive me?"

"Go right ahead. You've got me curious now."

"The Bible also says, *'Do not merely listen to the word, and so deceive yourselves. Do what it says.'* If all I do is read the Bible but don't obey it, what good is that? The only way God's Word changes me is if I do what it says."

"Okay, I guess that makes sense," said Vince. "Which is why you apologized for threatening us last year, right?"

"Right. I should've done it a lot sooner, really, Vince, but I'm glad we've cleared the air today. What I did by calling you last year might have made Andy and me feel good for a little while, but it was disobedience to God's commands—and that's sin. Sin separates us from God's love. It's what causes all the trouble in the world. The Bible says that every one of us has sinned and fallen short of God's standards for how we should live and act, and because of that, we've earned eternal separation from God when we die." David was on a roll, and all the boys were attentive, so he kept on going.

"That's why John 3:16—you know, the verse you see on signs at football games on TV all the time—says: *'God so loved the world that he gave his one and only Son, that whoever believes in him shall not perish but have eternal life.'*" He paused for a drink of water, and to let the boys ask questions.

"Is that what you believe, Andy?" Vince asked.

The boy nodded. "David said it really well."

"What about you, Jack?" Vince knew what Jack had said earlier, and he wanted to see him squirm a little.

"I know that's what the Bible says, Vinnie, and I want to believe that, but I admit that I have doubts sometimes," Jack replied.

Blake spoke for the first time in quite a while. "David, you said that sin causes all the problems in the world. Does that mean that I did something wrong to make my pop treat me like he does?"

"No, Blake. It means that the existence of sin in the world is the reason for all the pain, sickness, unkindness, crime, hatred, and everything else that's wrong. However, for the person that never says to God, 'I'm sorry for my sin, please forgive me and help me to change,' *that person* will be separated from God when he or she dies and won't have eternal life. Does that make sense?"

"Yeah, I think so. Thanks."

"Blake, just to make it clear about your question, *your* sin doesn't cause bad things to happen to *you.* It's not like getting caught in a speed trap by the cops and you get a ticket, or a teacher seeing you cheat on a test so you get a zero. What I'm talking about is the general effect sin has on everything in the world. God created everything and it was good. Sin breaks everything. Sometimes, sin *looks* or *feels* good, but in the end, it brings sickness, pain, and death. From the first time that people sinned, everything in this world has been suffering for it."

I felt like I was going to explode. *This! Why doesn't God do something about this??*

Vince must've seen the look on my face, because he spoke up and asked that very question. "So, David, if the whole world has been suffering for thousands of years or more, why doesn't your all-powerful God do something about it? Is sin stronger than God?" He winked at me after speaking.

To my frustration, David didn't miss a beat. "I'm glad you asked that, Vince. It's a question *and* an accusation brought up all the time. God *has* done something about it, Vince." He stopped and waited to see if the younger boy would figure it out.

"What? You mean, the whole Jesus-on-the-cross-thing? Looks like a failure to me, David. How could that have worked and we still have all the wars and starvation and crap going on? The Holocaust? I was right to begin with; you guys are full of bullsh—"

"Knock it off, Vince!" Blake interrupted. "You asked him a question and talked over his chance to answer. *Last warning, bucko.*" His eyes shot daggers at Vinnie, who immediately backed down. I'd never seen him look so cowed.

18. Crushed and Bruised

Content Warning

David gave a friendly wave as he said, "It's okay, guys. I understand how it looks and feels. Yes, Vince, Jesus is the answer to sin and suffering. No, that answer isn't a failure." He held up his hands again as Vince started to protest. "Just gimme a sec, and I'll explain what I mean by that. Okay?" How he kept his cool was a mystery to me. I would've knocked Vinnie's block off.

"When God created man and woman, he gave them a beautiful garden to live in, and told them they could eat the fruit of every tree except for one. For as long as they didn't eat from that one tree, they enjoyed a direct, face-to-face relationship with God. The book of Genesis says that in the evening, in the cool of the day, God would walk and talk with them. As kids, we always giggled reading about it because it also says they were naked."

The other boys and I snickered a little when he said that. "Yeah, I remember that from Sunday school," I said.

"Then came the day that the Devil tempted Eve to go against God and eat from that one tree so that she could be as wise as God. She decided to do it, and Adam did it, too, and they instantly regretted it, but it was too late. That evening, when they heard God walking to visit with them, they were ashamed of being naked, so they made clothes and covered up. God asked them why they did that. They confessed their sin to him, and he forced them to leave that garden."

"David, that sounds like a direct sin-and-consequence situation to me!" Blake interjected. "You said that's not how it works."

David nodded. "For the most part, it doesn't, Blake, but you're correct in this case. In the garden, there was a tree called 'Life.' They would never die if they ate fruit from that one after sinning. God knew that would cause even more pain and suffering for all of human history, so he banished them. But in Genesis 3:15, we see God's plan for fixing what Adam and Eve broke: *'And I will put enmity between you and the woman, and between your offspring and hers; he will crush your head, and you will strike his heel.'"*

"Whoa, whoa, whoa...this is..what? Enmity? Crush your head? Strike his heel? What the heck, David??" I couldn't contain myself any longer. "Who talks like that? What does this stuff mean? Don't you think you're getting in too deep here?? It was a simple question!" I didn't realize I'd jumped up and was pacing back and forth.

"Guys?" Andy spoke for the first time in a long while. "What say we take a little break?"

Everyone agreed. David took a walk in the woods with Andy. On their walk, David asked Andy what he'd learned about the situation involving Blake and his father. Andy said Blake had hinted there was physical abuse going on. His brother sensed there was more to it and gently prodded Andy about it while telling him to take his time.

The younger boy looked at his hero and said, "Yeah, there's more. He didn't get very specific, but the thought made him so upset that he started puking all over the ground. That's why it's all freshly dug up there. We had to shovel it clean before you arrived. He's hurting so much, David! He's losing hope for living—Jack told me that—plus he's afraid he won't have anywhere to go if his dad gets reported to child services. From what I've seen today, it seems obvious that his tough demeanor is a front for all the pain he's been through, don't you think?"

David stopped and pulled his brother into a half-hug. "I think you've hit the nail on the head with that observation, little brother. You've also reminded me of something I must tell Blake before we talk about anything else. I need to tell him that I'm a mandated reporter because of my work as a volunteer coach in Little League."

"What's a mandated reporter?"

"It means that if I hear about abuse—firsthand, not secondhand, so what you've told me doesn't count—then I'm legally required to report it to a higher authority. In this case, I would have to call the police or child and family services. So, I need to warn Blake about that before he trusts me enough to tell me something I may have to report. I don't want him feeling betrayed if he opens up to me and then gets his home situation disrupted."

Andy nodded thoughtfully before responding. "That's a lot of responsibility to have. What if you don't believe the story you hear?"

"It doesn't matter whether I believe it or not. If someone says they are being abused, or if they claim they are abusing someone else, I'm required to report it. If I don't, and it comes out later that I knew about it and didn't report it, I can be arrested or sued for failure to fulfill my responsibility as a mandated reporter. You're right, Andy. It *is* a lot of responsibility to have!" He smiled at his brother. "It's an important part of being a coach, though. I want my players to be safe in the game and at home, too."

They made their way back to the fort, where they found the others waiting for them. David spoke first. "Boys, there's something that Andy and I were talking about a few minutes ago that I need to let you know before we continue. Because of with coaching Little League, I'm a mandated reporter. Do you know what that is?"

"Yeah," said Blake. "It means that if one of us tells you something that involves harm to us or another person, you have to rat on us."

"Heh, I wasn't going to put it that way, Blake, but yeah, you could say it like that. If you tell me something bad is happening to you, or you're doing something bad to someone else, I'm required by law to report it to the proper authorities. I wanted you to know that before you tell me something serious about yourselves, all right? I don't want to go around being sneaky with you, making it look like I'm trying to stab you in the back by 'ratting' you out, all right?" He looked Blake in the eye as he made his final statement. "At the same time, if you need to let someone know what's going on, and you need help, please get in touch. Now, where were we?"

"Enmity, head crushing, and heel bruising," I said. "Care to explain that and get to your point? I'm totally lost."

"Heh, heh," David chuckled slightly. *Lord, help me bring you honor.* "God was speaking to the Devil and to Eve when he said those things. First, he said that there would be a state of war, 'enmity,' between them. Then, an offspring of the woman would come at some point in time that would crush the head of the Devil while being wounded by him in the process. Any idea Who that offspring is?"

I rolled my eyes. "Jesus?"

"Circle gets the square! Right you are, Jack." David grinned. "Genesis 3:15 is considered the first mention of the Gospel in the Bible. From that moment on, the Bible shows how God unfolds history to bring about his promised Answer to the question of sin and suffering—Vince, I haven't forgotten you! Where the *failure* comes in, Vince, is in the *people* that reject Jesus as the Answer."

"Oh, so it's *our fault?* How convenient! Put us on this earth, let us break his impossible rules, make our lives miserable, and then blame us when we don't get it right! Shutit, Blake, I'm sayin' my piece." Vinnie was at full lather and no warnings from Blake were going to stop him. "I was right in the first place not to trust you blathering religious nuts! *Christians!*" he snorted. "All you're good for is shoving your self-righteous crap down our throats while diddling anybody you freakin' want! GET AWAY FROM ME!"

I was stunned. I'd never seen Vinnie so worked up about *anything*, and he'd just screamed at *Blake* to leave him alone. *Blake,* the one kid that knew Vin better than anyone else, was trying to help our buddy, and the guy had reacted like the kid was lava.

"It's okay, Vin, buddy. It's just us. You and me, Vinnie." Blake soothed Vince's nerves with a soft voice. *"Nobody's touching you, Vin. Why don't you go to your tent for a bit, okay? You can listen from there if you want. If you don't want, just tune us out, bud."*

We watched in silence as Vince stepped away from us and wobbled to his tent. Blake turned to us and said almost inaudibly, *"He's had some horrible things happen to him. I'll leave it at that."* It was then I realized that Andy's and David's heads were bowed. No doubt they were praying. I felt a twinge that I should be, too, but I wasn't ready to trust God. He'd taken Mom. What was to say he wouldn't take these guys from me, too?

It was Blake that got us back on track. "David, I'd really like to know where you were going with your train of thought. You seemed to be saying that God made things good, we screwed 'em up, he sent the fix, and everything's still wrong 'cause we ignore the fix? How is it a fix if nobody pays attention to it? Present company excepted, of course. And what was that about the 'head crushing and heel bruising'? I don't get that at all."

"Thanks for the questions, Blake. I appreciate you hanging in for the long answers. Jack might've been right when he said I bit off a lot to chew." Everybody smiled with a slight chuckle. "The head crushing and heel bruising are about Jesus dying for sin and rising from the dead. He crushed the power of Satan, the Devil, by rising from the dead. Satan's power was Death, also called the wages of sin. The only way for that power to be defeated was for a sin*less* Man to die as a substitute for all the other sin*ful* people."

"And that's what Jesus did?" There was awe in Blake's voice.

"That's what Jesus did. He was the substitute." Andy piped in for the first time in more than an hour of our discussion. "The pain he experienced in the process was how Satan 'bruised his heel.'"

"Ohhh...that makes sense. Wow." After Blake's comments we all sat there, wondering what to do next. Then he said, "So, if that's how the Genesis 3:15 stuff worked out, how is that the 'Answer,' exactly?"

David replied, "When Jesus rose from the dead, he proved that he was stronger than death. From then until he returns from heaven at the end of time, he freely offers forgiveness of sins to everyone that asks God for it. When we're forgiven, we experience peace with God, which begins to change us into better people. By reading and learning the Bible, the Spirit of God helps us reject sin each day, which includes anger, jealousy, lust, pettiness, gossip, violence—and so much more. And when we sin again, God's grace and mercy are there to restore us and start again. Little-by-little, we grow up as Christians every day. Does that give you a better understanding, Blake?"

"It's a lot to follow, David, but yeah, I'm getting the picture. So, I guess the rest of it is that people don't want that kind of help? That's why they don't go for the fix? Geezum, seems kinda stupid to me not to take something that's free."

"People object to it because we want a genie in a bottle that will give us everything we want and nothing we don't want. We want a comfy life and pleasure all the time. We don't want to surrender control of our lives to Someone that commands obedience and trust. Yes, commands obedience. Those are strong words that people dislike and take offense at. But God expects his people to obey the Bible, which is the written way he reveals Who he is and what he expects of the people that believe in him. To *be* Christian means to repent of sin and believe that Jesus' death and resurrection were needed to pay for your sin." The older boy paused.

"Okay, now I see. That's much clearer, David. Thank you."

"You're welcome, bud. Do you have other questions I can help you with, any of you?"

The tent behind them rustled and Vince reappeared. His face was puffy, but the anger was gone. He shuffled to the circle and sat down. "I don't think I've ever been involved in such a heavy discussion my whole life," he said quietly. "I was so ready to blow you guys off, but Blake made it clear he wanted me here, so I stayed. Seriously, I wanted no part of this today, but I'm glad I'm hearing this. It's making my family make a lot more sense, and clearly *they're* the ones that are full of bull, not you two."

David and Andy just shook their heads and smiled. "If there's nothing else right now, how about taking a break and then playing a game of Uno and a round of s'mores? Is your tummy up to that, Blake?" Andy asked.

"I think it is, Andy," Blake smiled at his new friend. "A little fun would be good. David, please stay and play! It's been so serious around here lately, we need to lighten the mood, but I may have more questions for you in a little bit, if you don't mind."

"No, I don't mind at all," David said. "I love Uno, and I don't mind s'mores, either. Plus, getting time with Andy and his friends is always good. It warms the cockles of my heart to see the four of you together."

"It warms the what now?" I guffawed.

"The cockles of your heart?!" exclaimed Vince. "What the heck are those?"

"Heh, heh. It means the core of one's being." David laughed with them. "It's an expression our mom uses sometimes."

"Enough of the cockles, boys! Shuffle and deal," said Blake.

As they prepared to play the game, David took Andy aside and asked where the latrine was. On their way to it, Andy said, "Thanks for being here, big brother. What you did and said was cool. I know I referred to you as the 'giant killer' to prevent them from knowing who was coming, but

144

I think you slayed a giant problem with that testimony today."

"Thanks, Andy. Let's pray on our way back that God will use this time for his glory and their good."

When they rejoined the others, David said, "I've gotta say, boys, that's quite a fancy set up for a fort in the woods." He chuckled. "My buddies and I never thought of setting up something like that. How did you make it?"

Blake gestured to Vinnie. "He did most of the work. Dug a hole, set up the boards. I found the bucket to make it more like a seat so we weren't falling over and hurting ourselves." He laughed. "A few hits and misses later, and we seemed to have a working system. Jack helped us add the curtain later for privacy."

"You mean the interwoven branches that hang down from the posts set up around the hole? I like your name for it, 'curtain.' Well done, boys, really." David chuckled again. "Plus the fact that you have a bucket of water for rinsing your hands? Smart! Anyway, let's get the games going."

Several highly competitive hands of Uno later, the boys took a break from each other and broke out some snacks and drinks. Blake was still feeling the aftereffects of his sick session from earlier in the day, so he lay down for a brief rest. Jack and Vince played cards and kept an eye on the campfire. Andy and David strolled through the woods again, talking about the discussion held earlier in the afternoon. When they got back, David prepared to leave.

"Guys, there's something I want to tell you before I go, but before I do, I want you to know I've really enjoyed spending time with you this afternoon, and I'd like to hang out again sometime soon. However, I get the feeling that you're ready to have your fun without me, am I right? Okay, so I'll get ready to go in a minute."

"What were you going to tell us?" Vince asked.

"Jack already knows this since he's been to our place a bunch of times, but you and Blake just met me today. If you ever want a trusted older guy to talk to, I'm open. If you have questions about the Bible, or just need someone to listen to you, we're here. I say 'we' because I think it's best if it's not one-on-one. As a volunteer with Nolan's Little League coaching, we have a rule never to be one-on-one with kids, for accountability's sake. Therefore, if you want to talk with me in person, we'll always have someone else with us, all right?"

"Thanks for coming, David," the boys said in turn. "It was nice meeting you," Vince and Blake said, shaking hands with him.

"I hope you feel better soon, Vince. See you in the morning, Andy!" David hugged his brother and headed back to the Bannisters' house. No one else heard his comment to Vince.

When he got home, he told his parents about his time at the fort. As he finished his comments, he said, "I might be wrong, but I don't think we've seen the last of Blake Harris tonight. The Lord is working hard on that boy's heart, and we need to be ready for whatever happens, Mom and Dad."

19: A Touchless Hug

Content Warning

"I'm glad he's our friend now," Blake smiled at Andy. "I'm glad you're our friend now, too. I feel like my friend world has grown much bigger today, even though it's just by two."

Jack laughed. "Not by two, Blake! When you get Andy and David, you get their whole family, too."

"I do?"

"Yup. His mom's awesome. His dad's cool, too, but his mom is so sweet, you'll love her."

"Whaddya say, Vin? Are you happy to have two new friends today?" Blake looked at his best friend and suddenly frowned. "What's going on, Vin?"

Vinnie was sitting by the fire, locked in a stare. Blake went over and shook him by the shoulder. "Vin? Vinnie! Come on, snap out of it."

"Wha-what? I'm sorry, I kinda zoned out there for a minute. What were you guys talking about?"

"Are you happy to have two new friends today?"

"Two new friends? Oh, yeah, David and Andy. Yeah, yeah. Very happy. It's great. Listen, I'm gonna go home for the night. I'm not feeling so well, okay?"

"Jack, can you go with him to make sure he gets there safely? Just be careful..." Blake was anxious for Vinnie, but a thought nagged in his mind to say to Jack. He couldn't come up with it. "Oh, never mind."

"Sure, Blake. C'mon, Vinnie, let's go to your house and get you settled in, all right? You sure you're okay? All right, fellas, I'll be back in a while. Miss me!" Vince and I left the fort.

Blake turned to Andy and said, "I really *am* thankful that we became friends, Andy. I'm disappointed that we don't live closer and go to school together, though, because getting to hang out will be tricky. You have a very different personality than Jack. How did you two become such good friends?"

Andy explained to Blake how he and Jack met and became pals. He shared the ways that he had supported Jack as the new kid in the school, and how Jack stood up for him against his bullies. Their common interests in sports teams, similar senses of humor, and just enjoying being around each other had filled in the gaps. Andy admired Jack's work ethic and willingness to take on hard tasks, while Jack admired Andy's intellect and positive interactions with others. They fed off one another's strengths and helped overcome each other's weaknesses.

He smiled as he talked about his friendship with Jack, especially as he saw Blake laughing at the stories he shared. Then he said, "You know, Blake, I say all these positive things about our friend, but I'm not as naïve as people think I am. I know that he says and does things that I wouldn't approve of, using language I don't like and acting in ways I wish he wouldn't. I'm not as blind to it as he thinks I am."

"So why don't you call him on it?"

"For the same reason he doesn't call me on the things I do: Love. Not *that* kind of love, Blake! Maybe the better word is 'charity,' or 'kindness.' In the Bible we're told that 'love covers a multitude of sins.' It's the idea that we *could* nitpick each other's behaviors that bother us, or we can love, or care, about one another enough that we let these things go. Now, if Jack was doing things that were harming our relationship, then I'd have to challenge him and address them, but these other things are nitpicky, and not worth getting my boxers in a bunch over."

Blake nodded in comprehension. "That makes sense, Andy. And you're right about Jack not being as noble and upright as your stories make him sound. Then again, I'm nowhere near as good as that, either. I'm a rotten sinner is what I am. No-good, filthy, rotten sinner. What does your Bible have to say about that? What hope is there for someone like me?"

"In Matthew 11:28 Jesus said, *'Come to me, all you who are weary and burdened, and I will give you rest.'* Come to Jesus, Blake. He will give you rest."

"How do I know he won't turn me away like my pop does, or hurt me?"

Andy replied, "In John 6:37, Jesus said, *'All those the Father gives me will come to me, and whoever comes to me I will never drive away.'* And God tells us in First John 1:9, *'If we confess our sins, he is faithful and just and will forgive us our sins and purify us from all unrighteousness.'"*

"Okay, so say, for example, that I believe in Jesus and ask him to take my sin away and make me his," Blake began, "what happens next? Does Pop stop hitting and touching me?" He snapped his fingers. "It all stops, just like that?"

Andy looked at Blake and said, "No, I can't promise that it stops just like that." His voice was quiet, but still full of assurance and peace.

"Why would I bother believing in Jesus, then?"

"For your own sake, Blake. To be forgiven of your own sin, by God, so that your guilt would be taken away, and no matter what *anyone* does to you, you *know without a doubt* that God is your refuge and strength. Becoming a Christian is about you having a personal relationship with God, which Jesus made possible through his life, death, and resurrection. Asking Jesus into your heart brings God into your life, and you belong to Him forever.

"Romans 8:38 tells us that *'nothing shall separate us from the love of God in Christ Jesus our Lord.'* Jesus knows your pain, Blake. Talk to Him. Ask Him to be your God, your Savior. You won't find a gentler Father nor a greater refuge than the God of the Bible."

"How do I talk to him? How do I get what you have, Andy? I'm a thief, Andy. I steal from people. I'm dirty-minded; I watch porn and think about being with girls. I've *messed around* with girls. I'm a bully; I do everything I can to manipulate people into doing what I want. How could Jesus accept me? Why would he listen to me?"

"He'll do it because he died on a cross to save sinners like you and me. He will listen to you. He can't lie, Blake, and he always keeps his promises." Andy fell silent and prayed in his heart. *Lord, do your saving work in my friend's heart, for your glory, and for his good.*

A few moments later, Blake asked, "What do I say?"

"What do you want to say?"

Blake looked at Andy with desperation, and then he started talking. "God! Andy says you're real. His brother David says you're real, too. They certainly make a convincing case for you, so I'm gonna talk to you as if you're there, all right? Listen, God, you're probably aware of what

I'm like, but I think I should admit what I've been up to, and I hope I don't shock my friend Andy too much... Jesus, this is hard... I know I'm a sinner. I'm dirty-minded, God. I think about sex a lot, and I've messed around with girls. I don't know what the Bible says about this, but I'm gonna bet these things are wrong. I've got a lot of anger, God. I hate Pop. He's..he's *evil.* I just don't know another word for him. Jesus! My life is hell every day with him and I don't know where else to turn.

"I'm a thief. And I'm a bully. I'm sure you know all the people I've stolen from, and the kids I've beaten up or threatened to get what I want. That's selfish of me, and that's the opposite of what Jesus did, you know, dying on a cross for jerks like me. I mean, if he never did anything wrong, but he died so I wouldn't have to be in hell when I die? I know I'm a rotten kid, God, but all this talk about giving you my crap and you giving me your goodness sounds just fine to me. I'm really, truly sorry that my sin meant that Jesus had to die, and I'm asking you to forgive me. Please! Andy forgave me today, and that felt good, but if he forgave me because YOU forgave him, then you must be the real deal. And then his big brother, oh God! He asked *me* to forgive *him* for being angry at me for bullying Andy last year. *Who does that, God??* Who offers forgiveness before someone asks for it? Cuz David did that, too. Oh yeah, I guess You do that, huh? Anyway, God, *I'm* sick of living my life in fear. My Pop is so mean. He's my birth father, but he has never loved me, and I'm so tired. Jesus! Help me! Every day I just wanna die. I've started thinking about how to kill myself, God. I guess you know about that, too. My life has been hell, and I can't take it anymore. Andy says that without You in my life, my eternity will be in hell, and I can't face that. I'm a sinner. I'm empty. My life is going nowhere fast. How can I be so young and feel so hopeless? You know I've tried a lot of things to find happiness, God. None of it has worked, and I'm so fu—dging tired. Sorry about that one. Oh God, I'm rambling."

Blake took a deep breath. "Okay, God, here goes. Please, Jesus, make me yours. I want you as my Father, 'cuz my father here doesn't love me, and Andy says you will love me unconditionally." And then he remembered how Andy and David had prayed earlier. " In Jesus' Name, Amen." He didn't recall closing his eyes or bowing his head, but he must have at some point because he had to open them and look up to see Andy, whose eyes were glistening with tears.

"Are you okay, Andy?"

The Madison boy only nodded and smiled, unable to find his voice.

"I..." Blake's voice trailed away. "I've never felt so full of life, Andy! What am I feeling? Why am I so hopeful? Where is the despair I've had all these years?" He was at a loss for words for a few moments.

"Am I... Did I just b-become a *Christian*?" he couldn't stop himself from grinning, shocked as he was.

Andy's head bobbed up and down.

"Is that why I feel like I'm getting hugged, even though no one is touching me?" He saw his friend's smile grow even bigger. "Oh, God! Thank you! I never knew such love was possible! Oh, Jesus! My sin is gone. My guilt is gone! I feel *new*! *Andy, what is this?* Is *this* God's love?"

"Yes, my friend, *that* is God's love." Andy kept crying happy tears. "And what's more, Blake, is that now that you are in God's family, you and I are *brothers* in Christ Jesus."

"You mean that I didn't just gain friends today, but I also gained brothers? What a day!" He sat down again and sighed with a peace he'd never known. *What now?* He voiced that to Andy.

"We ought to tell someone!" Andy said.

"Well, I ain't telling Pop, that's for sure. I'd get a whuppin' if I told him that. He *hates* religious people. Who can I tell?" Blake spoke truthfully but nothing deflated his excitement. Then he snapped his fingers. "I know! Mr. and Mrs. Bannister! Let's go tell them!" He got thoughtful for a moment. "Speaking of which, I'm surprised Jack isn't back yet. I hope everything's ok. Let's leave a note for him, clean up a little, and head to his house."

Andy agreed with Blake's plan, and within fifteen minutes the fort was shut down for the time being. They headed for the Bannisters' house with their spirits high. When they arrived, Andy checked his watch before knocking. "It's 8:00," he said to Blake. "That's not too late to knock, is it?"

"Not for this time of year, Andy. Besides, I think they'll be happy with the news we have."

Andy agreed and was about to rap his knuckles on the wooden door when Joe opened it and said, "Good evening, boys! Come on in. Oh, where are the others?"

"Jack took Vince home because Vinnie wasn't feeling well. He should be back soon, Mr. B," Andy replied. "Blake and I are here to—"

"Oh Lord, are you all right, young man?" Steph saw the bruising and cuts on Blake's face. "I knew that one of you had gotten hurt, but I had no idea... . Come in, son. Let me take a look in the light. Yes, you need some antiseptic on these cuts. Sit here. I'll be right back."

Blake obeyed as Andy said to him, "It's best to do what she says, buddy. Don't worry, she doesn't bite." He smiled as she returned to the room. "Thanks, Mrs. B. We've had such an exciting day that I forgot about the bruising."

Joe Bannister pulled up a chair to join the conversation while his wife tended to the young man in front of them. "Andy, I believe you said that you and Mr. Harris were on a mission to see us?"

"Yes, Mr. B." He turned to Blake. "Do you want to tell them or should I?" Blake gestured to the nursing happening to his injuries and then to Andy. It was clear that Andy would have to explain.

"I'm not going to say it all because some of it is Blake's story to tell," Andy began, "but I would imagine that you're aware of his less-than-stellar reputation?" Their expressions confirmed his comment, so he continued, "You probably know more, or suspect more, about his home life than he realizes." Again, they affirmed his statement, surprising Blake. "Recently, Blake has become more and more desperate about his future, and he hasn't known who to reach out to for help. He was really close to giving up hope."

"And on life," Blake added, as Steph washed her hands. When their hosts gasped, he said, "You've no idea how awful it's been. Well, I guess my face tells you some of

154

it. Go on, Andy." As Andy continued the story, Mrs. Bannister finished treating Blake's facial wounds.

"In a last ditch effort to come up with some kind of solution, he got an idea yesterday from talking with Jack about *our* camping trip—and the Bible readings we did—that maybe I would agree to meet and pray with him, even though he has bullied me."

"You're aware of the arrangements for me to visit today, and for David to come out to the fort, too. By the grace of God, David and I made peace with Blake and Vince and forgave them. Then David sought forgiveness from them for threatening to hurt them after the bike incident last year."

Blake interrupted. "David asking *me* to forgive *him* for defending his little brother blew me away! I even asked him, 'Who does that?' I got my answer and more." He waved for Andy to continue.

"After Vince and Jack left, Blake and I talked some more. It seemed clear to me that the Holy Spirit was talking to Blake. After twenty or thirty minutes of our conversation, Blake started talking to God aloud. By the end of it, he gave his heart and life to Jesus!"

By this time, Steph was done doctoring Blake, and she was listening attentively. When Andy revealed the conclusion, Blake interjected, "My heart felt so full! It still does. I said to Andy it was like being hugged though no one was touching me, and he said 'that's God's love.'"

Mrs. B's eyes were brimming with happy tears. "Blake, can I give you a real hug?"

"I'd like that," he said quietly.

As she embraced him, she spoke softly in his ear. "Welcome to the family of God, young man. Mr. B and I have been praying for you, and we'll support you any way we can." There were tears on both faces when they separated. She smiled at him and Andy, and then left the room with her husband. "We'll be back in a couple minutes."

Andy turned to his friend. "What's that look for, Blake?"

"I don't remember the last time a woman hugged me," he said with awe in his voice. "She said that they've been praying for me, and that they'll support me any way they can. I had no idea God worked like that. I'm just... amazed." He was still smiling, but there were tears in his eyes, too. "I'm beginning to see why you and your brother were able to forgive me, Andy." He wiped his face with the back of his hand, wincing slightly as he forgot about his bruised eye.

"I'm so happy for you, Blake! This is one of the happiest days of my life, but I have an issue on my heart that is concerning me a little, and with your permission, I'd like to talk about it with you before Mr. and Mrs. B come back."

The other boy nodded, suspecting what was coming. "This, straight up, *is the* happiest day of my life, Andy, but I think I know what's on your mind, and you're right; we need to talk about my living situation. I know that God will take care of me, but he might not want me to go home yet. Is that where you're headed?"

"You know? For a new Christian, you have a lot of wisdom, Blake Harris."

"Sad to say, Andy Madison, experience has been my teacher for years, and it is only today that God's love has given me hope to keep living, so I'd like to know what you have in mind."

"I can't promise you anything, but I'd like to call my parents to see if they'd be willing to let you stay with us for a while. They don't like being put on the spot, and I haven't even asked if you'd be ope—"

"Please ask them!" he cut in. "I'm open to it," he added. "Given what has just happened to me tonight, being with other Christians all the time is probably a good idea so I can learn everything I can, instead of hanging out with the bad influences I'm always with."

"Okay. I didn't want to ask the Bannisters because their house is smaller and they have a baby on the way."

"I agree, Andy. Besides, Jack and I get along well, but he's not a Christian, and I'm not sure that living with him would be good for either of us. Let's talk to Mr. and Mrs. B. and see if we can use their phone."

20. What Blake Forgot

Content Warning

I wasn't sure what was going on with Vince, but it was clear that he didn't want to be at the fort anymore tonight. Was he sick or was he faking it? I thought he was faking. Still, Blake wanted me to make sure Vince got home safely. He said, what was it? *Just be careful.* Be careful of what? He looked like there was something he wanted to add before sending me off with Vinnie, but when he didn't say anything more, we left.

It wasn't far, but the sun had gone down, and Vince didn't have a flashlight with him. As we walked through the woods, I tried to find out what was up. He kept mumbling things about David and Andy and Blake. It didn't sound like he was angry, but since he wouldn't speak clearly, it was hard to tell what he was saying. I finally quit asking.

We were about two hundred yards from his house when he stopped walking and turned to me. "Jack?"

"Yeah, Vinnie?"

"What did you think about what went on there today?"

"You mean, with David and Andy and Blake?"

"Yeah."

"It was interesting. What are you driving at, Vin?"

"Andy and David weren't anything like I expected. Much cooler than I thought they'd be. Almost too cool."

I laughed. "How can somebody be 'too cool'?"

He mumbled again. "I dunno. I felt left out, though."

"Oh, is that what this is about? You felt left out, so you're pouting? What are we, five years old?" I mocked him. He made me regret that.

"You don't get it, *Jacko*," Vince growled, using the nickname only Blake used to call me. "Blake is *my* special friend." He stepped closer to me, invading my personal space.

"Whoa, there, Vinnie, that's closer than I want to be." I backed up a step.

"I've seen how you look at him," Vince sneered. "I don't want to be ignored, Jack."

My face registered recognition at last. "Now, Vinnie, I'm friends with both of you equally, you know that. Shoot, you stood up to Blake for me when he started razzing me about my mom dying. I've always been grateful to you for that." I wanted to appease my friend's anger without becoming sniveling, but this was a fine line I was walking.

He stepped closer again, and this time I couldn't back up; I was against a tree. He reached a hand to my face and caressed my cheek. I blushed with a mixture of embarrassment and anger and swatted his hand away. "What are you doing, Vince?" I demanded.

"Oh, come on, Jack." He blocked my path and pushed me against the tree again. This time, he pinned me, and I couldn't move. "Don't you want to be my special friend, too?"

My eyes opened wide with concern. "Vince Jackson, what the heck are you talking about?"

"I told you; Blake is my special friend. Don't you want that, too?" Vince's face was feverish, and I realized something was very wrong with him. I struggled to break free but couldn't move. He stretched out and put his hands on my chest. "You're very strong, Jack." Then he reached under my shirt.

"What are you doing, Jackson!" I hollered. "Stop that!" *Oof!* I was hit in the mouth with his forearm, stunning me into silence. Before I could defend myself, he landed another punch on my jaw, and everything went black.

When I came to, I was on the ground under the tree where Vince had pinned me, but he was nowhere to be seen. My whole head ached, especially my jaw, and I had no idea how long I'd been there. As far as I could tell, he'd left me alone after knocking me out. I struggled to my feet and trudged to his house. Surprisingly, for everything that we'd done today, it was still early enough in the evening to knock on the door without waking the household.

His mother answered the door. She told me that yes, he was home but that he was in bed with a fever. When she asked me about the bruises on my face, I mumbled something about "boys being boys" before I turned away to go home and get cleaned up. Sick or not, her boy had made the wrong move, and I was pretty sure I knew what Blake forgot to say.

21: Right Side Up

Content Warning

When I finally made it to my house, there were cop cars everywhere. How had I missed them going by Vinnie's house? He lived just up the hill from me. Oh, right, I'd been unconscious. I shuffled into the mix of family and friends and heard the cop talking to Blake.

"Blake, do you have any other relatives living in Maine?"

My friend shook his head. "As far as I know, it was just the three of us. I've never seen an aunt or an uncle or any grandparents. I don't know if any of them even exist."

"Officer, is there any legal reason why Blake would have to live somewhere other than with us?" Peter Madison interceded for the boy.

When did Andy's parents get here? Live with the Madisons? What's going on?

"Only a judge can say for sure, sir. Child Protective Services will have to verify your home as suitable, of course, but if they do that, you can be granted guardianship."

Guardianship? What the heck?

160

"How long does that process take?" Sarah Madison spoke this time.

"It can take several months, but I will ask them if they can expedite it somehow. The judge may be able to do what the bureaucracy cannot. Off the record, I'd say that if you're people of prayer, get that started to make the process work in your favor."

"We'll see what we can do. Can Blake stay with us for now?"

Wait, what? What's going on?? I fought the almost overwhelming urge to butt into their conversation with the million questions swirling through my already beleaguered mind.

"Yes, if that's agreeable to him. Is that what you want, Blake? All right. I'll have you fill out some paperwork with me tonight. Tomorrow, all of us will go see Judge Timberland at family court to see what the next step will be. Then you can go with the Madisons for the night, if not longer."

I watched all of this unfold in my kitchen and wondered what I had missed. *What happened at the fort after I left with Vince? Why does Blake look so different?* I'd gotten home just as the cops left the Harris' driveway with Pop Harris in the backseat of a cruiser. *I guess Mandated Reporter David Madison did his job, then.* "Blake? Are you okay?" I finally found my voice.

"Jack! I'm better than I've ever been before!" He looked at me closely. "Oh, no. What did Vince do? Mrs. Bannister? Jack needs some ice for his face. Vince hit him." Blake took the ice from Stephanie and put it on my face. "I

161

know it hurts, Jack, but it'll be worse if you don't ice it." *He knows what he's talking about, I'm sure.*

"How did you know Vince hit me?" My voice was barely above a whisper.

Blake lowered his voice to match mine. "Forearm before punch, right? Yeah, that's how he does it, right after pinning you to a tree?" He sighed. "I thought he was over that phase. I'm so sorry, Jack." His apology surprised me.

"Vinnie thought he might be g... Last year, Vinnie thought he had 'special' thoughts for me, Jack, and when he tried to express them to me, physically, and I didn't respond in the same way, he knocked me out like he did to you. Of course, given what happens with Pop, he felt totally horrible about it, and hasn't stepped out of line that way with me ever since, so I figured it was just a 'phase' he was going through and it was done with. I'm not sure that's the case, now. I think he's still figuring out what's friendship and what's more than that."

"So that's why he called you his 'special' friend?"

"He called me that?" Blake shook his head sadly. "For all the sins God has had to forgive me of, Jack, being Vince's lover is not one of them. I'm afraid that's all in his mind. I'm his friend, and he is mine. The friendship is 'special' only because he's been my friend longer than anyone else in my life, and he knows the horrors I've experienced for so long, but it's not because we're sleeping together."

"He asked me if I wanted to be his 'special' friend like you and he were just before he began to touch me." My lips were trembling as the reality of Vince's actions became real. "I can't believe he did that to me. I've never done anything to invite that, have I?"

"No, you haven't, Jack. Vince is confused about what's love and what's friendship. Watching porn has made it worse! I've heard people say it's destructive, and now I understand why. It makes it so hard to tell the difference between reality and fantasy, especially if you're like Vinnie and having a tough time sorting that out! The fact that he wasn't feeling well probably made it even tougher for him because he was 'out of his mind,' or lacking his usual self-control. Oh, God, what a mess my sin has made for you, my friend. I'm so sorry! Can you forgive me?"

"Your *sin*, Blake? What are you talking about? What did I miss at the fort??"

"Jack, I realize this may shock you, but I gave my life to Jesus tonight. I've asked him to forgive my sin and to give me new life in God. I can't begin to tell you how freeing it has been, how much peace God has given me, and how alive I feel. And I can't thank *you* enough for bringing Andy to our fort today."

My jaw hit the floor. *Blake Harris is a Christian now??*

"That's not all. When we came to the house, I called the police and reported my father to them. They came and arrested him for the abuse I've suffered for the last several years. The Madisons have offered to take me into their home so that I don't have to go into regular foster care. They are also going to try to gain legal guardianship of me."

My jaw went through the floor to the basement. *If Blake lives with the Madisons, does that mean he'd be at my school in the fall?*

We parted ways not long after that conversation. I murmured some baloney explanation for my bruises to Dad and Steph before going to bed, and the Madisons and Blake went home. They gave me the rundown later on what took place the next day.

On Monday morning, Mr. and Mrs. Madison, along with David and Andy, drove Blake to the courthouse in town. The officer they'd met the night before at the Bannisters met them at the door and ushered them into the building. "Judge Timberland is waiting for us in his chambers. There's a caseworker there, too."

They all fit into the judge's chambers, just barely. Peter and Sarah immediately recognized the caseworker and silently thanked God for his providence; the lady was from their church, knew them well, and had been to their home on many occasions. She was speaking to the judge as they arrived, so they waited until he called on them before saying anything.

"You are Peter and Sarah Madison?" Judge Timberland asked. "And who do you have with you?"

"This is our son David. He's 17. This is our younger son, Andy, who's 12. And this is Blake Harris. He is 13, Your Honor," Peter Madison replied.

"How long have you known the young Mr. Harris?"

"Your Honor?" Andy spoke up. "I'd like to answer that if I may. Blake and I became friends yesterday, but we've known each other for a couple of years. He used to bully me, but yesterday we met and he apologized, and I forgave him, and now we are friends."

"Hmm. That seems a little unusual for your family to be so eager to take him in, then, don't you think, Young Madison?"

"I can see your point, Judge, but we also became brothers yesterday." Andy suddenly wondered if he spoken out of turn in some way.

"And how did you become brothers?" Judge Timberland was intrigued.

"I-I became a Christian, Your Honor," Blake spoke for himself, "and the Madisons are Christians, and that means that we are part of the same family of God. So, if you think about it, even though I don't have any blood relatives here in Maine, David and Andy are the ones that explained to me about becoming a Christian. Now that I am a Christian, that makes us brothers in Christ, and their family, my family, don't you think, Judge?"

Judge Timberland sat back in his seat with a small smile on his face. "That is an interesting argument you put forth for yourself, Young Harris. I believe it is safe to say this in my chambers, because like you, I am a follower of Christ. In fact, you are in an extraordinary position today, Mr. Harris, since everyone involved in your case is a brother or sister in Christ. Yes, even the police officer and caseworker are Christians. From what your caseworker has said to me today, I believe your new guardians would call it 'God's providence' that this situation has played out in this way. However, as happy as you feel right now, Young Harris, I must caution you that the road ahead will not be all roses and buttercups."

The judge leaned forward. "Your father will be put on trial unless he pleads guilty. If he goes on trial, you will be called to testify. He will not be convicted without your testimony, Blake. If it comes to it, testifying against him will be terrible for you. You will have to recount the details of his treatment of you for others to hear, and his attorney will be sure to raise doubts about your trustworthiness as a witness, especially given your own history of vandalism, shoplifting, petty larceny, and assault. You didn't think I knew about that, Blake?"

Blake's face was serious. "No, sir. I was sure you did. I'm just very sad that I did all those things. I want to know how to make them right, if I can."

"If you mean what you say, Young Harris, then I will make arrangements with Mr. Madison for you to make restitution wherever possible. It is more likely to involve service than money, but serving others is a positive way to learn humility, a quality we all need. Wouldn't you agree?"

"Yes, sir. Thank you, Your Honor. Did..did Mr. and Mrs. Madison already know about my crimes when they offered to take me in?"

"When they offered? No. But when they heard about your crimes, they reportedly prayed about it and realized that having you with their family was more important than what you have done in the past. In fact, Blake, your life as a Christian has just begun, and it is wonderful right now. We all rejoice with you, but many changes are coming. Your routines will be different. Your neighborhood will be different. Your school friends will be different. As time passes, you will find that old habits will want to creep back into your life, and you will have to resist those temptations, especially because you're going to be held accountable by very loving parents. In Proverbs 13:14,

King Solomon gives the wisdom that 'sparing the rod spoils the child, but the father that loves his son provides discipline.' Peter and Sarah Madison are highly unlikely to use a physical rod on you, but you can certainly expect them to hold you accountable for your attitudes, actions, and words, just as they do with their natural born children."

The judge continued, "You have lived an undisciplined life, young man. For the first time in your life, you will not be left to run about on your own at all hours of the day and night, and it is going to feel restrictive. In fact, you'll feel as though you've been jailed. My advice to you is this: Your hope is in the newness of life in Christ that has been given to you. Grow in your knowledge and love of God like he is a drug that you crave, and you'll overcome every obstacle that comes to you. Mr. and Mrs. Madison will be your guardians until I say otherwise. Listen to them. Obey them. Honor and respect them and your new family. May God be with you."

"Yessir. Thank you, Your Honor. I'll do what you've said. I'm not saying I want to go to jail or anything, but this kind of 'jail' you just talked about sounds nice for a change. I've never had anyone that cared where I was or when I came home unless it involved hurting me. Everything was also the opposite of what it should have been, and I wondered what I did to turn things upside down. I think it's safe to say for the first time, I feel like my life is right side up."

22: "He *Let* Her Die?"

Content Warning

There was no getting around it: Blake's conversion changed everything for me, and I wasn't happy about it. Sure, I was glad that Pop Harris wasn't beating on Blake anymore, but that was as far as my happiness went. Once again, I found my life disrupted. Blake moved in with Andy's family, Vince had gone all weird on me and I didn't want to hang around him without Blake there. I was getting along with Steph and Dad better, but that kind of freaked me out, and I felt at odds with my life, just like I had in Portland before we moved here.

I wanted to talk to Andy about it but didn't know if the two of us could do that without Blake getting in on the conversation. I was shocked that I was beginning to look forward to the new school year, just to be able to see Andy, and possibly Blake, every day, but that wasn't for several more weeks. The emotional frustration was building up, and I didn't know what to do.

Vince hadn't been out of his house in more than a week. He had vague memories of the weekend at the fort, but his last one was telling his friends that he wasn't feeling well and was going home for the night. He couldn't recall anything after that. He'd woken up in his bed the next afternoon, his mother patting his forehead with a cool washcloth and observing him with more concern than he remembered her having for him in a very long time. She took his temperature, which was 101.2 degrees, and told him to sit up and take two aspirin. She asked about what happened between him and me after he left the fort, but his mind was blank about that; he had no idea what she was talking about. She had him lie down again, covered him, and told him not to worry about it. He asked about his camping gear. She told him that she'd call me and ask me to bring it over, but it was time for Vince to sleep.

When he drifted off again, she did what she said, and I showed up on Tuesday with Vince's sleeping bag, tent, and all the other gear he'd taken to the fort. She asked me what happened between me and her son, but no way was I gonna tell her. I shook my head and muttered something she couldn't follow, so she let it go. I asked how Vinnie was, and she told me he was sick, but that was the end of our conversation. Mrs. Jackson thanked me for bringing her son's stuff, and I left. I haven't seen or heard from Vin or Mrs. J since.

Andy and Blake called a couple of times, but they hadn't been able to visit yet. It was a hectic week at the Madison home. I'd learned that Blake was officially under the guardianship of Peter and Sarah Madison, which my dad had explained meant that Blake would be living with them until further notice. While it wasn't exactly foster care, it was weird that Blake was living with my best friend... *did I just realize that Andy's my best friend?* And that's when all the changes began to make sense to me. *Andy's my best friend from school, and Blake's my best neighbor friend, and now **they're** living in the same house, **away from me!***

The pain and frustration which that realization brought to me erupted volcanically, and I punched a wall in my room, breaking the sheetrock and hurting my fist. "OW! Damn it!" I gritted my teeth in pain and hoped the Dragon didn't come running down the hall to harass me about my language.

169

I was in luck. Steph Bannister was in the yard and didn't hear my outburst. I looked at my hand. It wasn't cut, but my knuckles were reddened and bruised. I brushed off the dust from the sheetrock and looked around for something to cover the hole. I found a Carl Yastrzemski poster I'd gotten for Christmas and hadn't put up yet, so I took a couple of push pins out of my cork board and used Yaz to cover up my misdeed. I was still upset, but under control now, and knew I needed to find some other way to deal with my anger. I left my room, found Steph, and said I was going to the fort.

When I got to the fort, I noticed that some of Blake's and Andy's stuff was still there. I carefully packed it up and stored it under the tarp. Then I realized that I was going to be all alone in the fort without my gang of friends, and the anger welled up once more. I grabbed the makeshift table I'd made and broke it apart, throwing it around in my rage. Not calmed by this, I grabbed the next thing I could reach— the tarpaulin—and began ripping it down, shredding it. I picked up one of the stump stools and threw it at the walls, trying to break them down. In my rampage, I didn't hear the boys arriving behind me.

"Jack! What are you doing?! Stop!!" Andy called to me, but I wasn't listening.

Blake ran up to me and tried to restrain me. "Jack! Stop it! It's me, Blake!"

It wasn't until Blake said his own name that I began to comprehend what was going on. I stopped thrashing and looked around me. The fort was trashed. It wasn't going to be our hangout anymore, but I wasn't sure I cared.

"What's going on with you, Jack?" Blake was still trying to get my attention.

"Everything's changed. You've gone to live with Andy. Vince got weird. I don't have friends anymore. I'm right back where I was when I moved here. I can't handle it." I was dejected.

"What are you talking about? You still have us, Jack! I realize we're all of two-and-a-half miles away now, but gosh, we're still friends, aren't we?" Blake prodded me to acknowledge them. "Okay, I get it. I'm not two houses over anymore, but Andy got a 3-speed bike this week, so we rode over today."

"You *rode* here??"

Andy's grin was a mile wide. "It's a lot easier when you're with a friend and not getting flipped off your bike," he joked, elbowing Blake good-naturedly. "And that 3-speed makes a difference, too." He chuckled. "It's further than I've ridden before, but not impossible. I'm looking forward to the long coast from here to Whitman's!"

I'd never seen Andy look so proud of himself, and I had to admit that I was proud of him, too. "Well, boys, this changes things! I won't say my mood's changed completely for the better but knowing that you two can ride here to hang out, man, I just... COOL!" We all laughed at me for stumbling over my words. "But wait a minute. What brought you guys over here today?"

"Stephanie called us. She thought you could use a friend or two." Blake explained the situation. "Clearly, you need a psychiatrist, too, bud." He smiled at me, but then it faded. "Jack, I'm sorry that my situation upset the friendship applecart for you. I'm sure you're glad that I'm not with Pop anymore, but I don't blame you for being sad not to have Vince and me around. It's going to be a long time before we see Vince again; he's really sick, and not all of it is physical." My friend tapped the side of his head as he said that about Vinnie. "Andy and I have been praying for him."

"So, you really became a Christian, Blake? What happened while I was following Vince home that night?"

"Yes, Jack, I have become a Christian. When you left to follow Vince, I was talking with Andy, and the more questions I had, the more answers he gave. It seemed that no matter what objections I raised, Andy had a Bible verse that talked about it. My life was spinning out of control, you know about that, and I was already planning to die soon. No, really. I had a plan to kill myself, Jack. Pop was truly making our home complete hell. He was abusing me every way possible including what you already know, plus emotionally and verbally. I just couldn't take any more."

Before I could interrupt, Blake held up his hands and said, "There's more to it, Jack. You see that last day we were there, when I went to put back that video, I accidentally opened the spare bedroom door instead of the room I'd gotten it from. It was scary to see what he had in there. That crazy man had a cage with handcuffs and chains, Jack! He was going to make me his prisoner in my own house! I only had that door open for a few seconds, but he caught me closing it. He knew I'd seen what was in the room. I had all I could do to get away from him. That's why he beat me so badly before I could join you and Vince at the fort. I knew I could never go back to that house, so if push came to shove, I was going to string up somewhere in the woods."

I trembled listening to Blake describe the horrors of his life and what awaited him if he had returned to his home.

"Since I had no control over my life, Jack, I tried to control others. I used bullying, scaring, and anything else I could think of to manipulate them—even you and Vince, to get you to do what I wanted. You know I was good at it."

I nodded knowingly.

"I'm sorry I was like that, Jack. I hope you'll forgive me. At any rate, at some point you brought Andy into our lives. Sure, we had picked on him before we knew who he was, but we didn't *know* him. When you introduced him, I felt threatened by him. I thought he was someone that would steal your friendship from me, and I'd lose control over another part of my life."

"But when Andy came here and said he'd forgiven me for bullying him before I even asked him to, it was like a light switch getting flipped on inside me, Jack, or the first in a row of dominos being tipped over. By the time you and Vin left, my heart was ready to give up control, and to let God take over. Nothing *I* was doing helped me, and David and Andy sure made it look like God could take care of me."

That's when I interrupted. "You'd think that, but he didn't take care of Mom! He let her die! He *failed*!"

"He failed? Did your mom trust in him?"

"Well, yeah."

"So, where is she now?"

"In heaven, I guess."

"You guess? Come on, Jack. Is she in heaven or not? If your mom trusted in Jesus, and she died still trusting in him, is she in heaven with him, or did God fail and now she's in hell?" Blake was arguing like his old, persistent self.

"SHE'S IN HEAVEN, YOU JERK! GOD DIDN'T FAIL TO TAKE HER TO HEAVEN. HE FAILED TO KEEP HER *HERE* WITH ME!" I broke down sobbing and fell to my knees. My voice became very small. *"I loved her so much, and I needed her, and he let her die!"*

Blake looked at Andy as if to say *Now what?* Andy shrugged his shoulders and mouthed 'I don't know.' His friend's eyebrows shot up. *What do you mean 'you don't know'?* they said. Blake wasn't used to Andy not knowing what to say. Finally, Andy gestured to Blake with his hands together, 'Pray.' Blake nodded, bowed his head, and began to pray silently for Jack.

Andy sat down next to Jack. "Jack? I'm so sorry that your mom died. I can't imagine what that feels like. I'm here for you, Jack. If you want to talk, or just sit, or feel like yelling at somebody, I'm here. Shoot, you can hit me, if that'll make you feel better." He went quiet and began to pray in his heart.

They sat there for several minutes. As he prayed, Andy felt that this situation was not going to involve him, but that it would be Blake and Jack that talked this out. He prayed that God would give Blake love and patience as he spoke to Jack, and that Jack would be open and listening.

Blake broke the silence. "Jack, I'm glad you can tell the difference between God not failing your mom and what you wanted."

I was lost in my thoughts. "What? What do you mean?"

"You said that God didn't fail your mother. You said that he took her to heaven when she died. Then you said that God failed *you* because he didn't keep her here with you. I'm glad you can see the difference because that's what I asked before you yelled at me."

That puzzled me and put me on my guard, but I wasn't angry. Not yet. "Go on, Blake."

"I was telling you that I decided that God could take better care of me than I was doing because of what I saw in Andy and David, but you didn't agree because of what happened to you. I'm sorry you lost her. When my mom was in my life, she didn't abuse me, but she didn't love me, either. When she left, the only thing that changed was that Pop started abusing me instead of her. Jack, I can't relate to losing a loving parent, because I never had one until I met God." Blake's voice cracked as he spoke the final statement, but he kept his emotions in check.

"Please don't misunderstand me, Jack. I'm not trying to manipulate you like I used to, okay? You asked why I became a Christian, and I'm trying to tell you. For as long as I've known you, I've had walls up to protect myself, and Jesus broke through them. He changed me, Jack. He forgave me and made me *his child*."

"I'm glad it's working out for you, Blake. I really am. But what does that have to do with me?" I couldn't figure out what all that had to do with my objections to the idea that God could be trusted.

When Blake spoke, I had to admit I was surprised by his patience, but he seemed to pound the same nail into the same pressure point in me. "Jack, again, you said your mom trusted God, and he did not fail her."

175

I was getting exasperated from hearing this over and over. "Yeah, Blake, that's right."

"She found him trustworthy."

"Yeah, Blake."

"She had taught you that he could be trusted and that you should trust him, too, and you believed her."

I gritted my teeth. *"Yes. Blake."* I spat out the words.

"So why are you disobeying her now?"

I jumped up and squared to throw a punch. ***"What are you talking about?"*** Spittle flew everywhere as I spewed out my words in utter fury. To my shock, Blake sat down and didn't say anything. "You—You—You can't just toss that out there and not answer my question, Blake!"

He just sat there with his eyes closed. "Are you *praying*?? I can't f-fu—" I remembered Andy was there before I finished the word. "I can't friggin' believe this! Blake-Porno-Harris is preaching and praying? I guess hell *has* frozen over!" And still, he didn't move. I gave up and sat down, too, though I was fuming inside.

Blake spoke again, quietly. "Your dad and Steph love you, right? And you believed your mom at the time when she told you God could be trusted, but now you don't, just because she died? You're still loved Jack! I don't get it." He shook his head sadly.

"You mean I'm supposed to accept that God *allowed* her death? And I have to *keep* trusting it's *better* for me in the long run that it happened that way?" I was incredulous.

"Yes, Jack, that's *exactly* what I'm saying."

"Blake, that's a load of crap!" I jumped up again. *This guy is nuts.*

"No, it isn't, Jack. No, you're going to listen. Sit down and listen. Please. You know what my life has been like for the last decade, Jack. I *never* received love from either of my parents. *All* they gave me was neglect and abuse. Just think about that for a minute, okay? While you're thinking about it, let me tell you that I haven't envied your life. But here's the thing: As awful as my home life has been, I'm beginning to understand it's better for me that it happened that way."

"Are you out of your ever-lovin' mind, Blake Harris??" I nearly sprang out of my seat. "Why would you say something stupid like that?"

"If my life hadn't been so full of hell, Jack, I wouldn't have asked God for help! *He took my hell and gave me heaven!*" The tears were flowing freely from my friend's eyes now. "Jack, if I hadn't known such pain on my own, I wouldn't understand such healing with Jesus now!" He looked me in the eyes and said, "You *must know* that God loves *you like he loved your mom*, Jack. He's waiting for you to return to him, I know he is."

I sighed. "Maybe he is, Blake. Maybe he does love me. Maybe he doesn't. I don't know. At least now I understand what you've been trying to say. I'll... I'll think about it. I will." I could tell my friends were hoping for a more emotional reaction, but I wasn't going to go into hysterics for them. If, IF God loved me like they thought, and was ready to welcome me back, he was going to have to prove himself to me.

This idea of taking an important person from my life "for my own good" was bullcrap, and it was time for God to prove that he wasn't as arbitrary as all that.

177

23. Probing Questions

Content Warning

    Junior high school was weird. About a week after Blake's "heart change," Andy told me about the new school he'd be going to. I couldn't blame him for switching after all the bullying he'd experienced at City Christian, and getting to have his mom as one of his teachers made me envious. I would've loved to have Mrs. Madison as a teacher! Naturally, with the Madisons as his guardians, Blake attended County Christian School, too.

    The final weeks of summer vacation involved some haying at Andy's place, but I had also begun playing soccer at City Christian, so I had practices three days a week for two weeks before classes started. My friends were busy getting their new school building ready when they weren't haying, and we didn't get to hang out much. I was beginning to resent Blake's new faith because of the separation it caused, and I didn't fully realize how much it changed my social life, at first, but without Andy around to help me stay in line at school for seventh grade, joining the soccer team gave me the motivation I needed to keep my grades up and watch my attitude in class.

    I was surprised to learn that Blake and Andy didn't become best friends. On the rare occasion that I saw either one of them, they described themselves as good friends and "brothers in Christ," but Andy still called me his best friend, and Blake was making great connections with kids at their church. They hung out with me as often as possible, but the dynamic was very different.

    Vince wasn't around much, either. When I did see him, he was shy and quiet, and I was careful not to spend time alone with him. He didn't act out again like he did that time in the woods, but I still wanted to stay safe around him. He had grown big and strong, and I wanted no part of what he'd tried to do that summer night.

Then my little brother was born, and I spent more time taking care of him than I did trying to hang out with my friends. It was awesome to be an older brother, and I wanted to learn everything I could about childcare. I'd never expected to feel like that, but it meant that I had to work harder to behave in school so that I wouldn't lose out on time with little Matthew. My relationship with Dad and Steph improved, and I found myself calling her "Mom" often, though not exclusively. To her credit, she didn't force me to.

By the end of 8th grade, I was a starter for the school soccer team, and I had a good shot at making the varsity team as a freshman. I was a sure bet to be junior varsity. I made the honor roll a couple of times and shown that I could do more than the bare minimum in the classroom, though boredom did kick in every now and then, which broought mischief along as its partner.

In the Madison family, Blake had been adopted and was officially Andy's brother. He was visiting me one day while Andy was away, and he filled me in on the latest news. From everything he told me, he attended one-on-one counseling every week, and the family went to counseling once or twice a month. He said that becoming a Christian had completely changed his view of life, and he insisted that without Jesus in his life, he'd already be dead. That shocked me. I couldn't imagine the world without Blake Harris in it.

I still wasn't convinced that God could make that much impact on someone's life, but there was no denying how different Blake's life had been the last two-plus years. It helped that his Pop pleaded guilty to the charges without making Blake suffer through a trial. Mr. Harris was sentenced to 40 years in prison for the crimes against his son, and I'd heard that state prison was not a good place to be for a man with his charges.

Blake said that even with God in his life, the years of neglect and abuse caused issues for him, so that's what the counseling was for. He did solo sessions to help him with his own needs, and the family went as a group to keep all of them helping one another. He didn't share details with me, saying it was confidential, but he told me that the counseling helped a lot.

Little by little, he was putting his early childhood in his past. That included his illegal activities, he added. Mr. Madison and Mr. Whitman were friends, he said, and "Dad Madison" helped him talk with the store owner about the shoplifting.

"You admitted to Whitman that you shoplifted? Are you nuts?" I couldn't believe my ears.

"I had to, Jack. The Bible says, 'You shall not steal.' I'd been stealing for years, and I needed to come clean. Dad Madison helped me by talking to Mr. Whitman first and then by going with me."

"What happened?"

"We went to see him. I introduced myself, and immediately apologized for what I'd done. I asked him to forgive me, and then I offered ways I could make restitution, such as working for him without pay."

"And?"

"He thanked me for admitting to him what I'd been doing. He said he'd known about it all along, and he'd been praying for the day I'd come clean to him. He said that it was an answer to many prayers to be talking to me about it that day! He told me he forgave me and accepted my offer to work for him without pay to make restitution, but he's going to pay me for some of my hours."

"I've already started. I work two hours a day three days a week after school and four hours on Saturday mornings. I offered to let him search my pockets before I leave work each time, but he told me he'll know if I steal again, and that he's giving me this chance to earn his trust."

My jaw went slack. "How in the world did he know and not prevent you from going into his store?"

He shrugged. "I haven't asked him that. Maybe when I get to know him better."

"Well, let me ask you this, then, Blake. You've given up shoplifting. What about smoking? What about porn?"

"What about them, Jack?"

"Are you still smoking?"

"No."

"Still watching porn?"

He laughed at me. "We don't even have TV!"

"Reading it, then?"

"No, Jack."

"Not even tempted?"

"I won't say I'm never tempted to smoke or look at porn, Jack, but God is helping me resist these sins."

"Oh, so smoking is a sin?"

181

"I'm not sure that it is, but it's against the law, so it's sinful for *me* to do it. Why are you so interested in these things?"

"I'm just trying to get a sense of how *Christian* you really are, Blake. You know, did you actually convert, or just for pretend?"

"Jack, do you know what it means to be a Christian? It means that I've been forgiven of my sin by God. It also means that God is helping me become more like Jesus every day. When I read the Bible, pray, worship God in church, study the Bible with others—these are actions I take to help me learn more about what God is saying to me through his Word, the Bible, so that I can love him and obey him more. When I don't get it right—when I fail and sin again, which happens every single day—and I ask him to forgive me again, he will. That is grace, and it is amazing. Maybe instead of mocking it, Jack, you should ask for it."

"Whoa, hey, no need to get huffy, Blake. I was just asking a couple of innocent questions."

"No, Jack, those weren't just 'a couple of innocent questions.' You were trying to see if I'm the same old Blake Harris underneath, scummy son of Pop Harris, the kid that swears, flips people off, bullies everyone, talks about screwing girls at school, smoking weed, and whatever else you can bring up. You don't fool me, Jack. You never have."

"Oh, I see how it is. I never fooled you, so you decided to fool me, right?"

"What do you mean by that?"

"You knew what Vince was like when he went without enough sleep. You *knew* how he'd act when he got 'sick.' And you *still* sent me after him that night at the fort."

Blake's face went pale. "That's not how it was, Jack, I swear. Not that night."

"Not that night? You mean there was *another* night you were going to do that? What kind of sick jerk does that?"

My friend—though maybe I shouldn't call him friend now—sat down and put his head in his hands. Finally, he looked at me. "I was going to tire him out another time and set you up, just to knock you down a peg or two, but I was going to follow you guys to make sure he didn't get anywhere with what he'd be sure to try."

"*That* night, though, I was so caught up in what was going on with David and Andy and me that I totally forgot about the situation with Vinnie, except that he seemed ill. I knew I had to tell you to be careful, but I couldn't remember what for. I am *so sorry*, Jack!" He ran his fingers through his hair. "Oh, God! What did he do to you?"

"Wow, you really were a manipulative prick. Did it give you jollies to think about Vinnie and me like that? Were you *that jealous* that our parents weren't cruel like yours?" I pressed him. *You're right, Blake. I'm looking for the old you. How hard do I have to prod and pry to find you? I'm looking for your breaking point, mister. Come on, just a little more, and I'll prove that your God is no match for the ol' Blake Harris temper!*

"Did it really twist you that much that our dads weren't screwing us like yours screwed you, Blake, so you tried to get our *friend* to screw *me*? You said it; it's all about having control, right?" *That ought to do it.*

Blake stood up and walked around. *God, my life was such a mess! I did so much that was wrong, so many terrible things. I'm trying to come clean with Jack, Lord, and he's so angry and hurt. He's doing everything he can to make me angry; I don't blame him, Father. I was angry for so long. Forgive me, Jesus. Forgive my friend; he doesn't know what he's doing. If he forgives me or not, I know you have. Thank you. And thank You for your love, Jesus.*

He broke the silence. "Yes."

"Yes? Yes, what?" I was startled that Blake was suddenly talking again.

"Yes, I really was a manipulative prick. Yes, sometimes it gave me jollies thinking about you two like that. Yes, sometimes I really was that jealous that your parents weren't cruel like mine. Yes, it really did twist me that other kids' dads weren't screwing them like mine did me, and that it made me a freak. Yes, I was going to try to get our friend to mess with you a little bit, but not to screw you like you're saying it. And yes, it was all about having control." He'd said everything so matter-of-factly but looked so sad.

It was my turn to fall silent. *I was just egging him on; I didn't think he'd actually answer me, and I especially didn't think his answers would be "Yes." We were friggin' twelve and thirteen years old back then, for goodness' sake. Kids that age aren't supposed to be dealing with issues like these. Shoot, we're fourteen and fifteen now, and these issues still shouldn't be on us. What the heck?*

My next thought blurted out before I could stop it. "Dude, are you straight?" *Did those words just come out of my mouth?*

184

"You know something, Jack? I don't know. I'm kind of young to know that right now."

I laughed. "Not the answer I expected, to be honest, Blake."

"No?"

"I would've pegged you for straight-as-an-arrow. Well, until our little conversation tonight, anyway."

He chuckled. "Because of the way Pop treated me, I did my best to convince myself and everyone else that I was straight, Jack. The truth is, though, I've always wondered where I stand. Still, I think it's too soon to know for sure one way or another. That's why I answered you the way I did a couple of minutes ago."

"You mean, 'sometimes get your jollies blah blah blah'?"

"Exactly. I'm not going to specify what 'get your jollies' means, but if you're asking whether the thoughts were ever attractive to me or not, yeah, sometimes they were. Sometimes they weren't. And that's the way I am every day. Some days I like girls, other days, boys. I don't know if my attraction is just wanting to be emotionally close or if it's something more. Since I'm only 15, I figure I have time to sort it out."

He continued. "Something I've been learning about in science class is that our brains don't completely mature until our mid-twenties, so our feelings and attractions will come and go for a long time. We can be 'certain' we're attracted one way now and in a couple of years, it has changed, so I'm in no rush to say one way or the other. Plus, the Bible is clear that a guy is supposed to marry a girl or be single, so I'm asking God to help me with that. I bet you didn't expect a long answer to such a short question, did ya?"

I shook my head. "No, and I'm not surprised you worked God into your answer, but I am a little shocked that Blake Harris would admit to being attracted to guys sometimes."

Blake looked at me for a long moment. "I'm not sure I ever would have said anything about that to you, Jack, but then you started asking very personal and direct questions. After I prayed and asked God for help answering you, it seemed the best answers were as direct and personal as you had been. As you know, I've disregarded other people's safety and well-being all my life while trying to control them for my own selfish reasons. Now I'm trying to be as open and honest as possible, even if it makes us both a little uncomfortable. Or would you prefer I go back to be sneaky and manipulative?"

I shrugged. "No, open is fine. Awkward, but fine." I laughed a little, and he did, too. "I'm glad we still know how to laugh at each other."

"Me, too."

I felt the need to redirect the conversation, which had gotten waaaay too serious. "Tell me, what's it like to live with the Madisons and go to school with Andy?"

"I'll answer you, but I wanna know how your family's doing, too, okay?" After I nodded my agreement, Blake told me more. "You've been over a lot, so you know what the family is like, anyway. Andy and I share a room, but the bunkbeds are getting a little small! I don't know what we're going to do, but Dad Mad—I know it sounds funny, but it's the nickname we use now—has talked about fixing up a different part of the house to make a larger room for us on the first floor, or possibly just completing another room on the second floor and letting me have my own room. The only problem with that is that I'm still having separation issues, so I'd rather not be alone. We're trying to figure out the best solution."

"Andy has been great, even though he was used to getting all the attention as the youngest and doesn't get as much as he used to. He's happy to be my brother, and we're both glad to have David as an older bro and mentor. Of course, David's in college now, so we don't see him as much as we used to, and that's a bummer. Dad Mad is glad to have extra hands for all the chores! Andy seems more motivated, too, since he's not working alone as much. That is, I help when I can, but I go to so many counselors and therapy sessions that I'm not always around to help, but when I am, he's happier. It's cool."

I broke in, "Ha ha ha. Andy *is* happier when he's not doing the work!" I laughed and laughed. "Oh, that cracks me up, Blake. He's a good worker, but he's not a fan of it, that's for sure!"

Blake grinned. "Yeah, he likes his breaks."

"Do they make you go to church and all that crap, too?"

"It's not crap, Jack, not to me. I'm thrilled to go to youth group, Bible study, prayer meeting, and church and Sunday school. I *get* to go, not *have* to go. I also get to go to Bible camp in the summer. It's just a week in August, but it's *awesome*. Hey, I'm not perfect, Jack, and I don't understand everything they talk about, but it's changing my life for the better, and I like doing it."

"How's the school? *That's* gotta be different from what you're used to."

"Yeah, it's been an adjustment. I'd been in the same school with kids from our town all my life, and then in 7th grade I was suddenly not there anymore. It was weird. I mean, just a few weeks before school started, I met Jesus, my dad got arrested, I moved to a new home in a new town, and I started attending a Christian school. Why wouldn't there be an adjustment involved? Especially since my new "mom" was one of my teachers *and* the school principal?"

"Wait, what? Mrs. Madison is the principal, too? I didn't know that!" I was amazed that Andy's mom held so many different roles at their school. *I'm more envious than ever! Wish I could go there!*

"I wish you could go there, Jack! It'd be so cool to have you in our classes." Blake had read my mind, it seemed. "But I know your mom...I mean, your stepmom would have to teach there, too, because of the rules at your school."

"It's cool, Blake. I call her 'Mom' more often than not now. You ought to see my little brother! He's two now, running around and talking. He's so much fun. My dad got a new job about a year ago. It has better pay and better hours. Steph doesn't have to work now if she doesn't want to. I wonder..."

"You wonder what, Jack?"

"Naw, I just realized that the only way they could afford my tuition at the school I go to now is that I go free if she works there. They'd never be able to pay for me to go to your school. Bummer."

"Hey! We could pray about it. You never know if you don't ask." Blake was in earnest.

I didn't want to throw cold water on his idea, but I knew the money wasn't there. "Tell you what, Blake. You pray. If your God wants it to happen, then he'll make it happen. I'm not holding my breath." No cold water, but he deflated a little. What can I say? I just don't believe like he does.

24: Jacked to Party

Content Warning

As excited as I was to be a varsity starter as a freshman, we weren't a big school, so I'd have to play exceptionally well to make a name for myself. I didn't mind. It was better than goofing off in class. No, really, for all the trouble I'd made in my first year or two there, now that I had a place on the soccer team, I was focused on my studies and stayed in line. Nothing was going to keep me from playing each week!

In our first game of the season, I scored two goals, leading the team to victory, 3-2. The local paper did a story on us, highlighting the youthfulness of our starting core, since there were five freshmen and four sophomores among the starters. It was cool to see my name in print; Dad brought home a couple extra copies of the paper the day the story ran so he could keep the article and send one to each of my grandparents.

Our second game was a blowout in which I scored a hat trick, and we defeated our opponent 10-2. Unfortunately, our goalie was injured late in the game. He finished playing; we didn't realize he was hurt until the game was over. Coach Williams asked me if I'd play that position in the next game, since I'd been a keeper some in junior high. I liked playing offense, but I was willing to do whatever it took to help the team, so I said I'd do it. I had no idea what effect that was going to have on us.

For the next three games with me in goal, we shut out our opponents and won each game. The newspaper sent their reporter to interview me. When she asked why I'd switched positions when I was scoring so often and so easily, I knew the words to say. "I just wanted to do what would help the team. Coach asked me to make the switch, so I did. This is a team sport, and everyone does his part." Of course, I couldn't help grinning like an idiot as others praised my level of play, especially 'for a freshman.' It was the first time since I started school there that I began to feel popular and accepted. It felt good. Really good.

There were only two seniors on the team, and they weren't starters. I'd wondered why, but one of the sophomores eventually told me that the two seniors had gotten into some trouble as juniors. As a result, they'd almost lost their spots on the team. "Their parents slid some extra money the school's way, and the guys were allowed to stay on the team, but they lost their roles as starters," he told me. I didn't know if that was all true or not, but I wondered what they could have done that would've caused so much fuss.

The sixth week of the season, we had a bye. Coach practiced us until Thursday, and then told us to take the weekend off, saying that we'd resume Monday with prep for our next opponent. As we left practice, the two senior guys, Cody and Phil, came up to me. "Say, Jack, what do you have going on tomorrow after school?"

"Nothing."

"Well, then, Mr. Soccer, how 'bout joining us and a few of our friends for a little get together?"

"What do you have in mind?"

Phil took up the comments. "Cody, here, has a great place just outside town. Huge house, indoor pool, grill on the patio, you get the picture. We were thinking it'd be fun to treat you to a little gathering to celebrate our success as a team so far and thank you for all your contributions to it. Whaddya say, Jack? You up for that?"

I began to nod my head. "Who else is gonna be there? Anyone else from the team?"

"Yeah, we've invited other guys. Don't know if they'll show up or not. We're keeping it kinda hush-hush, though, since the school kinda frowns on fun like this, y'know? Tell you what: You're a freshman, so why don't we invite you to stay over tomorrow night, so your folks won't be suspicious? We'll call it a soccer team social event, all right? That should work." Cody suggested the way to make it work for me to be there.

I liked their thinking. I didn't know what would be going on or who would be there, but it sounded a little rebellious, which appealed to me immediately. I loved playing on the team, yet I had to admit that all this rule-following was getting on my nerves. Life just hadn't been the same since Vince went weird and Blake got religion.

My dad was waiting in the parking lot to pick me up from practice, so Phil and Cody did the inviting in person. Apparently, he hadn't heard of them before, so no red flags went up for him when they introduced themselves, and he readily agreed to the plan they presented, in spite of the fact that they were three years older than I am, as I had recently turned 15. I don't think it ever entered his mind that they could be up to something less than wholesome, while I was hoping for just that. Then again, what I was hoping for and what happened weren't the same thing.

The next day when I got up, I packed my swimsuit, a towel, a change of clothes, and a few other items into my backpack, and then passed my day in eager anticipation of going home with Cody at the end of it. He drove a Camaro, which was also a rare treat to ride in for me, given that I typically rode in my father's Oldsmobile sedan, an ugly family car if ever there was one. I could sense that Cody wanted to show off the speed of the Camaro, but he behaved with me in it.

When we got to his house, he showed me around the first floor, so I'd know my way around, and then told me to follow him upstairs. "Here's the guest room you'll be staying in," he said. "Go ahead and put your stuff there. See that door on the right? That's the bathroom. And my room is the next one down the hall on the left. If you want, you can change now for the pool party. People should start showing up in the next hour or so."

I couldn't believe my ears, but I played it cool. My hopes of a pool party were coming true. Of course, I wanted to see if the 'elements' of a pool party would be involved, but I'd have to wait and see on those. I went into the bathroom and changed into my swimming trunks, tee shirt, and flip-flops, hoping I hadn't picked the wrong clothes for the evening. When I went downstairs and saw Cody and

Phil, I realized I'd chosen well. As their other guests began to arrive, I relaxed about my outfit, feeling foolish that I'd been concerned about it at all. This really was a pool party; people were trickling toward the water. It had been ages since I'd been for a dip, and I was ready for one today.

Cody was the first one in the pool, yelling for others to jump in, too. A couple of girls I recognized from school jumped in, plus some I didn't know. I cast off my shirt and footwear and joined them. "Ladies, this is our Mr. Soccer!" Cody called out. With that, a couple of the older girls came swimming over to me.

"Mr. Soccer!" they squealed. "Swim with us!" They giggled and flirted shamelessly. I laughed and swam across the pool with them. I didn't know what Cody was doing, but I went along with it. "Swim to the shallow end, Mister Soccer. We want to see your abs!" I blushed a little when they said that, but followed them, anyway. *Why not show off that I've been working out?*

I'm fifteen years old, and these what, 17- or 18-year-old girls are admiring my washboard stomach? I grinned and said, "All right, ladies, you'll have to take a picture and let me go. No hogging me."

"Awwww. Did you say, 'No hugging you?'" they whined.

I laughed again and shook my head. "Nope. Not what I said at all! I said, 'No *hogging* me.' You gotta share me with other people." I grinned at them again and opened my arms wide. Each one came alongside for a half-hug. "See? I'm willing to hug."

As we broke away from each other, I glanced at Cody. He had a look in his eye that made me stop smiling and wonder what was going on. *Did I just screw up badly? Wait, was this a setup? Oh, crap. I didn't think this through at all. I was so full of myself that when he and Phil invited me, I fell for it hook, line, and sinker. Have I just screwed my place on the team?*

Lost in my thoughts, I didn't see the senior boy swimming toward me. "Jack? Are you okay?" Cody tapped me on the arm. I jumped at the contact. "Jack, it's just me. Are you all right? You spaced out there for a couple of minutes." Cody's face creased with concern.

"Oh, I uh, yeah, um." I fumbled for words, unsure of what to say.

"Hey, I'm sorry if I put too much pressure on you, Jack."

"Too much pressure?"

"Siccing those girls on you like that. I've been telling them about your skills on the field, and they've been dying to meet you. I didn't realize they'd come on to you so strong."

I felt embarrassed again for some reason. *Probably because you were just thinking the worst of this guy, you idiot.*

"Jeez, Jack, why are you blushing? Was it something I said?" Cody laughed.

"Sorry, Codes. Is my freshman immaturity showing that much?" I groaned with chagrin.

He punched me in the arm. "Don't worry about it, kid. Seriously, though, what has you so flustered?"

I hesitated again, but then I came clean. "I hate to say this, Codes, but I got a little paranoid a few minutes ago."

Cody laughed again. "About what, kid? Oh, you think we're trying to trick you or something? Naw, man, this was just a little fun." He punched me in the arm again. "Come on, let's get out of the pool and get something to drink."

I wondered how he could tell so easily what my paranoia was about, but he seemed sincere. I brushed off my fears and followed him to the pool's edge. We climbed out, toweled off, and headed for the kitchen, where he handed me a cup of punch, cautioning me to drink it slowly. Didn't take a rocket scientist to figure out why he said that. I don't know what kind of mixed beverage it was, but it clearly contained alcohol. I was grateful for the word of caution and for the fruit juice that cut the potency of the liquor, but I knew from my first sip that this cup wouldn't be my last tonight.

Having never been to a party like this, I didn't know what to expect, except for what I'd seen on TV or in movies. Cody and Phil had arranged decent food, including pizza and sub sandwiches, and guests had brought the booze. I was hungry after being in the pool, and I found the subs most appealing. When I finished a six-inch roast beef sandwich, I grabbed some potato chips and went in search of my second cup of punch.

Cody saw me and said, "Be sure to drink at least one cup of water for every punch to avoid a raging hangover, kid. Otherwise, you'll get dehydrated."

I nodded, filled my cup with tap water, and downed it. Then I went for the alcohol. Not being a drinker *and* being so young, two cups of booze brought on a buzz quickly. I relaxed and looked around for my hosts. Not finding them, I refilled my cup with water twice more, drained it, and filled it again with the latest mix provided, vodka and orange juice. My body said, 'slow down,' so I listened, at least for a little while. I wanted to enjoy the party.

I didn't find Phil or Cody, but I did locate the pool girls. They were talking to boys from another school. As I glanced around the party, I realized that no other kids from our school were there. Aside from the two girls I'd seen in the pool at the start, I hadn't seen anyone I knew. Well, the guys did say they'd invited others but weren't sure if anyone would show up or not. Apparently, hanging out with these two wasn't something the 'good' kids did. *Screw 'em. These guys are fun.*

Naturally, if any word of what I was doing reached my folks or the coach, my season would be over, but in my buzzed haze, that wasn't part of my thinking. The pool girls came up to me again and wanted to hang out. I didn't see any reason why not, so we sat in lounge chairs near the pool and sipped our drinks while they talked about their school. To my surprise, I realized that they were from my town, and they were seniors at our town high school. If I hadn't been stuck at the religious school all this time, I'd have known them longer.

I asked them where they lived and who they knew from town. Turns out they lived about a mile from me, but their lives took place in the opposite direction, so our paths never had a reason to cross. As we talked, I finally asked their names. The blond-haired girl was Leslie, and the brunette was Lisa. I didn't know if I'd ever see Leslie or Lisa again, but if I did, I wanted to who they were. Before they left, each girl gave me a peck on the cheek and said I was "sweet." I blushed yet again and mumbled my thanks.

For mid-autumn, it was a remarkably warm evening. After visiting with Leslie and Lisa, I went outside to the patio, where I found Phil for the first time all evening. He was sitting there with a couple of his buddies. They all looked very relaxed, and a familiar aroma hung around them. "Hey, Jack, sit down and join us. Fellas, this is our Freshman Phenom I was telling you about. He can score for our team and keep the other teams from scoring against us. Shoot, Coach doesn't need Cody and me anymore!"

I shot Phil a look of surprise, and he realized what he'd given away. "No, Jack, no, don't worry about that. That's just me being a jerk. It's my own fault that I'm not starting this year, not yours. Really, Cody and I are happy you're on the team. You're a good player!" He fell all over himself apologizing. "Here, peace smoke?" He handed over his blunt and encouraged me to try it. I was only too eager. With a couple of puffs, though, I was choking on the smoke, and Phil and his friends were laughing. "Not the same as a cigarette, bud! Here, try again."

Within a few minutes, I was as stoned as they were. What a feeling! No wonder they'd looked so relaxed when I arrived. *This* was the way to live. No worries. No concerns. *Wow. Mary Jane, where have you been all my life?*

The good feeling didn't last long. The vodka, the other mixed drinks, the roast beef sub, and the pot overwhelmed my senses, and I began to feel queasy. One of Phil's friends noticed. "Phil, I think your friend's gonna be sick. Want me to help him find a bathroom?"

With that, he motioned for me to follow him into the house. He led me upstairs as he said, "Are you staying here? In the guest room?" As I nodded yes and tried not to lose my stomach contents too soon, he showed me to the bathroom I'd already forgotten my way to. "Quick. In here." He lifted the lid and helped me kneel just in time.

As my supper, drinks, and lunch returned in spectacular fashion, Phil's friend stood by, handing me toilet paper to wipe my mouth every few heaves and flushing the toilet when the smell became overpowering. He gently patted me on the back to make me feel better when I seemed to be nearing the end, but it just triggered a fresh wave. *Maybe that was his intention? Get it all over with at one time?* I appreciated his kindness. He even got me a glass of water from the sink.

When the drama was all over, he washed my face with a cloth from the cabinet, helping me to feel less gross, but that lasted only a few minutes. "Go sit on the bed for a minute. I'll be right back. I don't think you're ready to rejoin the party just yet." I was touched by his concern, not realizing what was on his mind.

While we were upstairs, Cody was downstairs looking for me, apparently. He found Leslie and Lisa and asked them if they'd seen me. "We talked to Jack for a long time. Did you know that we live about a mile from him? Same road, same town, and everything! If it weren't for him having to go to your school, we'd be in high school together! He's a sweet kid."

Cody nodded. "He is a sweet kid, and I want to keep him that way. Do you have any idea where he went after you got done talking to him?"

Leslie shook her head, but Lisa said, "I think I saw him head for the patio."

"Thanks, ladies. I gotta dash." Cody hurried outside. The only one there was Phil, stoned out of his mind. "Phil, buddy, where's Jack?"

Phil's eyes were glassed over. "Jack? ZJack?" he mumbled. "Youdon'tknowzJack!" he giggled. "WhozJack?"

"Oh, come *on*, Phil! Where is Jack?" Cody urged his friend. Still getting no coherent response, he slapped Phil across the face using his open palm.

"OW!" screamed Phil, putting a hand to his face. "WHAT DID YOU DO THAT FOR, YOU JERK?!"

"Phil, where is Jack? Who is with him? I need to know NOW!"

Phil's eyes rolled around, slowly focusing. "Jack'supstairswithKevin," he slurred.

"Kevin? Oh, shit!" Cody took off running.

Up in the guest room, Phil's friend Kevin had come back to check on me. "Ugh, Jack. You got puke on your swimsuit."

"I-I did?" My head was still foggy from the dope and drinks.

"Here, let me help you change. Your clothes are over here, right?"

I nodded groggily, though something didn't seem quite right about this. I couldn't quite put my finger on it. What was I missing? "My clothseses are in my backpack," I stumbled to say. Do you know how hard it is to speak clearly when you're drunk?

Kevin nodded. "Okay, Jack, just lie back and we'll get you taken care of. Lift your hips so I can slide those off you."

I was so tired from puking that I didn't think about what he was doing, at first, but then he made a mistake, and something clicked. *Did he just lick his lips?* Alarm bells began ringing in my head, and just as he began tugging at my trunks, I stopped cooperating. I tried sitting up. "I can change my own clothes, Kevin, thanks."

He didn't seem to hear me. Instead, he just pushed me back down and kept trying to get my trunks off me. When I tried to move, he pinned me down on the bed. The fog cleared from my brain instantly.

"What are you doing, Kevin?" I demanded. "What is wrong with you? Let me go!"

"Oh, Jack, I don't think so. I said I'll take care of you, and we're just getting started. You've already shown how willing you are, so this is all consensual."

"What?? No! This is NOT consensual! I do not agree to this, Kevin! Stop! You need to stop!" I began twisting and turning as much as I could to get away from him, but he was bigger, stronger, and in a better position to keep me captive.

"You said you would let me take your swimsuit off you, Jack. Why did you do that if you didn't want what's next?"

"I thought you were helping me change my clothes, Kevin. That's all I was expecting!" *This is a nightmare. How am I gonna get out of this?*

"There's no point in yelling, Jack. The music downstairs is so loud that no one will hear you, but if you're thinking of crying out, I'll stuff a sock in your mouth. If you're going to cooperate, no sock. What's it gonna be, sock or no sock? No sock? Good. Now, just lie still and let Kevvy

200

take care of you." The silky tones of this guy's voice creeped me out and made my stomach churn again, but I didn't know what to do.

25: The Party's Over

I shut my eyes and tried to ignore what was happening. That's how I missed Cody's dramatic entrance. By the time I realized that I was being rescued, Kevin was not much more than a bloody mess on the carpet, and I was covered with a blanket by an extremely apologetic Cody.

The party ended at that point. Cody sent his other guests home. I don't know what he told them, but they got the hint and left. Phil was incoherent the rest of the night. Cody kept Kevin locked in a spare room overnight so he and Phil could address him in the morning when they were all sober. I stayed in Cody's room, and Cody slept where I had been accosted by Kevin. My first party had been a success and a failure of epic proportions, but there was no way I was going to involve the police or my parents. The success had been too much fun to ruin it with the little discomfort that Kevin had brought to it. I'd settle that up with Cody's help, and then I'd get on with my life. Bringing my parents and/or the cops into it would ruin my new-found social life, which was the last thing I wanted to do.

By morning, the high and the buzz were gone, and I was left with questions about my attacker. I talked them over with Cody and Phil. Cody had known that Kevin could be like that, he said, but he didn't think Kevin would be so bold at the party last night. When I'd gone missing, though, Cody became alarmed and started searching for me. Once he realized that Kevin was with me, he was sure of what was happening and raced to find me before Kevin could complete his plans. He hadn't asked me last night, so he put it to me now. "What did Kevin do?"

I explained how the situation unfolded. "Ultimately, he didn't get very far. When I realized what he had in mind, I tried to get up, but he pinned me to the bed. He had just started to pull my trunks off when you burst through the door. I had shut my eyes so he couldn't see my reaction to what he was doing to me, which is why I didn't witness your daring rescue, Codes." I laughed slightly, trying to lighten the mood. "All I saw was a bloody mess on the floor."

"Speaking of that bloody mess," growled Cody, "where is it, Phil?"

Phil looked back nervously. "He's, uh, he's still in his room."

"Go get him and bring him here. NOW."

After Phil left, Cody turned to me. "I am so, completely, totally sorry for what happened, Jack. Kevin wasn't supposed to be here. Phil invited him. Phil was supposed to keep an eye on him. I'm as pissed at Phil as I am at Kevin, and Phil knows it."

Phil returned with Kevin in tow, arms bound with rope. They sat opposite Cody and me.

Content Warning

"All right, asshole," Cody growled again. "What's with the pedophile act last night?"

Kevin's eyes opened as wide as Buick hubcaps. "Pedophile act? What are you talking about?" He turned to Phil. "You told me he was 17 but looked young for his age."

202

Cody and I looked at Phil. Phil blinked. *"PHIL?"* Cody was outraged. *"You told* Kevin he could take a turn at Jack? What kind of sick fuck does that? Jack was a guest at my house last night!"

Phil shrugged. "Listen, Cody. I'm tired of playing second fiddle to this *freshman*. If you remember, *we* are seniors. *WE* are supposed to be starters. *I* am the best fucking goalie this team has ever had. When what's-his-name went down with an injury, *I'm* the one Coach should have called on to take over, not this Jack-in-the-Box. If you'd let my plan play out, the kid would be done, and you and I would be starting again, 'cuz Coach would have no choice but to play us."

He never saw what hit him. One moment he was standing there spouting his outlandish ideas, and the next minute he was on the floor, clutching his blood-spurting nose. "Get out of my house and don't ever come back, you filthy jerk! You come here again, and I'm calling the cops!" Cody was trembling with rage as he threw out Phil and Kevin. I sat down in the nearest chair, stunned.

Cody calmed down and asked me how I was feeling. I admitted that I wasn't sure, so he offered me some breakfast. Food helped a lot. It steadied my thinking and my nerves. I realized how little I knew my senior teammate, and we talked and laughed for about an hour. Then he surprised me for the second time that weekend. "Hey, Jack, I'd like to make up this crappy experience to you. You wanna stay another night? We could just hang out, drink a few beers, take a swim, grill some burgers, maybe watch a movie. Nothing big, just to make up for a lousy end to the party."

"Sounds like fun to me."

"Great! I'll call your dad and ask if that's okay." He got up and went to the kitchen phone. I overheard most of his end of the conversation, which seemed to go favorably. When he returned, he reported, "He said that if I get you home early Sunday afternoon so you can get your homework done before Monday, he's fine with it. Naturally, I didn't mention the 'drinking beers' part." He laughed. So did I.

"Thanks, Cody. I guess I don't really understand why you picked me to hang out with, but I'm enjoying myself. Well, for the most part." *Why do I enjoy his company this much? I've never been one to hang out with older kids. I mean, he's cool and all, but what is it? Oh, come on, Jack, no, that's not it. Get a grip.*

"Well, now that you're my prisoner until tomorrow, I suppose there's no harm in coming clean." He looked at me with a twinkle in his eye and laughed loudly. "Don't look so nervous, Jack!"

"Kinda hard not to look nervous after a comment like that and an experience like last night, Codes."

He chuckled again. "Say, I like your nickname for me, 'Codes.' Anyway, I *was* as upset as Phil about you being so good, at first, but unlike him, I'm willing to 'take one for the team,' as it were. I like winning, Jack, and with you on our team—along with the other young players we have—we're winning more than when Phil and I were playing as starters. Phil was a good keeper, no doubt about it, but once he found dope, he lost reaction time, and he wasn't as good anymore. Lay off it until you're done playing soccer, Jack, 'cuz it'll mess with your skills."

"And I knew Kevin played for the other team, so I didn't invite him, especially since he loses perspective and self-control when he's high. He's come after me—with no success—and he's gone after Phil. Phil plays whatever team he can get, and he'll use Kevin to intimidate anyone who gets too close to taking Phil's place on the soccer team. I don't know if you've decided which team you play for yet, but it's not Kevin's or Phil's place to force that issue with you. For Phil to suggest that Kevin even try that with you is out of line in my book; beyond my 'Code.'" He smiled wryly.

I nodded, finally catching on to what he said about playing for 'one team or another'. "I appreciate your frank comments about my place on the soccer team, Cody. I've been looking for somewhere to belong since I moved here several years ago, and this is the first time I've felt that. I had a group of friends when I first arrived, but circumstances changed and that didn't last. To be part of a soccer team—to be friends with you—is more fun than I ever imagined possible. Last night's party was great until it wasn't. Kevin was kind, until he wasn't. As for which 'team'...I've always figured I'd know that by now, and I even laughed at a friend a few months ago for not knowing himself on that. He said he'd figure it out as he went along, even saying that 'scientifically speaking, guys tend to take until their mid-twenties to sort themselves out ultimately, and they can go through cycles of liking one versus another several times till that point.'"

"Are you saying you see your friend's point?" Cody inquired.

"Mm. Yes, I think I am. How weird would it be if I told you–?" I stopped.

"Go ahead, Jack. I won't share with anyone else what you tell me. You know things that could get me jail time, remember?"

I realized that was true. "Okay, Codes. How weird would it be if I told you that if Kevin hadn't pinned me, I might have been interested in, I dunno? Never mind." I couldn't bring myself to say it because it still would've been wrong—illegal-type wrong, not to mention all kinds of weird to think about. Besides, I was pretty sure which "team" I played for, and it was coed.

Cody shook his head. "Not judging you here, Jack, but maybe we should just leave it there, huh?"

"You're a smart guy, Codes."

"Sometimes a guy learns from his mistakes, Jack, and sometimes a guy learns from other people's mistakes."

I sat there in silence, thinking about what he said. Cody stood up and stretched. "I think it's time for us to go play some soccer, don't you? I've got a field out back, and I think I have some cleats that'll fit you."

Ninety minutes later, Cody and I returned to the house, sweaty and laughing from our time on the pitch. I was impressed that his family owned enough land for him to have a full-sized practice pitch behind their house, and they kept it in top condition. Cody could see the admiration in my eyes, I'm sure, but he wasn't arrogant about the family wealth. He just mumbled something about his parents' success as doctors, and their willingness to give him the freedom to live almost entirely on his own during his junior and senior years. They came to see him about once a month or so, but he had the place to himself most of the time. I asked him if he got lonely, and he said no. He

206

enjoyed his solitude and invited friends over when he wanted people around.

We had battled one-on-one for about forty minutes, and then just practiced various skills for the school team. He took a lot of shots on goal to help me improve my play there, pointing out some weaknesses I had as keeper, giving me a private tutorial. Phil was right; Cody was a great player, and I was discovering a great admiration for his skills. *What could he possibly have done to get demoted to the bench?* I wasn't sure he'd tell me, but I was dying to know. I decided against asking him this weekend, though. I hoped to visit him again, and maybe he'd just open up and tell me at some point. Or not. I simply decided that this wasn't the time nor the place to rock this boat.

The rest of our day was fun, too. We swam in the pool to cool down after playing soccer. Leslie and Lisa came over and joined us. That made the time more enjoyable and a little less awkward, to be honest. In addition to swimming, we played *Uno*™ and *Monopoly*™, with the latter taking us right up to supper time. That's when we were treated to Codes the Cook! Man, that guy can grill a mean burger. After burgers, chips, and soda, the girls went home. I found out that when they'd told me last night that they live a mile from me, they didn't explain that they're not sisters, even though they looked a lot alike. They live across the road from each other and have been friends since kindergarten. I bet the only thing that would break up their friendship would be chasing after the same guy. Like, Cody, maybe.

When they left, Codes broke out the beer, as promised. "I didn't want to bring it out while they were still here, since they had to drive home, and I haven't had time to clean the spare bedroom for them to stay over," he explained. "Come on, Jax, let's go pick a movie and relax." He grinned at me, having rhymed his new nickname for me with 'relax.'

I carried the 12-pack of Budweiser and he brought chips and dip to the den. He waved to the TV cabinet. "Pick whatever movie you want, Jax." I moved to look at the shelves and realized that he had more than just known movies there. I turned and looked at him in surprise. *"Whatever you want, Jax,"* he emphasized again, smiling a little shyly. I read through the titles, unsure of what might show up on the tapes. Finally, after consuming a can of beer and gaining some liquid courage, I chose one and handed it to Codes.

"Are you sure? Don't do this just 'cuz you think it'll impress me, bud," he said. I thought about it a moment longer. Then I returned it to the shelf and selected an action film I'd been wanting to see. I hoped he wouldn't be disappointed. It turned out I had nothing to worry about. "Good choice, Jax! I love that one!"

I sighed with relief, and he punched me in the arm. "You don't have to impress me, Jack. I'm not Phil or Kevin, all right? I really just want to hang out with you. You're a cool kid with great soccer skills. I'm not sure we're destined to be best friends or anything, but before you fell in with those two, I wanted to make sure you knew what their game is and that I'm not on their team." He smiled at me. I smiled back.

"That's cool, Codes. Greatly appreciated, really. It's good to have friends in high places." We both laughed, reached for beers and chips, and settled in to watch the movie, a James Bond flick called *"Never Say Never Again."*

When the movie was over, we hit the hay, and before I knew it, it was early Sunday afternoon and time to go home. Cody drove me. I'd had a great time and told him so, thanking him. He demurred but seemed pleased. He apologized again for his friends' boorish behavior on Friday night, but I waved it off. "Don't worry about it, Codes. Nothing happened. They were high and drunk, and now they've revealed their true character to both of us. I'll watch my back around them; you'd better watch yours, too! No telling what crap they may pull on you, my new friend." I grinned at him before I clapped him on the back like a teammate hug after a goal or a save on the pitch and climbed out of the Camaro with my gear in hand. "See you at school tomorrow. Don't forget that we know each other now and go back to pretending I don't exist!"

"Just you wait and see, Mr. Soccer!" he called as he backed out of the driveway. When he saw the look of worry on my face he yelled, "Don't worry, Jax! I got our backs!" He laughed at his own rhyme again as he drove away, and I shook my head, smiling, as I turned to go into the house.

Dad and Matty were waiting for me when I arrived in the kitchen. My little bro toddled up to me. "Matty missed Jack!" he said, reaching for me to pick him up. I set down my gear and held my brother as I sat down at the table.

"What did you do while Jack was gone?"

"He played by himself, for the most part. We took him apple picking yesterday," Dad replied. "How was your weekend? From what Cody said on the phone, it sounded like you must have had a good time, given that he wanted you to stay an extra night."

I bobbed my head affirmatively. "Yeah, Cody's cool. He's got a nice house with an indoor pool, plus a full-sized soccer pitch out behind it. We played one-on-one yesterday for about 90 minutes. I had no idea he's so skilled at the game! I don't see him play much at school."

"He's a senior, right?" Dad asked. "Doesn't he start?"

"No, he did something that upset the Coach last year. Whatever it was, he rides the bench most of the time this season. Him and Phil." It didn't occur to me what I was revealing to my dad, which was weird. I *always* kept my guard up when talking to people in authority.

"Oh. Are there any other seniors on the team this year?"

"Nope, just those two."

"You said Cody's cool. What about Phil? Did you get along with him?"

I frowned and shook my head. "Phil and I had a disagreement on Friday night. He stayed till Saturday morning, but then he left. He made it clear that he resents that I'm a starter on the team and he's not, so whatever it is that he and Cody did to upset the Coach last year must've been big, because to hear Phil say it, when our starting keeper this year got hurt, Phil should've been the next one in line to take over, not me. He's sore that I was chosen for the role over him. I mean, he's wicked angry about it. Angry enough to pull a dirty trick on me Friday, but Cody stood up for me, and that was that. Cody threw him out Saturday morning when he figured out what Phil was doing. Then Cody and I just hung out on Saturday. It was cool."

"Just you and a senior boy." There was a question in his statement.

"Yup. Well, we invited a couple of girls over that were there on Friday evening. Oh, don't get all panicky, Dad. It wasn't like *that*." I blushed with embarrassment. "We swam in the pool, and then we played cards and a board game, and Codes cooked burgers for us on the grill. It was fun. Then the girls went home, and Cody and I watched a James Bond movie on VHS."

"What you're telling me, then, Jack, is that the 'team get-together' on Friday was, in truth, a party at Cody's house that involved girls, and I assume, illegal drinking, and probably sex, and that on Saturday, more of the same. Am I wrong?"

My mind reeled to hear dad's description, but then I realized he'd given me an out. I didn't have to lie, technically. "Yes, you're wrong," I said. "Cody said he invited other team members, and one or two showed up, but not most of them. Kids from other schools showed up, too, including the two girls I mentioned. They live just a mile up the road from us. There was alcohol there, and there might have been, uh, the other activity going on, but not for me. And Saturday it was just as I've already described."

"Jack," he gave me a stern, penetrating look. "Don't think you can fool me with things like this. I know all about Phil and Cody and why they aren't starting this year. I knew you were safe with Cody around, or I wouldn't have let you go to his house. I let you stay the extra day because when he called me yesterday morning, I made him give me an accounting of the evening before." He waved off my protests. "I don't know, nor do I need to know the details of what took place Friday evening between you and Phil until or if you're comfortable telling me, but I never would've given you another 24 hours there if I'd thought you'd be in danger. Still, mixing alcohol with hormones is a bad idea, Jack. Don't do it, or you'll end up doing something you'll regret."

This was one of the oddest lectures I could ever remember getting from my dad. He was undoubtedly serious in what he was saying, so I knew he meant what he said, but at the end of it, he stood up and gave me a big hug and told me he loved me and was proud of me. I understood the love but not the pride. I hugged him back and then went to my room to do my homework. Monday was coming fast, and I had a ton of work to finish.

26: It's a Match

At our game that Saturday, I tried to remember some of the tips Cody had taught me the previous week, especially regarding the weaknesses he'd seen in my play as the keeper. My streak of shutouts came to an end, but it was our toughest opponent yet, and regulation play ended with us in a 1-1 tie. Since it was a division opponent, the game went to overtime and a shootout. I managed to stop four of the five shots they attempted, but their keeper stopped only three of ours, giving us a squeaker of a win.

Our final goal was scored by Cody, who finally got into the game. I was stoked for him. I ran to meet him at midfield and gave him a big high-five. "Way to go, Codes!" I was grinnin' like a fool.

He grinned back, grabbed me in a bear hug, swung me around, and then dropped me on the field. "You remembered some of the moves I taught you, Jax! What an amazing game!" After saluting each other's level of play, we joined the rest of the team's celebration. Coach was looking at us with a raised eyebrow.

Instead of waiting to be asked, I thought it best to explain. "Cody showed me some holes in my game as keeper, Coach, and he was excited that I remembered what he taught me. And I was excited that he scored. I had no idea he was such a good player since I haven't seen him play that much." I knew I was treading on thin ice with that comment, but I figured this was the only way to plug him as a good striker for our team. "We could really use his leadership as the season progresses."

Coach smiled and said, "Today was a great team win. Everyone played hard and contributed to this victory. They were a tough team to beat—our toughest so far. Well done, men! Still, there were several scoring opportunities that we left uncapitalized on, so we're going to look at those and see how we can stay out of these dramatic finishes next time. Hit the showers, and I'll see you in practice."

That was it? He's not going to acknowledge Cody's victory goal at all? I was startled out of my grumbling thoughts by Cody himself. "Hey, don't sweat it, Jax."

"Don't sweat what?" I tried playing dumb.

"And don't play dumb." He laughed at me. "Coach heard you loud and clear, and he respects what you think."

"Then why didn't he—?

213

"You basically called him out in front of the whole team, Jax. You *disrespected* him. Is that *really* what you meant to do? I didn't think so. You were just excited and firing from the hip. If you want to lead, though, you have to consider how you come across to others. Pick your time and place, huh?" He elbowed me and laughed. "Hey, *I appreciate* what you were trying to do there, Jax. Just tryin' to help you see a better way to do it, right? Come on, last one to the showers is a rotten egg!" and he dashed off. I was the rotten egg.

After my shower, I dressed and knocked on Coach's door. "Can I talk to you, Coach?"

"Sure, Jack, what is it?"

"I, uh, I'm sorry for being disrespectful on the field after the game, Coach. That's not what I was trying to do."

He waved his hand to the chair opposite his desk. "Have a seat, Jack. I appreciate you saying that, and I accept your apology. What *were* you trying to do?"

What was I trying to do? I shifted in the chair and looked at him momentarily like a deer caught in headlights. "Well, Coach, since I don't know why Cody isn't a starter, and since I recently found out how good his skills are, I guess I was trying to see if you'd let him be a starter again. I was hoping there'd be some way he could get a second chance. Isn't that what this Christian school idea is supposed to be about?"

Coach closed his eyes for a moment and then opened them. "Jack, it's not my place to explain why Cody isn't a starter on this team. Ultimately, the only person that can tell you that is Cody. As for his skills as a soccer player, no one I've ever coached in the last 22 years with better skills than he has, and only one or two that would be his equal." He paused, and before he could continue, I burst in again.

"If he's so good, why doesn't he start playing more??" It seemed so illogical to me that I was apoplectic in my confusion.

Once again, Coach's eyes closed and reopened before he spoke. "I haven't spoken to your last point yet, Jack, regarding second chances and Christianity." He sighed slightly. "Sincere Christians have some disagreement on what this means, Jack, so I am going to do my best to tell you what I believe these ideas mean and what I believe this school believes. I will leave it up to you to decide if these beliefs are the same or different."

"We know that the Bible teaches that all people are sinners who need their sins forgiven by God. We all know that anyone who asks God to forgive them will be forgiven because they trust that Jesus died for their sin. With me so far? Good. We know that when we become Christians, we still fight against sin's power in our lives, but Jesus promises us ultimate victory in the end, right? Therefore, we fight sin every day, winning and losing battles. We sin every day and ask forgiveness every day, but only become a Christian once. Still with me? Okay. This means that as long as we *fight* sin, we're getting those 'second chances' you talked about, even if it's not 2nd chances, but 3rd, 4th, 100th, or whatever. We just have to be *fighting against whatever the sin is.*"

"That's what I believe the Bible teaches, Jack. If we fight sin as Christians, God will forgive us again every time we slip up. If we're not fighting sin but deep-diving into it without guilt, then we probably aren't Christians to begin with. Does that make sense to you, Jack?"

Oddly enough, that *did* make sense to me, but what did it have to do with Cody? The puzzlement must have shown on my face.

"What does this have to do with Cody? Where the school factors into this, Jack, is the administration's belief—I say this according to the actions they've taken, not according to their words—that there's a limit to forgiveness of one kind of sin or another. According to their actions, Cody fouled up one too many times, and his punishment led to his not being a starter for our soccer team ever again, no matter how good his skills were. Even if playing him was the only way to field a team, the administration would force us to forfeit rather than let him start. As I said a few minutes ago, I leave it up to you whether these views are the same or different and whether this school is acting on its beliefs."

I was blown away to listen to my coach say these things. It seemed obvious to me that he disapproved of the discipline shown to Cody, but he hadn't said that plainly, so I wasn't ready to hang my coat on it. "If you feel that strongly, Coach, why are you still working here?" *Did I just say that out loud??*

The man smiled tiredly at me. "Good question, Jack. It's crossed my mind many times, although I'm never certain that I feel that strongly nor do I know if I agree or disagree with the administration. You see, it's one thing to hold an individual belief, but it's another matter to establish an institutional value. What I may personally judge myself capable of forgiving may not be acceptable for my business to forgive. If you were a swindler, for example, I could possibly employ you in a job where stealing from my company wouldn't be possible, but if my job were as a bank manager, I certainly wouldn't be able to employ you at the bank! I'm not going to put a drunk in charge of a bar, or a drug user in a pharmacy. We must use wisdom when addressing disciplinary concerns."

It was clear that he wasn't going to say anything more about the situation, so I thanked him for his time and left. I remembered something I wanted to add, so I poked my head back through the doorway. "Coach? Next time I have an idea like I did today, I'll try to remember to just bring it to you instead of spouting off in front of everyone else."

"Good idea, Jack. Thanks. See you next practice."

Dad wasn't waiting for me in the parking lot like he usually was. I was surprised not to see him, but a familiar voice called my name. "Jax! Over here!" I turned to see Cody leaning on his Camaro. I jogged to him. "While you were talking with Coach, your dad came to pick you up. He seemed to be in a hurry, so I told him I'd bring you home. In fact, I told him I'd be your ride from now on, at least till the end of the season, just to spare him from having to wait around. He seemed to appreciate that. He's a nice guy, isn't he." It wasn't a question the way Cody said it, even though he used the words of a question. I smiled at him as I got into his car.

"Thanks, Codes. Yeah, my dad's a nice guy, for a dad." Then I laughed. "He knows more about you than you probably realize. Shoot, he knows more about you than I do." I was chuckling, but when I looked at Codes, his eyes were wide with what, fear? Shock? Worry? "Chill, dude,

217

what's wrong? He said I'm safe with you. I am, aren't I?" I punched him in the arm. "Codes?"

My new senior friend chuckled a little nervously, though. "What does your dad say he knows about me?" His voice quavered a little. He still hadn't buckled up or started the car.

"He just said that he knows why you and Phil aren't starters anymore, that's all, Codes. Jeez, relax, would you? He knows that, but I don't, and have you noticed that I haven't asked you for that information? That's your business, not mine. I haven't heard *anyone* spill the beans on it, Codes." I laid my hand on his arm to calm him down, but that startled him, apparently, because he jumped. "Sorry, dude. Didn't mean to startle you." I pulled my hand back and buckled up. "Anyway, Cody, I don't know why you're not a starter, even though I've never seen a more skilled soccer player than you in person or on TV. And I'm not asking you to tell me your business, okay? We're teammates, and we've become friends. Let's just enjoy that, Codes. Take me home, please. I'm hungry, and I have a crap-ton of homework to do."

Thankfully, that made Cody laugh more naturally, and we headed for my house. Our talk turned to our next opponent and what we knew about them. Cody said that they evenly matched us last year, but several of their best players graduated. Still, they had a strong freshmen class like we did, so we'd have to be ready. Maybe I should come over and do some extra practice with him sometime in the coming week? I agreed. A few of the new skills he'd tried to teach me weren't second nature for me yet, and I wanted to be the best keeper I could be, even as a freshman.

Our plans fell through. Coach was willing for Codes to spend a little time with me on keeper stuff during regular practice time, and he even authorized us to go out during Phys ed one day in place of what we would've been doing, which we both realized was a nod to the positive effect Cody's coaching was having on my play as keeper.

27: Connecting the Dots

Content Warning

I hadn't seen Phil since the morning after that party, but no one commented, so I kept my thoughts to myself. It was clear that Coach Williams would never bring it up, so there was no point stirring that viper's nest. Then, just when it felt like I was rid of that slimeball, he showed up on a day that Cody was absent for a doctor's appointment. I did my best to avoid Phil during practice, but he caught up to me at the end as we walked to the showers. He forced me to hang back from the others.

"I hear you've been getting 'extra coaching' from *Cody*," he hissed into my ear. "Is that your special word for it?"

"What are you talking about, you creep? He's been teaching me how to be a better goalie, Phil." I tried to move away, but he stepped closer and tugged on my practice jersey. "Get off me!"

"Ooh, you want me to get it off you, Jackie? Are you inviting me? How cute is that?" He was egging me on, and I didn't know what to do. The rest of the team was too far ahead of us to catch on to his disgusting game. "You thought *Cody* would   make *you* his *keeper*? I was   his *first keeper*, Jackie! *ME! NOT. YOU!*"

"WHAT are you *talking about*?" I hissed back, and then it hit me. "OOOHHHHH. You and Cody were....ooooohhhhhhhhhh!" I couldn't help it; I started laughing. Oh, God, did I laugh. I doubled over, gasping for air, threw my head back, and laughed even more, until tears streamed down my face.

"You—were—his—KEEPER!!" I screamed with laughter again. *He thought that Cody and I were 'together'!?* And just like that, I stopped laughing. *He believed that Cody and I were in love, which drove him crazy with jealousy, which means...he and Cody were...and THAT's why they didn't start for the team anymore. OH.MY.GOD. The VHS tapes at Codes' house. His understanding attitude toward me that day. But why was he so upset with Phil and Kevin?*

Phil's fingers were snapping in my face. "Earth to Jack! Earth to Jack! Come in, Jack! Jeez, Jack, you went from a laughing maniac to a silent psychopath. Now *you're* freaking *me* out. What's gotten into you?"

The rest of the team had gone into the building to shower, but we were still outside. I pushed him to the ground and sat down beside him. "I'm gonna talk and you're gonna listen. You're not gonna interrupt, Phil. If I get something wrong, you'll correct me when I give you the chance. Did you get it? Good." I took a deep breath and started spouting my theories.

"All this weird talk today is because you're jealous of my relationship with Cody. You think I've stolen him from you, and it angers you, especially because you and Cody were more than just friends. The thing is, you were raised in Christian homes where you learned that being gay is a

220

sin, and even though you believed it was a sin, you took your friendship to that point anyway, and then you were caught, which is why you aren't starters on the soccer team anymore. It also explains why you hate Christianity so much and have rebelled against it in every way possible. How am I doing so far?"

Phil's jaw was slack. He was about to answer when another voice spoke behind me. "Sounds like you've hit most of the points so far, Jax." *I thought I'd heard a car door. Should've turned around to check.*

"I've got more, Codes. The VHS tapes at your house, the ones you said I 'didn't have to choose to impress you,' are explained more fully in this scenario, and your understanding attitude toward some other things I said in conversation that day."

"I think you've hit all the nails on the head, my young friend. Why are you shaking your head no?"

"It doesn't explain why you were so angry with Phil and Kevin."

Cody gestured to Phil. "You want to answer this one, or shall I?"

Once again, Phil shrugged. "It doesn't matter now, I guess. Today's my last day in this school. I've been expelled. Might as well come clean to you, not that it'll make any difference to my life. Whatever. Kevin is 19 and isn't a student here. He's a known predator of middle-teen boys. I know this because that's how I became hooked into his racket. I was 15, lonely, bullied, and he befriended me at another school. I didn't know this at the time, but he was grooming me for the moment he'd take advantage of me, and then he turned it around on me, convinced me I'd wanted *that*, when all I'd really wanted was friendship and kindness." Phil looked defeated.

"In turn, I hooked in Cody, except that he resisted better than I did. He showed me great affection as a friend, and occasionally let it go a little further than that, but he never seemed to buy into the whole 'lovers' idea, at least never when Kevin was around, and rarely any other time. We got caught doing minor displays of affection that we couldn't brush under the rug as mere childishness, and the school gave us a second chance to straighten up."

His laugh was brittle when he said that. "Straighten up. Ha ha. Then it happened again, and we were given another chance, and so on. Finally, the school administration made it clear that our 'childishness' had to stop, that they were putting their collective foot down. We didn't believe them, and one day last year after soccer practice, we got carried away. We were the last ones left in the showers, thinking we were the only ones in the building and that all we had to do was turn off the lights and leave."

Cody picked up the narrative. "We didn't realize that Coach was still here. While showering, we decided it was time to experiment a little. We'd wanted to for a long time but never got the chance to at each other's homes because there was always someone there to interrupt—my parents were still around a lot at that point, and Phil has a bunch of siblings. Again, thinking we had some independence and freedom, we shared a shower and got careless. We didn't do anything 'ultimate,' but we shouldn't have been doing what we were doing, especially where we were, and we were caught. By Coach. He tried to dismiss us from the team quietly, but our parents wouldn't go along with it. We wouldn't tell them what we'd done—they would have killed us! We weren't, and aren't, out to them! And Coach refused to reveal what he knew. He simply told the administration that we had broken team and school rules too severely to remain on the team or in the school. When the school tried to follow through with expulsion from the team and the school, our parents threatened to sue. Coach backed down on one condition: " We could never be starters again, even if it meant forfeiting a game."

That's where *I* interrupted. "Actually, Codes? That's where *you're* wrong. Who told you that *Coach* backed down on that condition?"

"The school administration. Why?"

"They're liars. *Coach* was ready to suspend you for a time, *bench* you from starting for a few games, and then start you again, but the school administration wouldn't let him. He *still* wants to start you, but he can't. Why do you think he keeps showing us favors for practice time? And *no, Phil,* it's not so Cody and I can go screw each other on the pitch. He really is trying to help me be a better soccer player."

Cody, who had been standing while I talked, collapsed to the grass. "Shit! What a bunch of *losers!* Oh my god, I can't believe this! All this time, I've held a grudge against Coach because I thought *he* wouldn't start us again for anything in the world, and it's just the opposite?? What a prick I am!!"

"I don't know about that, Cody," Phil groaned, "but what—'DON'T SAY IT!' Cody shouted over Phil—"you have."

Cody's attempt to drown out Phil was laudable. Still, his reaction made me laugh so hard I almost puked. "I'm not part of this conversation!" I jumped up and moved to the door. "You two say whatever you have to, to each other. I'm getting my shower and I'll be back in a few minutes, Codes."

When I got to the car, Phil was gone. On the way home, Codes explained that Phil had gotten expelled for telling the school principal what he could do with the disciplinary plan and himself. Phil would try public school next, Codes said, but he'd have to be careful about revealing his love choices. Public schools weren't known for their tolerance any more than Christian schools were. In fact, many were much more dangerous.

Cody also confirmed that his anger about Kevin at the party was that he knew Kevin was a predator towards kids my age, and since Phil had agreed to monitor Kev and didn't, Codes figured out that he had brought Kevin for the purpose of messing up my life, and he couldn't stand for that. He wasn't a fan of mine until that point, then he realized that he liked me, *as a friend*, he emphasized, and he wasn't going to let anyone mess with me like that.

That gave me something to think about, since that was twice now that guys had tried to mess with me "like that," and I'd been spared. I wasn't ready to "thank God" yet, but I knew what my old friends Andy and Blake would say.

Wow, it had been months since I'd thought of or talked to them. I wondered how their freshman year was going. Maybe I should be in touch? Would Cody like to meet them? No, that'd probably be too weird. Then again, maybe they'd like to come to one of my soccer games?

"What's on your mind, Jax?"

"I was just thinking about something you said, Codes, about not letting anyone mess with me 'like that.' That's the second time in my life I've escaped from that. I was just thinking that I'm not ready to 'thank God' just yet, which made me think of my old buddies Andy and Blake and what they'd say. And *that* made me realize I haven't thought of or talked to them in months—they go to County Christian High School—and wondered how their freshman year is going and whether I should invite them to one of our games sometime soon. You know, stream-of-consciousness-type thinking."

Cody laughed. "Wow, that's more like a river." Then his tone got serious. "So, you wonder about your relationship with God, too? Mine comes and goes. I used to have a strong one, I thought before Phil came along and introduced me to these attractions that I didn't realize I had. And then I'd pray every day that God would take them away, but when he didn't, I thought maybe he didn't care enough or that I was supposed to live with them, or that I was supposed to follow them. I don't know. It's been very confusing. But I don't dare talk to my parents or pastor because I've heard how they talk about gays, and it's very condemning and hateful, you know what I mean? If they think I might be one, they probably won't love me anymore, and then where would I be? Where would I live?"

We were both silent for a few minutes until Cody spoke again. "Say, what are Andy and Blake like? I'd like to meet them. Invite 'em to a game, and then we can chill at my house."

"Okay, but no booze or porn. Andy and Blake are hard-core Jesus followers."

Cody tensed next to me.

"Don't worry. They love Jesus, but they love people, too. They aren't judgy. At least, they haven't been in the past."

28: A Missed Sign and the Big Game

It was a little weird to be socially involved with a senior like I was, given that I was a freshman and that we had only known each other a couple of months. We'd been at the same school last year, but junior high and high school students had classes in different buildings, and unless you had younger/older siblings in the other levels, you'd never know the goings-on of the rest of the secondary school. That's how it was for Cody and me; he was an only child, and I was the eldest in my family. our paths and social circles didn't cross until I began soccer practice freshman year. If it hadn't been for his hormones getting the better of him in his junior year, I never would have made the varsity team, much less as a starter, and it seemed highly unlikely that this slightly odd friendship would even exist. *I should focus on making friends in my own grade. He's going to graduate next spring. Who will I hang out with then?*

Granted, I didn't exactly come up with that thought alone. Dad and Steph planted it. They were a little concerned that all my attention and spare time were being spent with Cody lately. I hadn't even mentioned the possibility of visiting Blake and Andy in weeks, and while Cody and I were friends at Christian school, I don't think Dad and Steph fully trusted our friendship to be healthy for me. They knew a little more about Cody's situation than I did. As much as I tried to defend him to them, they diligently watched for signs that my relationship with him remained ultimately 'appropriate,' as they called it. However, given that I'd talked to Cody about it already anyway, I decided to call the Madison house and see how my friends were doing with ninth grade.

Mrs. Madison answered the phone. She sounded a little tired, which I wasn't used to hearing with her, but her voice perked up when she realized who was calling. "Hi, Jack! How are you? It's been a long time since we've seen you, hasn't it? How's freshman year going?"

"Hi Mrs. M. I'm fine, thanks. Freshman year's going okay. As a starter, I made the varsity soccer team, so that's been fun."

"Oh, wonderful, Jack, congratulations! How's your little brother? He must be growing so fast."

I grinned so much when she asked me that. "Matty's great, Mrs. M. I love being a big brother."

"I'm so happy for you, sweetheart. Of course, you didn't call to be grilled by me now, did you? Who do you want to talk to?"

"No, ma'am, but I like talking to you, Mrs. M. You're always so kind to me." I was blushing, even though she couldn't see me. "May I speak with Andy, please?"

"Of course, you may. He's right here, Jack."

I heard her hand off the phone to Andy and whisper, *"It's Jack Bannister."*

"Hi-ya, Jack!" Andy's cheerful voice came over the phone line. "Long time no see or hear! I've been thinking of calling you recently. Just hadn't done it. Sorry. It's been a little busy here."

"Hey, Andy, it's good to talk to you!" I realized it *was* good to talk to him. "It's been way too long. How've you and your family been?"

"Well, we've been, um..." I'd never known Andy to struggle to answer that question. "The Lord is with us," he finally said. His voice shook slightly as he spoke. "We are in his hands, and there's no better place to be. How about you, Jack?" He finished stronger than he began.

"Oh, I'm fine, Andy, just fine. I'm having a pretty good year so far, even though I miss you and Blake like crazy again." *Just a little white lie.* "I made the varsity soccer team as a starter, and it's been a great season so far. I was hoping you and Blake could come to a game sometime soon."

"A freshman starting varsity? That's GREAT, Jack! Congratulations!" I heard his muffled voice as he covered the phone with his hand and yelled to someone else in his house. Moments later, I heard Blake next to Andy.

"Way to go, Jack!" Blake called to me. "That's exciting! I'm so happy for you."

I beamed. "Thanks, guys! Do you think you two could come to a game next weekend? We play on Friday, and then my teammate Cody wants you guys to join us at his place for an overnight party. No booze or anything like that, just hanging out with us type of thing."

Andy spoke for them. "Hey, that sounds fun, Jack. We'll talk to Mum and Dad and let you know as soon as I can. We'll talk to you again soon, all right?"

"Sure thing. Have a good night, guys."

"You too," Blake and Andy chorused.

A few days later I heard from Andy. He and Blake were coming to see me play, and then he was coming to

Cody's house. Blake had an appointment after the game and another one first thing Saturday morning, so he was going to miss the sleepover. Plus, he wasn't sure he was ready for something like that, he said. He had reached a point in his therapy where he had identified behavioral triggers that negatively affected his recovery, and new social situations could be troubling for him. He understood his own needs well enough to know that going to Cody's house overnight wouldn't be healthy for him, so he chose not to do it. I was impressed with his progress, but it didn't ease my disappointment much. It made me wonder what had happened to my rough-and-tumble childhood pal. *Will he ever recover?* It nagged at me. *What difference does Jesus make if a kid can't be whole again?*

The day of the game arrived, and I couldn't wait to see my friends. I didn't realize it, but we had a half day of school that Friday, so Coach provided pizzas for our lunch, and then we took our time dressing and prepping for the game. It was going to be a 3 PM start—an hour earlier than usual since it was getting late in the season and the weather was much cooler. Plus, darkness fell sooner, and our field had no lighting, so we had to be sure to finish in the daylight available.

The skies were overcast, but not threatening rain, and game time temperature was about 62 degrees. We got word just before the game started that we didn't have enough starters, though, and it looked like we were going to have to forfeit. I don't know what happened to the guys that should have been there, but with players missing, it looked like another plan was going down the tubes.

Then Coach did something I never expected. He told Cody to go in as a starter. Cody and I looked at each other, and then at Coach, but we kept our traps shut. We led the team onto the field to the cheers of our fans, and the game began. At first, it seemed like we were going to run away with it. By half-time, we were up, 5-0. The other team, supposedly a powerhouse, had managed only four shots on goal, and I had stopped all of them. Cody had scored two for our team and assisted on the other three. What a leader he was! He was all over the field, encouraging our teammates, calling plays, coaching while playing, really. It was so much fun; I couldn't believe we'd been deprived of this all season.

At the break, Coach had one of his assistants run through some plays with us and remind us that our opponent was known for its aggressive second-half play. I looked around for Coach, and finally spotted him. The principal was talking to him, and neither man looked happy. I began to get a sour feeling in the pit of my stomach. I soon forgot it, though, because as we prepared to retake the field, Blake and Andy hollered to me from the sidelines. Their smiles lit up my face, too, and I eagerly took my place in goal, ready for the rest of the game, or so I thought.

Thirty seconds into the half, our opponents scored on me. Twenty seconds after that, they scored again. Less than a minute later, again. In fewer than two minutes, our 5-0 lead had shrunk to 5-3. Our defensemen were playing well, but I'd been caught with my brain somewhere else. *I was dwelling on the conversation between Coach and the principal. Was Coach in trouble for starting Cody? I need to talk to Codes!* I needed to get my head back in the game, and the only way I could talk to Cody during the game was if he thought I was hurt. *I'm gonna have to fake an injury so he comes to check on me. Oh, brother.*

On the next run at our goal, I faked a collision with someone on our team and flopped. Hey, I didn't want to penalize anyone. I just needed to talk to Cody. I must have convinced the referee, though, because he blew his whistle. Sure enough, Codes came over to check on me as I rolled around, groaning.

"Jax, you okay, man?"

"I'm fine, Codes, but listen up," I hissed between clenched teeth.

"Wha–?"

"Shut up and listen. I faked this so I could talk to you. OOhhh…" I groaned loudly again but waved my arms.

Cody caught on. "He'll be okay in a minute, Sir. He got the wind knocked out of him and banged his knee. No, he doesn't need the trainer. Just a moment or two, please, Sir." He spoke to the ref, who motioned for me to take a few more moments. "What is it?"

"During half time, Coach and the principal were talking. Both looked upset. I'm worried about Coach."

"That's why the other team scored so easily? You were distracted by that? Look, Jax, we'll deal with that after the game. Now, get up and play. We need to win." Codes was insistent, but I appreciated his tone and support.

With his help, I got up slowly, acknowledged the cheers of the crowd, and thanked the ref for the time to gather myself. Then I returned to my place on the field to resume play.

From that point on, my mind stayed in the game. We regained the momentum. Cody scored twice more, giving him four for the game, and he helped our team to a 9-3 victory. I was so proud of him I thought my heart would burst. My teammates lifted him on their shoulders to carry him off the field. They had no idea how happy that made him.

I hadn't been paying attention to the schedule. This was the final game of the season, and we'd gone undefeated! I was so focused on seeing Andy and Blake that I'd lost track of the number of games we had left. It took a teammate pointing out our record to open my eyes to the situation. Holy cow!

Our school had never been undefeated in the regular season before! I looked around for my friends but came face-to-face with the newspaper reporter almost immediately. "Congratulations on your first undefeated season, Jack!" she said. "What was the secret to your team's success?"

"Uh, teamwork and coaching. Coach has been awesome this year, and he's supported players like Cody James," I was cut off by the principal, who walked into the conversation.

"Mr. Bannister, please come with me." He didn't look at the reporter or me. He just gestured away from the crowd. I followed him a few steps and then stopped. He turned around and said, "You are prohibited from speaking to reporters. Do you understand? If you speak to them again, your stepmother will be fired." Then he spun on his heel and stormed off.

I stood there with my jaw hanging open. Someone tapped on my shoulder. As I turned around, the reporter said, "Jack, you were saying something about your Coach and Cody?"

"No comment." I walked away. I had to find my friends and escape this bizarre situation. *Can I tell Dad and Steph about this?* Cody ran up and slapped me on the shoulder.

"Can you believe it, Jax? What an amazing game! You played awesome the rest of the half, bud. Those stops, dude! Oh my god, you were *fabulous. What a keeper!*" In his excitement, he gave me a giant hug. Then he dropped his arms and jumped back. *"Dude! Sorry about that. Didn't mean to get carried away."* He whisper-hissed.

I looked at his pink-tinted face and laughed. "Relax, Codes, it was just a friendship/teammate thing, right? *RIGHT?*" When I emphasized the word the second time around, he blushed beet red.

"YES, of *course!*" he protested. He looked flustered for a moment, but then he seemed to remember something. "Say, where are those friends of yours?"

"You mean Andy and Blake?" He nodded so hard I thought his head would fall off his shoulders. "They're right behind you." He jumped, and I burst out laughing again. *This poor kid. He's a senior, but he acts like a 7th grader half the time.*

I stepped over and hugged my friends. "Andy, Blake, this is Cody, my teammate and good friend. Cody, the Madison brothers."

"*The Madison* brothers?" Cody's eyes widened. "I've heard of you, but I thought one of you was, like, six years older?"

Blake laughed. "That's our older brother, David. He's away at college. How have you heard of us, from Jack?"

Cody shook his head. "Nope. I heard about the older brother who stood up for his younger brother against some town bully and threatened to hurt him if he ever messed with his younger brother again. Which one of you was he talking about?"

Andy and Blake laughed. "Both of us," they said in unison.

"Huh?"

"David is the older brother that stood up for his little brother Andy," Blake explained, "against the bully named Blake," he pointed to himself. "None of us knew that I'd one day be adopted by the Madison family and become David and Andy's brother, too!"

"Wow, that's weird! How the hel... heck did that happen?" Codes was intrigued.

"I'd love to tell you my point of view sometime, Cody, but I have to get to an appointment with Dad. Andy can tell you his side of things tonight if you're that interested. It was great meeting you. Congratulations on your game today, guys. Hope to see you again soon! Bye, bro." Blake headed off to the car, and Andy followed to get his gear.

"Nice catch on the language there, Codes," I smirked.

"Hey, I'm trying," he whined back.

29: A Revelation

Within moments, Andy returned with his gear. "Dad says hi and congrats on the win. He said there's no urgent timetable for me to get home tomorrow. I gave him your number so he can call if something comes up, Cody. Thanks for inviting me. I'm looking forward to this!"

Cody gave a thumbs up and led us to his car. I took the back seat, knowing that Andy gets a little motion sickness sometimes. He admired my friend's ride as we got it. "Sweet ride, Cody! I've always wanted to ride in a Camaro. Is this an '80 or an '81? It's an SS, right?"

My older friend smiled. "It's an '80, and you're right. It's an SS. How do you know so much about cars, Andy?"

"Oh, don't be too impressed," he said smiling and turning a little pink from embarrassment. "I'm not mechanically minded, so I read car magazines to sound more knowledgeable than I am. It keeps me from being bullied a lot of the time, and I find it easier to be conversational with more people."

I chuckled, and so did the other two. "Not a bad idea, Andy. Don't you agree, Codes?"

He nodded. "It's too bad you have to do it to avoid bullying, Andy, but I'm impressed that you know the differences between a 1980 and a 1981 Camaro!" He smiled again at my childhood friend. "You won't be bullied by me. That's not my thing." He glanced at me in the rearview mirror. "What should we do for supper tonight? Do you guys like Chinese food? I'm kind of in the mood for it."

Andy turned and looked at me. "I've never had it, but it sounds yummy." I agreed with the idea.

"Great. Let's get to my house so Jack and I can shower, and then we can use a takeout menu to call in an order. It'll be my treat. Did you bring swim trunks, Andy? Good. We can swim while we wait for the food to arrive. I know we're all hungry, but the place I order from is slow. It's worth the wait, though."

It wasn't long before we were in the pool, laughing and having a good time. There were no girls this time, though. Cody figured it wasn't a good idea to have Leslie and Lisa there when Andy was around. I was disappointed but couldn't blame him for being careful. I was the one that told him to be cautious about other things, after all. I had checked the movie cabinet when Andy was in another room, and to my relief, all the gay pornos were nowhere to be found. I didn't know if that was because Andy was going to be there, or if Cody had just stopped watching them. Part of me wanted to ask him, but the rest of me just said to leave him alone about it.

When the food arrived, we learned that Cody hadn't exaggerated. It did take a long time to arrive, but the wait was worth it. Each of us had second, third, or possibly, fourth helpings, though we all acted like roly-polys the rest of the evening. I finally had to ask Cody for a Rolaids tablet to settle my stomach.

Content Warning

At some point after supper, Cody returned to his question about how Blake and Andy became brothers. I had secretly hoped he'd forget about that. He didn't, and I settled in to hear Andy's explanation yet again.

"I'll tell you as much as I'm comfortable saying, Cody, but a lot of this is my brother's to tell. Blake grew up in a horrible situation. When he was 13, he asked for help getting out of it. By that time, he had been my bully for a few years while being Jack's friend at the same time. Jack suggested that Blake talk to me, so one day, I went over to Jack's house and met with Blake and another friend of theirs."

"When Blake and I met that day, he apologized for bullying me, and I forgave him. Later that day, my brother David joined our group and apologized for threatening Blake and the other kid for a time when they had done something to me. The other kid *said* he forgave David, but Blake really did forgive him. Throughout the day and in our conversations, David and I explained how forgiveness comes from God as a gift because of Jesus being raised from the dead, and that we forgive because he first forgave us."

"By mid-evening, Blake told me that he was ready to stop trying to control his life, and that he wanted Jesus to be in control, instead. He asked me to help him pray and ask Jesus to forgive him for his sin, that he wanted to be changed by God and to live the way God wanted him to, not the way *he'd* always wanted to live. Blake wanted to give up the lying, cheating, stealing, violent ways he'd known, and be given the love, truth, and peace of God in his life."

"We prayed, and he told me afterward that he felt a joy and lightness in his heart he'd never known before. He suddenly knew he was *loved* with everlasting love, and the joy of Jesus in his life has completely changed him. That same night, he called and turned his father in for the abuses he had suffered for so many years. When his dad was arrested, Blake was left homeless because he didn't have any relatives. By the grace of God, my parents arranged for

Blake to stay with us. Eventually, we adopted him, and he's my brother as a Madison and my brother in Christ." Andy's face was beaming with joy and glistening with tears as he finished speaking.

I couldn't help but choke up a little, too, despite my usual cynicism. It *was* a beautiful ending to a tough story. Then I heard a sniffle. *Cody* was crying. *What in the world?*

"Codes? Are you okay?" I walked over and put my arm around his shoulders. "What's wrong?"

He shook his head and grabbed a tissue to blow his nose. *"That's love."* He whispered. *"I've always been looking for love, and that's it."* He cried some more. "I'm sorry, Andy!"

"Don't be, Cody," he said. "You don't need to apologize for being moved by love."

Cody looked up at Andy and shook his head. "You don't understand, Andy. I'm gay."

Andy looked back at Cody. "You don't understand, Cody. I'm not bothered by that."

I looked at both of them. "What the fuck!?"

Andy gasped. "LANGUAGE!"

I blurted out, "Who are you, Vince?"

"Who's Vince?" Cody queried.

"Long story." Andy replied. "Best left untold." Then he giggled.

That got me. I giggled, too. Pretty soon we were all giggling, followed by all-out laughing.

When we'd caught our breath, Andy said to Cody, "What difference does your being gay make to the fact that you finally figured out what true love is, and why should I be bothered by it?"

Cody spluttered, "Well, I-I-I, um, well, I, uh…"

"Exactly. You don't know. Listen, Cody, having the temptation and acting on the temptation are not the same, all right? If I'm tempted to lie, for example, but I tell the truth, I haven't committed the sin. If I'm tempted to cheat on a test, but I don't cheat on a test, I haven't done anything wrong, no matter how strong the temptation was. If I'm tempted to kiss a boy or make out with him, but I don't do it, then I haven't sinned. If I'm tempted to do those things and I pleasure myself while thinking about those things, then I *have* sinned, but I'm not condemned forever if I ask God to forgive me and to help me be stronger the next time those thoughts enter my mind. Being tempted is not the sin. Giving in to the sin is the sin. *Jesus* was tempted, Codes, but he didn't sin. Consider that. Until we get to heaven, we're going to have temptation to deal with."

"Andy, you've thought about this a lot, haven't you?" I posed to him.

"Yes, Jack, I have. These are not new issues in my life. Blake and I have talked about these and other issues many times."

I understood. I recalled my conversation with Blake during summer vacation, but I didn't bring it up. I just nodded my head a little. "What does Blake have to say about it?"

"Well, he's been studying what the Bible has to say, Jack, so he brings up Old Testament and New Testament references about homosexuality."

Cody interrupted Andy. "He ought to be careful with that, Andy. A lot of those references have been shown to be outdated or vague or not meant to be used against homosexuals today as they are. I've been studying the issue, too, and fundamentalist Christians today twist a lot of those Bible references to say things they weren't meant to say."

Oh, boy. Here we go. This was supposed to be a fun sleepover, but my extremist friends are going to have a knockdown, drag-out debate of epic proportions. I sighed heavily without realizing it.

"Is something wrong, Jax?" Cody paused his rant to gaze at me. I glanced at him and then noticed that Andy was looking at me, too.

"What's on your mind, Jack?'

"Guys, I was eager to have a fun time with two of my best friends tonight, but instead, you two are about to have a big theological dispute over being gay and being Christian!" I was whining, but I didn't care. "If this is how tonight will go, count me out!" I got up and stormed out of the room. *Real mature there, Bannister.*

Andy and Cody looked at each other and shrugged. "I was just trying to answer his questions," Andy defended himself.

"And I was just putting in my two cents' worth," Cody added. "What's his problem?"

They sat quietly for a moment, but then Andy had a lightbulb go on in his head. "This happens with me around," he whispered.

"What happens?" Cody asked curiously.

"Jack invites me into a situation where he has other friends that don't believe the same things I do. We get talking, and before long, I've started a conversation about God and the Bible, and Jack's sidelined, completely left out, and whatever fun plans he had for the visit are out the window."

"Really?"

"Yup."

"So, why does he keep inviting you into situations like this?"

"I dunno."

"I think I know."

"You do? Could you please enlighten me, Cody? I constantly feel like I'm upsetting Jack's applecart of fun."

"Oh, you're definitely doing that, Andy."

"Gee, thanks."

"You're welcome."

Andy punched Cody on the arm.

"What was that for?"

"You still haven't 'enlightened' me, 'Codes,' to use Jack's nickname for you. I like that nickname, by the way. It's cu... I mean, cool."

Cody looked startled for a second, but he said, "Thanks. I didn't like Jack at the start of the season. He was a freshman playing varsity *and* starting, taking a role on the team I thought I should have, but when I saw his skills and realized he wasn't doing it to show me up, I decided I should support him and maybe even become his friend. When we became friends, he gave me that nickname, and I started calling him 'Jax.' Maybe it's weird, that a senior and a freshman hang out as much as we do, but I dunno. He's laid back, and I like that."

"Jack's been a good friend to me, too. I'm glad you've discovered friendship with him, Cody, even with the difference in grade levels. I have friends that are older than

I am like that. It's no big deal. You know what's a big deal? You haven't told me why Jack keeps inviting me into situations like this." Andy grinned at Cody.

"Wow, you're like a bloodhound, aren't you? All right, Andy, here's my theory. Jack invites you into situations like this because he wants to hear what you believe the Bible has to say about different issues. He trusts you, Andy. He doesn't trust anyone else to explain the Bible to him. He's looking for a reason to believe that God is worth listening to, *and for a reason to justify ignoring God for the rest of his life.* I can't say as I blame him, Andy. The adults in my life have lied and cheated and misused the Bible with me, so why should I believe them when they talk about it? If a friend explains and lives what the Bible says, then maybe I'll trust God again."

Andy shook his head. "I'm not a model of Christian virtue, Cody. If you or Jack were to look closely enough at my life, you'd see just as much hypocrisy there as you see in the adults you're talking about!"

Content Warning

"But you're not shoving it down our throats like the adults do, Andy!" Cody protested. "You're gentle with your tone, and you're kind with your attitude. They could learn a lot from you! Seriously! Stop shaking your head!"

"Listen, it's been a long time since Jack and I hung out together. He doesn't know me as well as he used to. Did you see his reaction to my comments about Blake and me talking a lot about the same sex attraction issues?"

"Yeah. Why?"

"I can guarantee you he thought I was referring to what Blake expressed to him during summer vacation about

242

not being sure if he was straight or not. But Cody, I wasn't talking about *Blake's* attractions. I was talking about *mine*. Blake has been studying what the Bible says about them to help *me* understand how to address *my* temptations, not his."

Cody realized he was angling forward in his seat as Andy talked because his new friend was speaking so earnestly. When the younger teen finished revealing his secret, Cody leaned back and relaxed with a deep breath, nodding his head in comprehension of the evening's developments. *That explains a lot.* "That's why you emphasized temptation versus acting on temptation." It was a statement, not a question. "And you placed yourself in the example because it's been true of you, not because you were being polite." Another statement, followed by another deep breath. "When are you gonna tell Jack?"

"I don't know how to tell him." Andy's shoulders slumped, and he looked miserable.

30: Under the Influence

I don't know what I expected when I stormed out of the room. Were they supposed to stop me? Follow me? I didn't process that; I just needed separation from the drama taking shape in the den.

My first destination was the bathroom, and then I went to the kitchen. Feeling thirsty, I opened the fridge to see what Cody had on hand. To my delight, he had beer. I didn't care that Andy was nearby, I was pissed at him for starting another Bible fight, so I opened a bottle and began sucking it down. It was nasty, and it made me think of the joke Cody had made one time about this brand of American beer: "How is this beer like making love in a canoe? They're both f**king close to water." It's a stupid joke, but I laughed then and now, and I choked on my drink. When I'd recovered, I finished the bottle and opened another one.

My dinner had settled, for the most part, but it still cautioned me not to drink too much. *Beer and Chinese food are not a good mix down here,* my stomach warned me. I didn't listen. It was becoming a common theme in my life.

The alcohol was calming me down, so I looked to see if Cody had anything better than this horse water. In the back of the fridge, on the lowest shelf, I found a higher quality brew. I pulled that out and began chugging a bottle of it. My tolerance had increased since my first time at Codes' house, I noted, since I wasn't staggering after my third bottle.

Better slow down, though, Jax. No need to antagonize Andy. Speaking of Andy, where is he? Thought he would've come looking for me by now. Maybe I should go see what's going on.

I walked quietly back toward the den. As I got closer, I could hear Codes and Andy talking. Apparently, there would be no theological throwdown tonight. I was about to burst in on them when I heard Andy say something about Cody still not telling him why I "keep inviting Andy into situations like this" or something like that. *This is curious. What are they talking about? I'll just sit here and listen for a little bit.* Boy, did I get an earful!

Was Cody right? Did I invite Andy so I could hear his thoughts on the Bible for various issues? Was I looking for a reason to believe or an excuse not to?

Wait, what did Andy just say? **He** *was the one he was talking about?? Oh.my.god. What a jerk I've been!*

Before I realized what I was doing, I stumbled into the den and fell onto the couch next to Andy. I leaned over and gave him a hug. "I'm sorry," I mumbled. "I haven't been around for you, and then I blamed you for tonight not going the way I wanted. I'm sorry, Andy."

Then I got up and walked over to Cody. I motioned for him to stand up. When he did, I gave him a hug, too. "I'm sorry, Cody. I've been impolite and insensitive to you, too. You've been a great friend to me. I really appreciate it." He hugged me back, messed up my hair, and sat back down.

"I forgive you, Jax. It's a good thing you're Mr. Soccer." He grinned at me. He pointed at Andy. "I think he forgives you, too, but how long were you eavesdropping?"

I went crimson. "Only the last few minutes, guys, honest, but I heard some important things from both of you. You've made me do some thinking, and you know how much I hate that. On a more serious note, of course, Andy, is that I'm sorry that you've been dealing with this temptation, but I'm glad Blake's been helping you."

Andy nodded solemnly. "Thanks, Jack, I appreciate that. I've been dealing with it for a long time, and the older I get, the more intense the battle seems to get. God seems to give me victory for a while, and then I fail for a time, back and forth. If that were the only thing in my life..." His voice trailed off, and regret washed over his face. "Do you guys mind if I hit the hay? I'm tired."

"No, not at all," said Cody. "Let me show you to your room. I'll be back in a few, Jack." He and Andy left the room.

245

"I'm glad you came over tonight, Andy. I can see why Jack values you as a friend."

"Thanks, Cody. Likewise. I'm relieved that Jack has you in his life. He's suffered too many losses for his young age, and he needs solid friends like you to keep him positive."

Cody was visibly moved by Andy's comments. "Wow, Andy, that is probably the kindest thing anyone has *ever* said to me. Thank you." Impulsively, he gave Andy a half-hug around his shoulders and kissed the top of his head. Instantly embarrassed, he reddened and said, "Sorry! I'm a hugger and a top-of-the-head kisser."

Andy smiled. "It's okay. I appreciate the encouragement. I'm a hugger, too." His smile broadened into a full grin. "Good night, Cody. See you in the morning." He turned and went into his room.

"Good night, Ands," Cody said quietly. "Sleep well, my new friend."

On his way back to the den, Cody stopped by the kitchen, where he observed the empty bottles I had left behind. He opened the fridge and grabbed the rest of the six pack and joined me in the den. "One for you and three for me," he said.

"Fair enough. So, what do you think of him?"

"I like him."

"Yeah, I do, too."

"How did you two become friends?"

"We met on the bus first day of school in sixth grade. He offered me a seat on the bus, introduced himself, and by the time we got to school, we were friends. He helped me behave in school, and I stood up to his bullies. We both liked

Boston sports teams. His parents liked me, and my parents liked him."

"Has he always been so religious?"

"Yup."

"Always so conflicted?"

"Nope."

"What changed?"

"Probably puberty. I dunno, though, really. We stopped being classmates after sixth grade, so we haven't seen as much of each other since then.

"Now, you were the one that invited him into your neighborhood friend circle—the one where Blake ended up becoming a Christian and leaving the neighborhood, right?"

"Yup."

"And you were the one that wanted to bring him over here tonight, right?"

"Yup."

"Is my theory wrong, then?"

"Probably not."

"Uh-huh."

"What's that supposed to mean, Codes?"

"It means that you're looking for a reason to believe or an excuse not to, *Jax*. Don't you already have those?"

"Hmph." I was tired of the subject, so I changed it. "Hey, Codes, am I supposed to like beer this young?"

Cody gave me a wry smile. "I dunno, Jax. How young is your beer?"

"Really?"

"Ambiguity, Jax, the Devil's volleyball."

"What's that supposed to mean?"

"Hey, you're the one with the misplaced modifier, my friend. You want a straight answer, don't give me a crooked question. Did you want to know if you should like young beer, or if you should like beer when you're so young?" He was laughing at me.

"Ha ha. Very funny. You know what I meant. Should I, at just 15 years of age, be liking beer as much as I do?"

Cody shrugged his shoulders. "How should I answer that, Jack? Do you want me to go all moral on you? As a 'mature' adult, I'd say, 'No, Jack Bannister, you should not be drinking alcohol at such a young age, nor should you enjoy it as much as you do.' There, is that what you wanted me to say?" He seemed annoyed that I asked.

"When did you start drinking?" *Why am I so obsessed with this tonight?*

He sat there with his eyes closed. I didn't disturb him because I could tell he wasn't sleeping, and I didn't want to upset him more than I already had. Finally, he looked at me. "A-after Phil... y'know..."

I had to think about what he was trying to say without saying it. *After Phil what? What had Cody told me about Phil that he didn't want to say again?* I thought back to my run-in with Phil and Kevin the first time I came to Cody's house. That didn't remind me, but then...OH! It took just a few moments of my stream-of-consciousness memories to spin forward to when Phil accosted me heading to the showers a few weeks after that. *What had Phil said? Kevin groomed him, and then, 'I hooked Cody.'*

My eyes widened as realization dawned in spades. "You really didn't want to mess around with Phil, did you? You went along with it to keep Kevin away from you!"

Another wave hit me. "And that's when you started drinking and partying, because you felt that you were betraying the boy you'd grown up wanting to be. You lacked friends, and the only one you had made you feel that you had to do physical favors for him, or he'd bring Kevin around to keep you in line? Dude, I'm sorry, but that's fucked up!"

As I uncovered the harsh reality of my friend's existence I was whispering, but the injustice of it brought my emotions out and I was almost yelling by the end of it. I was also crying. And then I thought of something else, but I kept it to myself. *He's not gay. Or is he?*

The red haze of fury cleared from my eyes, and I could see Cody again. He hadn't moved an inch since saying, "A-after Phil...y'know...". I glanced down at his hands and could see that he was white knuckling his grip of the armrests on his chair. *Is he afraid of what I've figured out? Afraid of me?* I lifted my eyes to meet his. There were pools of tears threatening to spill down his cheeks. *What have you done, Bannister? Have you broken Codes?*

"I, uh. I'm." *At a rare loss for words is what you are, Bannister. Grow a pair, Jack, and apologize to the man.* "I'm sorry, Cody. That was out of line for me to presume like that. Will you forgive me?" I hung my head.

"No." Hearing his barely audible yet firm response, I put my head in my hands and sat there, unable to move. *I finally found a great friend, and I've ruined it, again. What now?*

Moments later, Cody's hands were gently shaking my shoulders. "Show me your face, Jack. Look at me." I was too slow to respond, I guess, because he switched from a

249

request to a command. "NOW, Bannister! Look me in the eye!" *I've heard this before from someone else.*

I raised my head and was surprised to see Cody taking a knee in front of me so that we were eye-to-eye. His voice dropped to conversational level again, demonstrating that he didn't want to assert dominance in any way. I felt the tension in my body drop in response. *What does he want?*

"Do you remember your last statement to me, Jack?"

That took a quick think. I'd thought some questions—What does he want? What now? Where have I heard this before?—but I hadn't voiced those. Then I recalled it and the answer he gave. "Yeah. 'Will you forgive me? Or the one before that, that you went along with Phil to keep Kevin away?' I remember you said 'no' to forgiving me, Codes, so where do we go from here?"

"No, Jack, not a question. A statement. What was your last *statement* to me!"

I racked my memory. Cody prompted me further. "Just before you asked if I'd forgive you."

The bulb lit dimly in my brain. "That it was out of line for me to presume?" I asked him weakly.

"That's the one, Jax. *That's what I said 'No' to.* You weren't out of line, and yeah, it's screwed up that I felt I had to do those things with Phil to keep Kevin away." His voice had dropped to a whisper and cracked with emotion as he finished speaking. "Everybody sees me as this confident athlete, Jax, like I've got life all together. Money, nice car, freedom to come and go as I want—but I'm empty inside, Jack. The only reason my life has anything positive in it is

250

this freshman I met a couple months ago, a kid I call Mr. Soccer. He's been a friend, not trying to get in my business, not judging me for my past, just willing to hang out."

"Codes!" I began. "I—."

"Shut up. Come with me." Cody stood up and walked out of the den.

31: Was That Out Loud?

The following day, I woke up with an odd feeling. *Where am I?* Oh, at Cody's house. *Who else is here?* Andy and Cody. *Okay, but whose room am I in?* No answer for that one. Just then, the bathroom door opened, and Cody walked out in a towel, having freshly showered.

"Mornin', Jax," he smiled at me slyly. "Did you enjoy last night?"

Enjoy last night? I don't remember? "Uh, what are you talking about, Codes? We were talking about some serious stuff, and then you told me to follow you, which I did, but then you said we'd talk today and that it was time to go to bed. Why am I in your bed?" I was beginning to get a little nervous.

He smiled again. "You were acting a little weird when we said good night, and saying something about not wanting to be alone, so I said you could sleep in my room with me."

"I slept with you? I mean, not like *that*, but in your bed at the same time?" My face felt hot, so it must have been fire engine red.

Cody roared with laughter. "Dude, you're hilarious! It *is* a king-sized bed, y'know, so it's not like we were *anywhere close* to each other. You need to lighten up, Jax. Seriously, though, you were upset about something, you slept in here, nothing inappropriate happened, end of story. But it was impossible not to mess with your head this morning. Let's go see how Andy's doing."

I didn't have anything solid to toss at him, so I just threw a spiteful glare his way before chuckling at his joke. I crawled out of bed to use the bathroom and took a two-minute shower before checking on my other friend. When we went down the hall, his door was closed, so we knocked first.

"Come in." We entered to find Andy sitting on the made bed, reading his Bible. I shouldn't have been surprised, but it had been so long since I'd seen a friend doing that it caught me off guard.

Content Warning

"Whatcha reading, Ands?" Cody blurted out before I could stop him.

"Ephesians 2."

"Read it to me. Please. I haven't heard or read any part of the Bible in a long time."

"Okay. Here are some key parts of the chapter, beginning with verse 1 and then reading verse 4 and part of verse 5:

> *"And you were dead in the trespasses and sins in which you once walked."* Andy paused and said, "Next are two of my favorite words in the whole Bible, because they tell us how much God loves us." *"But God,"* he stopped again. "Isn't that amazing? After he tells us our natural condition because of sin, he explains where our hope comes from!"

252

"But God, being rich in mercy, because of the great love with which he loved us, even when we were dead in our trespasses, made us alive together with Christ..

"That's just a few verses of Ephesians 2, but I love how much they show the love of God for me," Andy said. "I was a spiritually dead sinner, and God made me alive together with Christ as a gift, not by something that I did or earned. Now *that's* love." His eyes were shimmering with emotion. Suddenly, he bowed his head. *"Dear Lord, thank you for loving me and forgivng me for my sin. Fill my heart with your Word that I may not sin against you. In Jesus' name, Amen.*

"Amen," said Cody. "Thanks for letting us sit in for that, Andy."

"You're welcome. Actually, I kinda forgot you were here." He blushed slightly. "To God be the glory."

I could see that Cody was intrigued by my other friend's faith and persona. I wasn't jealous, was I? Either way, I *was* hungry. "Hey, guys, I'm sorry to interrupt, but could we see about scrounging up some breakfast?"

My friends laughed. "Sure," said Cody. "I've got eggs and sausage available. Who's cooking?"

Andy's hand popped up. "I can cook sausage."

Cody laughed again. "I can cook eggs. I guess that leaves setting the table to you, Jack. Let's hit the kitchen."

When we had finished breakfast, we thought about going outside to play some soccer, but the weather wasn't cooperating, so we felt at a loss for plans. "Do you happen to have *Return of the Jedi* on VHS?" Andy suddenly expressed interest in a movie, and that rather surprised me. "I noticed you have a VCR and some other movies."

"As a matter of fact, I do have that one. Let's watch it!" Cody led us back to the den, where he and Andy took the couch. I sat in the chair this time.

"When did you start seeing movies, Andy?" I was determined to find out about his interests in this area.

"Oh, two years ago, I guess. My parents organized movie night for the family about once a month. We got a VCR and a TV—we still don't watch many programs—and for movie night, we rent a movie we all agree on, watch it, and then discuss the biblical ramifications of it. It's quite a lot of fun, really. Don't roll your eyes, Jack-oh!" he laughed at me, using Blake's old nickname for me with a slightly different emphasis. "It helps us understand the underlying messages in movies so that we're not just accepting whatever Hollywood says. We still enjoy the entertainment, but we try to learn from it, too."

"That sounds like an interesting family activity," Cody inserted into the conversation. "It must be especially important with social issues of today."

"It's interesting, all right, particularly when everyone's home for it. Some of my siblings are in college now, and one of my sisters is married, but the older ones are beginning to express their own views of life more and more, so they aren't just parroting our mom and dad's views on everything, and that adds some spice to our discussions. Plus, Blake is still newer to Christianity, and he's got some unusual ideas and experiences to share with us. We learn a lot from him. But the other thing is, Cody, that it's not just about current social issues or movies. There are inappropriate messages from Hollywood films made thirty or forty years ago, too. We've watched movies that are considered 'classics' that have anti-Christian or at least ambiguously moral messages. Many Christians today think of those films in nostalgic ways as more 'acceptable' than today's movies, but if they looked at them closely, they'd see those movies are just as damaging to Christian faith as these are, *if* we don't understand them for what they are."

"And what are they, Andy?" I queried.

"Entertainment from a worldview that believes humankind is king of the world and master of their destiny. Hollywood's ideal is that people hold the key to their success in their own hands, that we answer to no one but ourselves, and that morality is what we choose to make it. 'Good' versus 'evil' is whatever society has decided it should be. If society says that segregation based on skin color is good, then it becomes evil to fight for integration. If society says that abortion should be legal at any point during pregnancy, then it becomes evil to oppose it. If society says that what God calls sin is not sin, then it becomes evil to preach the Bible as truth. Look what happens in the U.S.S.R. Communists have declared that worshipping God is illegal, and they throw people in prison for defying them."

"Why bother watching them if they're such trash?" I was getting a little irritated by his moralistic superiority.

"Because they aren't trash, Jack. You remember how I used to write stories during sixth grade? Well, I dreamt of making some of them into movies someday. The people that make movies are gifted at their craft, and I love the stories they weave through script, makeup, cinematography, and all that. I *enjoy* their finished product, but I also pay attention to the message they're delivering and filter it through what I know from God's Word to see if there's a message that runs against the Bible or not. If not, then no harm done. If so, then what is that message and how do I respond to it? One reason that Christians struggle against sin is because it's presented to them as something appealing. That was Eve's problem in the Garden of Eden, and it's my problem here. She saw the fruit as attractive for tasting and revealing knowledge, and I see Cody as handsome and kissable. Thankfully, I'm not going to do anything about my attraction to Cody, because, oh CRAP, DID I JUST SAY THAT OUT LOUD??"

I glanced at Cody, who was turning beet red, and back at Andy, who was past beet red and going for purple. I'm sure I was some tint of pink, at least, but my most significant concern was the horror on my peer's face. I jumped from my chair and made a beeline to the couch, landing next to him and burying him in a bear hug. He was all sloppy tears, sobbing, and trembling. I'd never seen him such a mess. I rubbed his back soothingly, trying to calm him like I'd seen him comfort so many others over the years. He began to calm down, but I needed to get to the restroom. I looked to Cody and motioned for him to take over the comforting. His face registered concern, but when I mouthed, "I h a v e t o p e e," he comprehended the situation and reached over.

"Come on, Andy, it's okay, bud," he soothed. He gave my friend a half-hug around the shoulders and left his arm there, rubbing Andy's arm. As the younger boy quieted, Cody couldn't resist the urge to tease him a little. "So, I'm handsome and kissable, huh?" he kept his tone light, trying to brighten the mood. "Andy? Look at me, please."

The boy looked up at Cody, who said, "Kiss me on the cheek. Come on, now, before I chicken out."

Andy sat up straight, leaned over, and kissed Cody on the cheek. He blushed again but didn't cry. "Why did you tell me to kiss you on the cheek?" he whispered.

Cody whispered back, "Because I love you in Christ, Andy, and I will not lead you on sexually. I know I said I'm gay, but I'm not, because I've been reminded that I'm a new creation in Jesus. The only kiss you can give me is on the cheek, like Christians used to give each other in ancient times, and the only kiss you'll get from me is on the top of your head. I know you're struggling with same sex attractions, my dear brother, so I'm going to help you, all right?"

For the second time in two days, I witnessed an exchange between Cody and Andy that left me puzzled. I had seen Andy kiss Cody on the cheek, and then they'd held a whispered conversation. At the end of it, Andy had nodded his head to whatever Cody had said, they'd hugged, and Cody had kissed Andy on the top of the head. What was going on with my friends?

I coughed before returning to the den. "Are we watching a movie or not?"

"Uh, sure, Jack. Let's watch it." Andy sounded like he was feeling better. "We can talk more after, ok? There are some things we need to air out, I think."

"Sure."

When the credits were rolling post-movie, Andy was the first to speak. "I really liked that one! I've been dying to see it. I wanted to see it in the theatre, but every time I made plans, they got ruined."

"I agree, it was good, but I'm getting pretty hungry. Codes? Any ideas for lunch?"

"Burgers? I'll grill." With that, he got lunch going.

As we ate, I said I needed a nap afterward. "Can I trust you two to keep your body parts to yourselves?" I gave them the evil eye. My lack of a smile startled them.

"Jack, we're not going to be getting hot 'n' heavy as soon as you conk out!" Andy objected to my insinuation.

"Or at any point," added Cody. "What makes you think we would?"

"Just saying, guys. I saw the kisses and the whispered conversation earlier, so I wanna make sure we take Andy home still a virgin." I didn't see it coming, but I sure felt it. Andy can pack a wallop in that right hand of his! I'd forgotten that for all his typical tenderheartedness, he worked on a farm, so his hands were rough and calloused, and the open-hand slap caught the left side of my face with a full palm. Man, that stung!

"Go take your nap, Jack." I'd never heard Andy speak so icily to anyone. I stood up and left the room. As I did so, it occurred to me that I'd been doing that a lot this weekend. *Screw 'em.* I went into the guest room that I hadn't used last night and stretched out for a snooze. I wondered what had freaked me out so bad that I couldn't sleep alone the night before, but before I could figure it out, I was dozing contentedly. When I woke up and looked at my watch, I was surprised to see it was 1:30, and I'd only been out for an hour. I felt a lot better, though, until I remembered Andy hitting me and the ice in his voice. My gut clenched, and I hurried to see what was up with him and Cody. I was in for a shock.

32: Justice, not Revenge

"What are *you* doing here??" I couldn't believe who was sitting at the kitchen table. *Why in the world were Kevin and Phil in the house?* "Where are Cody and Andy?"

"We're right here," Cody said, as he and Andy came up from the den. Just then, the doorbell rang. "Jack, get that, will you? We're expecting a few more people."

I nodded numbly and went to the door. Opening it, I was surprised again. "Uh, hi. Come in." In walked Coach Williams and Principal Stephens from City Christian.

Just as I was going to close the door, I heard a familiar voice. "Jack, I'm coming in, too." I turned, and Blake was jogging to the door. *Blake? What does he have to do with this?* I held the door open for him. "Thanks."

We went to the kitchen together, where it was evident the table there was too small, so we moved to the dining room. I hadn't been in that room before, despite visiting the house so many times. The table there was plenty big enough, I observed, so we took seats there and waited to find out what was going on.

Andy came and went with cups and pitchers of water for everyone to help themselves, followed by Cody with platters of crackers and cheese and freshly cut fruit. *They did all that while I napped for an hour?* I glanced at the clock on the wall. It showed 2:45. *2:45?* I looked at my watch again. *Dangit, I forgot to wind it.* So, I'd slept for two hours, not one. Well, their arrangements took longer, then. That makes more sense, but arrangements for what?

Finally, Cody and Andy returned to the dining room and stood at one end of the table. Blake sat at the same end, close to Andy. Cody spoke first. "Good afternoon, everyone. As you know, I'm Cody James and this is my house. I appreciate that you've taken the time to come over today. Please let me introduce a couple of guys to you. First, the young man standing next to me is Andy. He and I just met yesterday, but we've become fast friends. I think you already know Jack, too. He and Andy have been friends for several years."

Cody gestured for Blake to stand up next to Andy. "This is Blake, Andy's adopted brother. I mention the adoption because it's such an important part of their lives. Blake knew Jack because they were neighbors, and they hung out all the time. During a rough patch in his life, Blake asked Jack for some help. Jack brought Andy into the situation, and with Andy's influence, Blake's life took on new meaning, including becoming his adopted brother. They can tell you their story sometime if you want to hear it." Blake sat down again.

I fidgeted in my seat. I raised my hand and Cody called on me. *What am I thinking? This ain't school.* "What's going on here, Cody? Why is everyone here?" I gestured to Phil and Kevin, Coach and the principal, whose name constantly escaped me.

"You'll see, Jack. I'm going to ask a favor of you, though."

"What's that?"

"Keep your trap shut."

Phil and Kevin snickered. Even Coach and the principal cracked smiles. "Fine." I snapped back.

"Good. Now, Coach Williams and Mr. Stephens, I believe I've already briefed you on what will occur next, right?" Both men nodded. "And you're willing to witness this?" Nods again. "Thank you. Please take up your positions." The two men moved to the doorways. I thought this was getting a little weird, but it seemed odd that Mr. Stephens was at Cody's house and wasn't holding a cross towards him to ward off the evil spirits, so I held up my end of the bargain and 'kept my trap shut.'

Content Warning

"Phil and Kevin, you're next. Do you remember what I threatened to do the next time you showed up here?"

The other two thought for a moment. Kevin snapped his fingers and said, "Oh yeah. You said you'd call the cops! So much for that!" he laughed obnoxiously.

"Really?" retorted Cody. "Do you know what our coach does for full-time work? I'll give you a hint: He's not a coach 40 hours a week."

"This is entrapment, Cody. You can't *invite* me here and then call the cops with the story that I showed up."

"This isn't about you showing up uninvited, Kevin. Say, you had a birthday recently. You're 20 now, right? This ought to be extra special for you, then. The last time you were here, you attempted to rape one of my underage teammates. Do you remember that? No? Maybe this will remind you." Cody stepped over to the sideboard and pulled out a cassette player. He pressed "play" and turned up the volume.

"Ugh, Jack. You got puke on your swimsuit."

261

"I-I did?"

"Here, let me help you change. Your clothes are over here, right?"

"My clothseses are in my backpack."

"Okay, Jack, just lie back and we'll get you taken care of. Lift your hips so I can slide those off you."

Rustling sounds.

"I can change my own clothes, Kevin, thanks."

More rustling sounds, with some struggling obvious.

"What are you doing, Kevin? What is wrong with you? Let me go!"

"Oh, Jack, I don't think so. I said I'll take care of you, and we're just getting started. You've already shown how willing you are, so this is all consensual."

"What?? No! This is NOT consensual! I do not agree to this, Kevin! Stop! You need to stop!"

"You let me take your swimsuit off you, Jack. Why did you do that if you didn't want what's next?"

"I thought you were helping me change my clothes, Kevin. That's all I was expecting."

"There's no point in yelling, Jack. The music downstairs is so loud that no one will hear you, but if you're thinking of crying out, I'll stuff a sock in your mouth. If you're going to cooperate, no sock. What's it gonna be, sock or no sock? No sock? Good. Now, just lie still and let Kevvy take care of you."

[A loud crash is followed by the sounds of punches, grunts, whimpers, and confused conversation.]

Cody stopped the tape play. He looked at me apologetically and then at Kevin, whose face had paled considerably. All bravado was gone from the 20-year-old's

262

features. "I'm not done playing tapes, so why don't you sit there and consider admitting that you're a predator before you get in hotter water by lying to a police officer, Kevin?"

He turned to Phil. "Your turn." He took a tape out of his pocket, put into the other side of the tape player, and pressed 'play' once again.

"What did Kevin do?"

"Ultimately, he didn't get very far. When I realized what he had in mind, I tried to get up, but he pinned me to the bed. He had just started to pull my trunks off when you burst through the door. I had shut my eyes so he couldn't see my reaction to what he was doing to me, which is why I didn't witness your daring rescue, Codes. All I saw was a bloody mess on the floor."

"Speaking of that bloody mess, where is it, Phil?"

"He's, uh, he's still in his room."

"Go get him and bring him here. NOW." Footsteps can be heard receding in the background.

"I am so, completely, totally sorry for what happened, Jack. Kevin wasn't supposed to be here. Phil invited him. Phil was supposed to keep an eye on him. I'm as pissed at Phil as I am at Kevin, and Phil knows it."

Footsteps can be heard coming closer to the recorder.

"All right, asshole, what's with the pedophile act last night?"

"Pedophile act? What are you talking about?" The voice turns away from the recorder. "You told me he was 17 but looked young for his age."

263

"PHIL? You told Kevin he could take a turn at Jack? What kind of sick fuck does that? Jack was a guest at my house last night!"

"Listen, Cody. I'm tired of playing second fiddle to this freshman. If you remember, we are seniors. WE are supposed to be starters. I am the best fucking goalie this team has ever had. When what's-his-name went down with an injury, I'm the one Coach should have called on to take over, not this Jack-in-the-Box. If you'd let my plan play out, the kid would be done, and you and I would be starting again, 'cuz Coach would have no choice but to play us."

The sound of flesh and bone crashing together can be heard, followed by a body falling with a thud.

"Get out of my house and don't ever come back, you filthy jerk! You come here again, and I'm calling the cops!"

Click. The cassette player stopped again. The room was silent.

"Coach?" It was Mr. Stephens who spoke first. "I've heard enough, haven't you?"

Coach nodded. "Mr. Stephens, do your duty." Mr. Stephens stepped out of the room and went to the phone. Coach Williams turned to the others in the room. "Kevin and Phil, if you know or know of a defense attorney, you'd better get ready to call him. You are going to need one."

I must admit that I was struggling to keep my mouth shut, but every time I was tempted to open it, I'd glance at Cody, and the look he'd give me would freeze me. On the one hand, I was relieved to see these two scumbags getting what was coming to them, but on the other hand, I knew

Cody was going to catch hell for the partying, furnishing alcohol to a minor, and probably some other charges, too. Why was he doing this?

We all sat there for about fifteen minutes, nobody really saying anything, and then Phil started getting antsy. It was almost as if he hadn't been paying attention earlier and was just now realizing how much trouble he was in. I was so focused on him that I didn't see Mr. Stephens return or the uniformed men who followed him into the room. Phil didn't see them either. He was too wound up.

"Who the fuck do you think you are, Cody? Here you are, pretending that what Kevin and I did was so wrong, but you did it, too!"

"No, I didn't, Phil."

"Yes, you did, Cody. You couldn't *wait* to get your hands on me. My god, you practically stripped me in the showers after practice that day and begged to –."

"No, Phil, I didn't do that. You *wanted* me to do that, but I didn't do it. You and I did a lot of messing around, but there's a lot I didn't do. Yes, we got caught by Coach, and I'm glad we did, because if he hadn't caught us, I would've ended up doing too much, and I'm not sure I could've come back from the world you dragged me into."

"The world I *dragged you into*?? You were *cruising, Cody!* All I did was teach you what you wanted to know! Don't give me this crap about not wanting what I gave you. *You.couldn't.get.enough. Admit it!*"

"Phil, I did what I had to do to survive." He put up his hands defensively toward his former friend. "I'll admit that I enjoyed it sometimes, Phil, but I knew that if I didn't do what you wanted, you'd bring Kevin into it, and he's too strong for me. You're so dense, Phil; it's written all over your face! How many times do I have to tell you that I never wanted this??"

"What are you talking about, Cody?? You were so *eager* and *willing* when I first met you!"

"I was eager and willing to have someone pay attention to me and be *my friend, Phil! MY FRIEND!* DON'T YOU GET IT?? I.HAD.NO.FRIENDS!! Jeezum, Phil! You came into my life, paid attention to me, and I was so desperate for a *friend* that I was willing to do whatever it took not to lose that 'friend.' By the time I got my emotions under control and realized that no true friend would manipulate me like that, you had already hooked me into your scheming ways, and my life was further off track than before I met you." Cody had gone from zero to sixty and back to zero emotionally in less than two minutes. It was impressive. Then he issued the zinger. "That's when I installed the audio recorder in my room and the den for whenever you came over. I needed proof that it wasn't just in my head that I kept saying 'no,' and you kept insisting 'yes.'"

"Phil, you're a year older than I am. You were 17, and I was 16 when this started. You complained to *me* about how Kevin preyed on you, and then you turned around and did the same to me. The two of you tried to get me to do that to Jack, and when I wouldn't go along with it, you called Kevin to come to the party that night, I'm sure of it. I wouldn't do that to Jack because I'm not a predator, Phil. I don't know if you ever intended to be or if that's just Kevin's influence on you. Either way, it's what you've become, and you need help, and you need to be held

266

accountable. I know I'm not the only guy in town you've hit on, manipulated, assaulted, and then blackmailed to keep us quiet. I'm telling you today that it's over, and I won't be shamed by you anymore."

"This isn't the first time Coach and Mr. Stephens heard me say these things. I called them earlier today and admitted what I've done. This afternoon, I was expelled from the high school where I've had an awesome career as an athlete, and it's due to what I've confessed to, but Mr. Stephens agreed to help me today because I'm trying to turn over a new leaf with the help of my new friends. In addition to being expelled, I have to answer to the police for illegal things I've done. You and Kevin must answer for your lawbreaking, too. Since both of you took advantage of underage boys when you were of age, you'll have adult felony charges to deal with. If you had shown any remorse for your actions, maybe it wouldn't have come to this, but you kept justifying yourselves, and I'm standing up to you for myself and my friends. Mr. Stephens?"

Mr. Stephens stepped forward. "Phil and Kevin, allow me to introduce you to members of the Maine State Police, both of whom are graduates of our school and have been keeping an eye on recent reports of predatory behavior and underaged pot smoking. I was fairly certain there was a connection with the two of you, and when Cody called today, I was more than willing to notify them of this opportunity to 'kill two birds with one stone,' as it were. They'll be taking Cody's tapes in as evidence—Phil, you'll be happy to hear, I'm sure, that Cody's version of not welcoming your advances as he claimed a few minutes ago are affirmed multiple times over on the other tapes he has from your visits here over the last several months."

Wow, I didn't know Mr. Stephens could be sarcastic, but there it was! Phil was definitely *not* pleased to hear that. Within a couple of minutes, Phil and Kevin were escorted out by the State Police, and the house *felt* cleaner. I raised my hand again, but Cody shook his head. I sighed and motioned zipping my lips. He nodded and smiled slightly.

"Mr. Stephens, Jack here is very confused by my expulsion. Can you explain to him what I've told you and how it all works out?"

"Sure, Cody. By the way, well done with the situation earlier. I'm impressed."

"Thank you, sir. I appreciate that very much."

"Jack, I can truly see that you're bewildered by today's events," Mr. Stephens began, "and I'll do the best I'm able to explain the situation, but some of it will have to be sorted out by others that are present, okay?" I nodded but stayed silent.

"When Cody called today, to say I was surprised would be an understatement. When the first words out of his mouth were, 'Mr. Stephens, this is Cody James. I'm calling to apologize to you and to ask you to forgive me. I've just given my life to Jesus,' I was blown away."

That explains it. "Mr. Stephens?" I couldn't stay silent any longer.

"Yes, Jack?"

"You don't have to say any more. You've just explained all of this."

"I have?"

"Yes, sir. I don't know everything Cody said to you today in detail, but I'm betting he came clean about a lot of things he's done, and because of that, he just can't stay in our school. The rules of the school have no flexibility to allow for that. In fact, I'd say that even though you're thrilled that he's given his life to Jesus and is finally getting his life on track, your hands are tied by the organization you work for. Instead of showing mercy and grace to him, you're forced to be judgmental in your actions, throw the book at him, expel him, and as a result he'll end up in public school, where he won't have Christians around to disciple him in his newfound faith, all because of the rigidity and legalistic ways of your workplace. Am I right?"

"You're absolutely, 100% right, Jack!" hollered Coach, "and Stephens knows it! The only way that school will ever change is if men like Stephens stand up to the bosses and tell them *they* are the problem! I would've been *glad* to stand with him in that, but I got *fired* last night, so my voice has been silenced in this fight."

"Wait, what?? Fired? Who fired you??" I was trembling with a mixture of anger, disappointment, and fear.

"I did." I didn't even have to look to know the voice. It was Stephens.

"WHY?"

"For starting me." Cody spoke quietly. "Coach and I talked about it already, Jack. There was no way to play yesterday's game without starting me. Your friends were going to be there, it was the last game of the season, and Coach had had it with the hypocrisy of the bosses at the school. He *knew* I should be a starter, and instead of forfeiting the game, he started me. Remember that angry-looking conversation you saw between Mr. Stephens and Coach at half-time? It was Coach being told he was fired when the game was over."

"Coach?" my voice cracked with emotion.

"It's okay, Jack," he said. "I don't have any regrets about starting Cody. In fact, I seem to remember a fantastic young player telling me once that Cody should be a starter! I started him, knowing that without him on the field, we'd forfeit the game, but with him on the field, I'd forfeit my job. I'm okay with that trade-off because I don't coach for my glory, Jack. I coach for God's glory, and I coach to teach the game to young men. It's been the greatest honor of my life to coach here, and the greatest joy to hear Cody testify that Jesus is now his Lord and Savior."

I didn't like it, but I respected it. Still, there was one more point to settle. "Mr. Stephens, I'm going to try really hard to be respectful here, but I have a legitimate bone to pick with you."

"Really, Mr. Bannister? What is that?" His helpful tone was gone, and the arrogance was settling back in.

"Why did you threaten to fire my mother if I talked to the reporter last night?"

He looked like he'd swallowed a chicken bone wrong. It was my turn to be sarcastic. "Oh, *I'm sorry*, perhaps you thought I didn't hear you? Or that I'd forget? Tell you what. Don't threaten my mother's job again, all right? Find something else to threaten, and make sure it's not an empty threat." I spun on my heel and walked away. *Asshole.*

I heard Coach behind me saying, "You threatened to fire his mother if he talked to a reporter? What kind of jerk are you? I ought to report you!"

"Who are you going to report me to? You don't work there anymore, and they don't like you, anyway."

Cody spoke up for the first time in a while. "Mr. Stephens, thank you for helping today. You and I will probably not cross paths again in this life, and we *might* in the next one *if* we both get to the same side in it. You're welcome to leave now."

I turned and smiled at Cody for the "most polite get-out-of-my-house-before-I-throw-you-out" invitation I'd ever heard. When he left, I glanced at Andy and Blake. My curiosity got the better of me at last and I said, "Okay, I get why Andy's here, but why did you have Blake come?"

"It's been killing you to find out, hasn't it?" Blake grinned at me. "Ask him." He pointed at Coach.

"Coach? Why am I asking you?"

"Because I'm Blake's counselor. He was with me for an appointment when Cody called to see if I could come over for this, and since Blake's Dad had asked me to give him a ride here after the appointment anyway, I was just— as Mr. Stephens said earlier—'killing two birds with one stone.'"

"Wait, wait, wait. So, you're not a cop?" I was totally lost.

Coach laughed. "Never said I was! For the record, Cody never said I was, either. He insinuated it, but Phil and Kevin just bought into the idea and acted accordingly. Now, as a certified counselor, I *am* a mandated reporter, so

271

hearing what went on required me to report it, which I did, by telling Deputy Stephens."

"Deputy Stephens?" This was confusing me even more.

"Oh, you didn't know? Principal Stephens is a part-time deputy with the sheriff's department in the county where he lives. It's not the same county as the school, so he had no jurisdiction to arrest Phil and Kevin, which is why he called in the State Police. Well, that, and he wanted to get some decent publicity for the school out of this mess by showing off the 'good' graduates catching the misbehavior of the 'bad' students."

"Coach, I have a serious question." Cody's face was troubled.

"Sure, Cody, what is it?"

"I don't mean to be stepping on anyone's toes with this, sir, but it doesn't seem appropriate for a counselor to be giving a ride to a client, if you follow what I mean, sir."

"I agree completely, Cody," Coach said, "which is why we weren't alone in the car. On the ride here, Deputy Stephens was with us. He and I rode in front, and Blake was in the back. Leaving here, I'll call a cab for myself, and Blake can ride with Andy. Oftentimes, I ask my wife or daughter to come along for the ride so that I'm never alone with a client. Does that make you feel better?"

"Yes, sir, it does. Thank you." Cody's face changed, as if a light bulb went on in his head. "Coach? Can I become your client? I have a lot I need to talk to someone about, and I think you're the best man for me to talk to. I don't mind these guys hearing me say this, Coach; they're my best friends, and they want what's best for me. I've just lost my team, my school, my social circle—which isn't a bad thing, but I still have to find a new one—and my parents have no idea what's been happening in my life, and even though I'm a new creation in Christ, I could use some trustworthy adults in my life to keep me on track, you know? I'm thinking you'd be a good one to start with."

Coach Williams smiled warmly at my older friend. "I'd be honored to be your counselor, Cody." He barely got the words out when Cody was embracing him, burying his face in the man's shoulder.

"Thanks, Coach. God has used you so much in my life, even when I was dead in sin and didn't know it. You're like a spiritual dad to me. Thank you!" Sniffles could be heard around the room, and I was glad not to be the only one with them. The two-man embrace quickly became a swarm hug, as we all got in on it. As we began to drift apart, Coach lifted his voice toward the ceiling and began to sing:
Praise God from whom all blessings flow!
Praise him all creatures here below!
Praise him above ye heav'nly host!
Praise Father, Son, and Holy Ghost!
Ah—-men!

33: Going Public

Content Warning

My soccer season was over. We'd finished undefeated, but Principal Stephens notified the League that we would be forfeiting our place in the playoffs due to 'internal circumstances.' He really didn't care how that impacted my teammates and me, but without Coach Williams and Cody around, I didn't feel like playing, anyway.

I was happy for Cody that he'd found the peace he'd been looking for but upset that I was left in the dust yet again. He'd tell me to 'trust God already,' but I guess I'm too stubborn. I just wasn't *there*, yet. And I suppose the fact that I'm saying 'yet' shows I'm getting there? Maybe?

At any rate, after the drama at Cody's house that day, I felt compelled to tell Dad and Steph about the confrontation with Principal Stephens. The next day, Dad and Steph went to Stephens' office. Later, they told me how it went.

"Principal Stephens, Jack tells me that you threatened to fire me if he spoke to a reporter at the last game. Is that true?"

"Yes, Mrs. Bannister, that's true. I didn't mean it, of course, but I was trying to get Jack's attention,"

"That is entirely improper for you to do, Mr. Stephens. Here is my resignation, effective immediately." She handed him a letter. "I have filed a complaint against you with the pastor, as well. Good-bye." She and Dad left the man's office and went to her classroom. She collected her personal things, said good-bye to her students, and took her stuff to the car. Then they called me out of class to talk to me.

"Jack," Dad said when I joined them in the hall, "we're going to give you a choice that we'll talk about tonight at home. Mom has resigned her teaching position here because of Principal Stephens' threat to fire her if you talked to that reporter, and she's done here. If you want to finish the school year here, we'll find a way to pay for it, but if you'd rather go to County Christian or to Newtowne High, we'll see about those options for you. Think about it. If you're not going to stay here at City Christian, be sure to clean out your locker today. Love you, son." He hugged me and left.

My mind was swirling when I returned to class. *Stay here? Go to school with Blake and Andy? Switch to NHS? Decide today??* My best friends weren't at City Christian, and I needed to talk to *them* to help me decide what to do. I knew right away what had to happen. The upsetting nature of this information made it easy to fake being ill, though I waited until Dad and Mom were sure to be home, and then I raised my hand. When my teacher called on me, I asked if I could go to the office. When I received permission, I headed there immediately.

At the office, I requested permission to call home, saying my father had given me some bad news that had upset me, and I wasn't feeling well. The school secretary was a nurturing woman whose personality was completely opposite Mr. Stephens', and she quickly gave me the privacy needed to make my call.

I dialed Cody's number, and to my delight, he answered. "Hey, can you pick me up, please? I'm not feeling well. Yes, I've been given permission to leave early today. I'll meet you at the other entrance. I'll have quite a lot of stuff with me. Thanks. Bye."

After thanking the kind woman, I went to my locker. I took my backpack out and started sorting my books. Everything that belonged to the school stayed in the locker, and everything else went into the bag. I went back to class for a moment to let the teacher know I was getting picked up. I grabbed my stuff from the desk, returned to the locker, got my backpack, and went to the far entrance.

My handful of years at City Christian were coming to an end. I'd had a few good teachers, but I was glad to be leaving. Daily chapel services and constant haranguing to 'give my life to Jesus' and to 'let Jesus be your Lord and Savior' were sickening—not because they weren't true, but because the people saying them were frauds. They'd say that one minute, and the next minute they were sucking face with people of the same gender (*sooooo* against their supposed beliefs), or cheating on their boy/girlfriend, or having sex (fornication is a sin!), or committing adultery (also a sin!), or gossiping (sin), or backstabbing (bearing false witness is sin) or some other shitty behavior. God, it's exhausting to be around fake Christians!

I'd rather be with Vince Jackson or Phil or Kevin. At least I *know* what to expect from them. Better yet, put me in company with the Madisons or Cody James. They're Christians, sometimes irritatingly so, but they don't pretend to be perfect. They're a little *too open* about their struggles with sin, ya know? But I *definitely* prefer that to these City Christian School Fakes.

C'mon, Codes, where are you? What's taking you so long to get here? An authoritative voice behind me startled me from my thoughts and self-reflection. "Just what do you think you're doing, Mr. Bannister?"

I turned to face the speaker. "Principal Stephens. Uh, well, I'm leaving."

"Leaving?"

My first, stumbling answer gave me time to recover my wits. "Yessir. My dad spoke to me when he was here earlier, and he told me something disturbing. It really upset

276

me, and I received permission to leave early. I'm getting picked up shortly."

"Why this door and not the main entrance?" *Deputy* and Principal Stephens was suspicious.

"I had some stuff to pick up from just down the hall, and since I'm carrying so much, I didn't feel up to carrying it to the front entrance, and I'd already arranged to be picked up here." I lied as smoothly as I could, hoping this was the last time I'd have to speak to this dreadful man.

He sighed. "Fine. Take care of yourself."

"Thank you, sir." As he walked away, I exhaled slowly. I glanced to my right as something in my peripheral vision moved, and I saw a familiar Camaro SS pull up. I hurried out the door, motioning for him to remain in the car. I swung open the passenger door, shoved my stuff into the back seat and said, "Let's blow this popsicle stand. I'm quitting City Christian School today!"

Cody peeled out of the parking lot in celebration.

"What's going on, Jax?" Cody looked at me as we laughed after speeding from the school parking lot.

"D'you remember when Stephens threatened Mom's job if I kept talking with that reporter at our last game?" When Cody replied that he did, I said, "I told her and Dad about it. She resigned from her teaching job today, effective immediately. Dad came and told me during class and said it's up to me if I want to stay here, go to County Christian, or switch to Newtowne High for the rest of the year. It was a no-brainer that I'm done with City Christian, but I needed a ride. I was going to call Dad, so I got permission to go to the office to do that, but at the last minute, I rang you, instead. Thanks for coming to get me."

Cody chuckled. "That was one weird phone call, dude. I decided to just go along with whatever you were saying and get the facts later. Glad I did. Now what? Take you to your house?"

"Yeah, but I need your help deciding where to go. Where are *you* going, by the way?"

My friend chuckled again. "Funny you should ask, Jack. I'm transferring to NHS to finish my high school career, so if you were to go there, too, that'd be very cool. Of course, if you chose County Christian, I'd understand."

"Boy, you made that choice easy, Codes! I *knew* talking to you was the right decision!"

"Well, Jax, now we'll have to see if Newtowne High School will takevus."

Dad and Steph were talking in the kitchen when we arrived at my house. "Hi, Cody, what a pleasant surprise!" Steph said, winking at me.

"Hi, Mrs. B, Mr. B. I, uh, hope it's okay." Cody stammered slightly.

Dad guffawed loudly, startling both of us. "Just as I predicted to Stephanie while we drove home, isn't it, honey? 'The boy's gonna call Cody James for a ride,' I said to her. The only question was whether you'd come straight here or go to Cody's house. She predicted you'd come here." He was grinning widely. "Of course it's okay, Cody. You're practically family in this house." He reached out and shook my buddy's hand. "Thanks for bring Jack home safely all these times. You boys want a bite to eat, or are you going to head out for an afternoon of safe shenanigans?"

Cody and I glanced at each other. "If it's all the same to you, Dad and Mom, I'd like to change out of my old school

278

dress clothes and hang out with Codes for the rest of today," I said.

"Fair enough. You go change. I'll talk to Mr. James."

I took my gear to my room and got ready. I wondered if I'd ever find out what they talked about.

In the meantime, Dad and Cody moved to the living room. "You told me that Jack was scared about something last time at your house? Any idea what that was about?"

Cody shook his head. "No, sir. It was bad enough that he didn't want to sleep alone. He slept in my room, Mr. B. In my bed. I know that's not ideal, but he was really upset. And it's a king-sized bed, so we weren't anywhere near each other."

"You were in the bed, too, Cody? I'm not sure I like the sound of that, mister."

"Mr. Bannister, it wasn't like *that*, okay? Besides, Andy was visiting, too. Do you seriously think I'd be that brazen? You just said I'm like family! Do you trust me or not?"

"You're right, Cody. That wasn't fair of me. I do trust you. You understand why that doesn't *sound* good, though?"

"Yessir, I do. It's not like I want to advertise it. I just thought you ought to know that I'm not trying to hide stuff from you. You and Mrs. B. have been so good to me, and I don't want to break your trust."

"Fair enough, *Codes*. Thank you. Let's see what's taking Jack so long."

Dad and Cody walked down the hall to my room and found me in the middle of the floor, trembling. Dad was about to speak when Cody stopped him. *"This, Mr. B,"* was all I heard him say.

Cody sat down next to me, and Dad perched on my bed. "It's okay, Jack. We're here for you. What are you seeing?" Cody's voice was low.

I just shook my head and put my arms up in a defensive pose. Then I heard a voice saying, *"No! No, that's not it at all! What are you doing? Stop!"* Silence followed for a few moments, and I realized I was lying down. The voice continued, *"What are you doing?? Stop! NO! STOP!!"* It was plaintive in my ears. Why was he begging? Wait, is that *my voice?*

Half an hour later, I woke up. I was still on the floor of my room, but I had a blanket over me. I got up and went to the kitchen, where I found Cody and my parents talking over a cup of coffee. My friend was the first to notice my arrival.

"How're you feeling, Jax?" His casual tone didn't completely mask the concern in his face. "You still up for hangin' with the Code-man this afternoon?"

Despite the wrench thrown into our plans, I chuckled at his self-titled nickname. "Code-man? Come up with that yourself?" I offered a winning smile. "Sure, let's go." I hugged Mom and Dad and headed out the door. I could talk with them later.

Our afternoon of hanging out was much more subdued than expected, but it helped me process the odd episode at home earlier. Cody told me today's episode was like the one I had at his house when Andy stayed over after the last soccer game of the season. I recalled some of our topics of conversation from that visit and realized that some long-suppressed emotional scars were cropping up at inconvenient times. I was beginning to piece together what it was all about, and it was scaring me half to death.

34: Anxiety Attacks

My stepmom, Stephanie Bannister, confronted Principal Stephens and resigned from her position as a teacher at City Christian School because of his behavior toward me at the last soccer game of the season. She did so knowing our family income was secure with only my dad working, but also that they couldn't afford the tuition at the high school I'd been attending. I found out later that he and Steph were pleased that I had my chance to get out from under Stephens' thumb on my terms just a little bit by calling Cody James to pick me up.

Unlike Stephens' claim that he "hadn't meant" that he'd fire Stephanie if I kept talking to that reporter after the game, she did file her complaint with the church's pastor, who was the de facto superintendent of the school. He was furious that Stephens had cost the school one of their best teachers. After conferring with the other members of the church leadership team that helped oversee the school operations, Stephens was fired.

His dismissal did little to assuage the pain he'd caused us Bannisters. Dad and Steph had already left the regimented and legalistic church to find one that emphasized the grace and mercy of God. I lobbied to go to the same church as the Madisons, but my parents weren't in agreement with enough of their views to be entirely comfortable there. However, they found another warmer church, though a little smaller, and had a good group of high school kids who loved to hang out together and study the Bible.

I still wasn't enamored of attending church, but my parents expected me to go on Sunday mornings, and I discovered that this new church was more interesting than the old one. Surprisingly, I even *listened* to the preaching sometimes, which annoyed me, especially when it made *sense. It's not supposed to make sense. God, what are you doing to me?? Can't I hate You in peace?*

In between Sundays, I began attending Newtowne High School. I was surprised by how easy the work was, but I had to take an extra class to make up for missing out on material most freshmen take in public school, and I hadn't since I'd been in Christian school. As the second half of my 9th-grade year played out, I realized that I worked about as hard at NHS as I would have at CCS, just for different reasons.

Content Warning

I occasionally saw my old friend Vince Jackson, but not often. We didn't talk much. It seemed Vinnie was quiet and withdrawn all the time. I felt very sad for Vin; we'd been good friends at one point in time, but when Vinnie had tried to express romantic feelings for me, our friendship had ended for all intents and purposes. It's not something I'd thought about much in the years since, but as I saw Vinnie in school now, the memories of that night flashed in my mind a little strongly. In fact, I was taken aback by how much it bothered me. *It didn't bother me then, so why's it giving me so much trouble now?*

My go-to emotion when things like this happened was anger, and I blamed God. Every time I did that, however, all I could think was, *"God protected me from greater harm that night. If God hadn't been with me, Vinnie might have done more than he did."* That realization bothered me, too, because I was used to blaming all my anger on God. He was supposedly in charge of everything, so why did he allow crap to happen to me, even if it didn't go as far as it *could?* Why not just prevent it altogether, God? Geez, Louise.

While I was trying to rationalize my anxiety about the night Vinnie came on to me, I began thinking about earlier this school year when Kevin tried to rape me at Cody's house. *What, am I that good-looking that guys really want me??* My self-deprecating humor fell flat. *Seriously, why do other guys keep hitting on me? I **know** I don't indicate that I want that kind of experience with them. Am I gonna spend the rest of my life defending myself against predators?*

The more that I tried to rationalize the irrational behaviors of others, the more I got stuck in my head and thoughts, and the more intense my anxiety became. Getting up for school became almost impossible. My parents thought my anxiety was connected to all the changes in my life in recent years. They didn't know anything else was going on because I wouldn't tell them.

Finally, they decided I needed to see a counselor, and I agreed to it. I even said I'd go to one that NHS had just hired, a man I knew better as Coach TJ Williams.

It was one of the weirdest signs I'd ever seen on a school office door, but there it was. I don't remember there ever being a sign on his door at CCS at all, but he was only there for a couple of hours a day. I guess he was moving both of his practices—hahaha—to the school, his new employer. I took a deep breath and knocked on the door.

"Come in!" A voice I'd heard on the soccer pitch welcomed me to his office as I opened the door and entered. "Jack Bannister! It's good to see you." He stood, smiling, while he shook my hand. "Please, sit wherever you like."

I looked around the room. It wasn't fancy, but there were a couple of faux leather easy chairs and a matching couch to one side with a coffee table between them. There was also a conference table in the middle of the room, lined with better-than-average chairs. I chose an easy chair and he sat opposite me. "Hi, Coach, uh, is it okay to call you that?"

"That's fine with me, Jack. Or you can call me T.J., Doc, or Mr. Williams. Whatever makes you most comfortable."

"Oh, okay. I'll, um, see how it goes, I guess. Thanks for seeing me today, Coach."

"You're welcome, Jack. How is the transition to NHS going for you?"

"Pretty well. I had one class to pick up and catch up on from mid-year and that's kept me busy, but the work itself is easier than at CCS. I've made a couple of friends, but mostly I hang out with Cody, Leslie, and Lisa, and I knew them before coming here."

"Good. I'm glad to hear you're doing okay with those things. I hope you plan to try out for soccer here. You'll find there's a lot more competition for getting on this team than there was at CCS, so you'll need to do a lot of training in the offseason to be ready, but Cody should be able to help you with that."

"Isn't he graduating?"

"I'll let him tell you what's going on with his plans, but he can help you either way." Mr. Williams walked over to his desk and picked up a file folder. "Now, let's take a look at what's really on your mind, Jack, ok?"

I nodded. "Am I supposed to start talking, or do I wait for you to ask me questions?"

"This is your time, Jack. You decide how this goes. What do you want to do?"

"I have some stuff on my mind, Coach, and I need to give it to you to help me sort out, okay? I've never told my parents this stuff, though, and I want to make sure you won't tell them. You're not going to, are you?"

"What you tell me is not mine to tell them, Jack."

"Good."

"After we've talked about it, you may decide to tell them yourself, and that would be healthy for your relationship with them, depending on what it is."

"Yeah, I suppose it might be." I sat and thought about it for a moment. "Well, here goes. I think you need to know some history, so I'll start with that."

'When I first moved to this part of Maine, Blake Harris—now Madison—and his friend Vince

285

were the first two kids my age that I met and became friends with. You know Blake, of course. He and Vinnie had been friends since they were little kids, and I was 10 when we met. They were rough-and-tumble kids, which I could be, too. We went to the corner store in Nolan, close to where Andy lives, where I bought some things, and they shoplifted. I didn't know at the time that's what they were doing, but later I found that out.

'We three guys had a fort in the woods behind my house. It was in a little clearing among the trees where we had nailed some boards together to make an enclosed space. At some point we tied a tarp over the top so we could camp underneath it. It became a hideout for Blake when his dad was beating and abusing him, as well as our secret fun place when we wanted to get away from older kids.

'Blake was a bully to Andy back then. He and Vinnie hurt Andy real bad during our sixth-grade year, and I was pissed about it, but they were my neighborhood gang. We'd gone fishing, swimming, and stuff together, and I wanted to stay friends with them. Andy understood; he remained my friend while letting me be friends with his bullies. He's truly an amazing guy!

'Well, this one day in the summer before 7th grade, Vince and Blake told me it was time to choose between them and Andy. They made me shoplift from the corner store to show my loyalty to them. Then we biked to Blake's house where he showed us a porn video that his father had. Unfortunately, we

lost track of the time and stayed in the house too long. Blake sent Vinnie and me to the fort to wait for him while he returned the video to his dad's room.

'His dad got home before Blake could get out of the house, and we heard him hitting Blake. We took off for the fort. When Blake showed up later, his face was a mess of cuts, bruises, and blood. That night, he told me he wanted Andy to come over the next day to pray for him. I went to my house to arrange for that to happen. That next afternoon, Andy (and his brother David) showed up. During the afternoon, they shared the gospel with Blake and Vince.

'To Vince's surprise, Blake hadn't invited Andy over to humiliate him or me. He'd actually wanted to find out if Andy could offer him some hope for his life, because Blake had been considering suicide! Sometime after David left, Vince spaced out. Blake recognized that Vinnie was overtired and that he was going to get sick. He knew that when Vince got like that, he could become unpredictable, too, but in his own unhealthy condition, Blake forgot about that part about Vince, and he asked me to make sure Vinnie got home safely in the dark.'

Here, I stopped and asked for a drink of water.

Content Warning

Williams spoke, "You're about to get to it, aren't you?" His voice was gentle and full of understanding. I nodded.

'Vinnie was ahead of me, and neither one of us had a good flashlight. It wasn't that far to his

house, though, and we were almost out of the trees—I could see his back door from where we were—when he appeared in front of me suddenly. He put his hands on me and started accusing me of trying to steal Blake from him. He said that he and Blake were "special" friends and I wasn't going to interfere with that. Then he asked if I wanted to be his "special" friend, too. He forced me up against a tree and kissed me. When I broke free from him, he reached under my shirt and rubbed my chest, trying to touch my nip—'

I'd done all I could to maintain my composure, but out of nowhere, it seemed, I was overcome by emotion, and as I relayed to a trusted, even admired adult about what had happened two years prior, I melted into sobs of shame, guilt, and disgust. I cried for several minutes, uninterrupted except for my therapist handing me tissues. When I felt like I could continue, I wanted to finish it.

'He, t-touched m-me under my shirt-t. I, I fought him off. I y-yelled at h-him, and h-he hit me with h-his forearm, a-and then h-he punched me h-hard e-enough to kno-ck-ck me out-t.'

I took a few deep breaths, letting each one out slowly, trying to regain control. I sipped my water. *'When I came to, he was g-gone. I checked my clothes, and it didn't appear that he'd done anything else to me...you know...my belt... sigh.. I got up and went to his house. His mom said he was in bed with a fever. I went home from there. I never told my parents what happened.'*

"How does it make you feel to talk about these things now, Jack?" Doc asked a question that was both sincere and routine. As the client had been speaking, the clinician had been listening and observing, as he always did, while ruminating on what he already knew about this young man. In this case, the boy had revealed being sexually assaulted just two years earlier. Yes, it qualified as such, even if it went only as far as Jack described it. *Unwanted contact of a sexual nature.* That's all it took to define the situation as assault. Per a common experience, sad as it was, the incident occurred at the hands of a trusted friend. The fact that they were both about eleven or twelve years old when it happened was even more troubling.

As a clinical psychologist, his job was to help patients work through their concerns in a manner that put them in the driver's seat, as it were. He equipped them with the tools for addressing the situations they faced so that no matter where they were or when the troubles arose, they could work their own way out. A *problem* he had in his work was that he *cared.*

He had asked the Lord to use him to help young people, and the Lord had placed his clinical practice inside a public high school. NHS also needed a soccer coach, so Doc was able to build rapport with the student body through coaching, and he understood that where God led, he needed to follow. For some reason, three of his clients were from the same circle of friends, and two of them were—or had been—on his soccer team. He didn't know if there was a significance to that or not. Time would snitch on that.

Back to this young man. As a starter on his soccer team the previous fall at another school, he impressed Doc with his on-the-field presence and attitude. Off the field, however, he displayed a tremendous disdain for authority. Late in the season Williams discovered some of the reason for that, and he couldn't blame the kid for feeling that way. Still, Jack needed to learn better ways to channel his energy, and Doc did what he could as a coach to teach him what he had to figure out.

This was different. Jack was attacked, as a twelve-year-old boy, in the private matters of life that should never be touched without permission. Then he'd hidden it for two years. Today was probably the first time he'd ever cried about it. He talked about his rough-and-tumble friends, which they may well have been, but he was their equal and then some. This young man built his walls higher and higher, keeping out all love and tenderness so that he could never be hurt again. Doc prayed, *"Lord, teach me to help this boy!"*

"It's, uh, kinda weird, to be honest with you, Doc. You're the first adult I've told this to, and only two other people know besides you. That's—"

Doc Williams cut me off. "I don't need to know names, Jack. If the other people you've told aren't adults, then you need their permission before naming them to me."

"Oh. Okay."

"Are these other people trustworthy? They'll keep your secret safe?"

"One hundred percent, Doc. They aren't the type to go around talking to other people about anyone's business."

He nodded thoughtfully. "Okay. You want to be careful choosing the people you confide in, Jack. Is there anything else you want to add to today's discussion?"

"Not today, Coach. There's more, but I..not today. Can you help me?" I pleaded with Doc Williams. "I keep seeing this kid around school!"

That startled my counselor. "Is that why these memories have been stirred up?" When I nodded, he continued. "Correct me if I'm wrong, Jack. You really haven't seen this other boy since that day, but now you're seeing him at school? Do you feel unsafe around him?"

"Yes and No. Yes, I didn't see him much since then. No, I don't feel unsafe around him. Whoa, too many double negatives, Coach! I've avoided him in the neighborhood, but he also just hasn't been around much. I think he spent some time in an institution for some mental issues. Anyway, he's at this high school. It's sad to see him now, honestly. He was a funny guy when we were younger.

"Blake told me once that *he* felt guilty about Vinnie's behavior, saying he'd corrupted Vinnie by *his* bad behavior. Vinnie stood up to Blake for me a couple times when we first got to know each other. Now, he always looks sad, but I don't trust him enough to hang out with him again."

"That *is* sad, Jack, but I agree that you shouldn't be around him. Your intentions, no matter how good, could easily be misunderstood by him, and that could lead to more aggressive misbehavior."

I nodded my understanding. "Is that it for this week, Coach?"

"Almost. I have some homework for you. Between now and next week, whether you just think about it or write it down is up to you, as long as you come prepared, here it is: *'Is there anyone in your life that you feel especially close to that understands you and that you can talk to? If so, who is it? Does that person know that you consider him or her trustworthy like that?'* And that's your homework! Let me know if you have any questions or concerns between now and then. You have my business card, so you know how to reach me. Take care, Jack."

"Thanks, Coach. It helped to talk about it. I look forward to next week."

Author's Note:
If you or someone you know have/has experienced sexual assault, child abuse, or domestic violence, please reach out for help:
National Sexual Assault Hotline: Confidential 24/7 Support
<u>800-656-4673</u>

35: That's a "No"

Content Warning

Talking to Doctor "Coach" Williams helped a little, but I needed to process my thoughts and emotions more when I got home, so I went out to the fort. As I walked, I processed more of my thoughts and emotions about my friends.

Seeing Vince at school wasn't getting any easier. I was increasingly torn between wanting to talk to him to see how he was doing, curious to find out if he still felt *that way* about me or if those feelings had passed, and wanting to punch *his* lights out like he'd done to me two years ago.

Seriously, how do you confront someone over something like that?

The more I thought about it, the more confused I became. Did I *want* him to still feel that way about me? No, I decided, I didn't want that, so what would I do if he said he *did* have those desires for me? React with violence? *That* wouldn't be helpful. Sigh.

And what about his relationship to Blake? Does Vinnie even know what's been happening there? Or is he completely clueless about the fact that Blake isn't a Harris anymore, that he's a Madison now? Yeah, talking to Coach released *some* of the anxiety, but my emotions hadn't calmed down completely when it came to Vince Jackson.

I used to trust Andy Madison. I could tell him *anything*, and he'd clam up about it. He was amazing that way when we were in sixth grade (I was about to say, 'when we were kids'). I guess we *were* 'kids' then. He and I were ten when I first moved here. That's young if you think about it.

But back then, we hung out *all the time*, and our friendship was uncomplicated by everything that's happened since. I mean, since Blake moved in as part of Andy's family, the Jack 'n' Andy Show hasn't been a thing. I haven't processed it like this before!

I'm just realizing how much I lost when Blake says his life turned "right side up." I don't have him as a next-door friend anymore, and I lost Andy from my daily school life. I know I've made a great friend in Cody, but he's *older*; I don't have other people in my peer group that I trust like I trusted Andy and Blake, and at one point, Vinnie.

God, this is so hard! Why? Why does this have to be so hard, God?? What is it with you, anyway? Why do you hate me so much?? Sigh. *You **always take away** the people I love.* I wanted to punch something. "GODDAMNIT!! I FUCKIN' HATE YOU!!"

"Who're you screaming at, Jack?"

The quiet voice startled me, but I recognized it instantly, and I whirled around to face Vince.

"What are you doing here, Vince?" I demanded.

He shrugged. "This used to be our fort. I come out here sometimes when I need to be alone and clear my head." He looked at me. "You haven't answered my question, Jack. Who were you screaming at?"

I sighed heavily. "God." I expected Vinnie to laugh at me, so when he didn't, I wanted to know why.

"Oh. I thought maybe. Why?" There was no taunt in my former friend's voice at all.

"Not sure I want to talk about it right now, Vin."

"Okay. No pressure, Jack."

We had sat down by that point on whatever stumps or seats we could find. It seemed that neither of us fully trusted the other, but neither of us wanted to be the first to leave, so we just sat there in silence for a few minutes. Finally, Vince spoke up.

"Jack?"

"Yeah, Vince?"

"Can we talk?"

"I guess so. What's on your mind, Vince?" I braced myself.

"I'm sorry for what I did to you, Jack, you know, assaulting you the way I did that night. It-it's h-hard to c-call

294

it that e-even now, but I know that's what it w-was." He drew a giant breath and released it through his teeth slowly. "I've spent so long fighting my attraction to guys, Jack. I became jealous of your friendship with Blake—even though he and I weren't a couple in any way at all—and I found *you* attractive because of your confidence for living life without appearing to care what others thought of you, not to mention that you've always been good-looking."

"That weekend, after all the stress and trauma, I wasn't feeling well *at all*, but I knew perfectly well what I was doing when I hit on you. I was secretly hoping you'd be attracted to me enough to respond positively to me, but when you didn't I got scared, so I knocked you out so I could get away and be in bed before you could beat me up. Jack, what I did to you was *so* wrong, and I'm *so sorry!*"

I was flummoxed. I don't know how else to put it. I just sat there, not knowing how to respond. After a lengthy delay, I spoke.

"I'm not sure how to respond, Vin. You're right about what you did being so wrong. Dude, kissing me? Touching my body against my wishes? Especially when I'm telling you not to? I'm not gonna lie, Vin; that messed me up, big time. I'm going to counseling now because of what you did. Did you... Did you do anything to me while I was knocked out?"

He couldn't bring his eyes to meet mine. *He couldn't bring his eyes to meet mine??* "What did you do while I was knocked out, Vince??"

"I'm so sorry, Jack! Please, *please* forgive me!" His eyes were wide, full of tears, and pleading for mercy.

Oh, God, NO! "Tell me, Vinnie."

Fighting back the tears, the boy in the broken-down fort described how he had touched me where he had no business doing so. *Despite my unconsciousness, he tried some things but stopped when his mother called for him from the back porch.. He'd carefully reassembled my clothes so I wouldn't notice anything amiss when I regained consciousness. It's no wonder I'd felt so violated and betrayed!*

"Why *now*, Vince?" It's all I could come up with to respond to this horrifying revelation. "You've had two-and-a-half years to tell me the truth! We were friends!"

I couldn't tell if I was angry or if I would be. Maybe I was just in shock that this *friend* had done this. I couldn't complete the thought; it was so revolting. *I was 12! I was unconscious! How could he do that to me???* I shuddered with revulsion and fought the urge to vomit.

He didn't seem to notice, or if he did, he didn't care. It didn't matter; our friendship was over. Suddenly, it wasn't important to hear why he was sorry. I just wanted him gone from my life, but he pressed on to explain his situation. I should've let him go when I had the chance.

"I've been in and out of juvie, Jack."

"Juvie? Juvenile jail? For what?"

"Yeah, for indecent behavior. I was caught with a classmate from school. He and I were, well, fooling around in the middle school locker room after school and we got caught."

"Really, Vin? What happened to him?"

"Nothing, Jack."

"Why not?"

"I'm older, so they pinned it on me, saying I was taking advantage of a younger student. We were both sixth graders, but he was a month shy of twelve, and I was twelve. Ma agreed that I needed to 'learn a lesson' so I was sent to juvie.

"All I learned there my first time was how to be more devious. During 7th grade, I got sent again, but this time my 'special friend' went, too. He was an 8th grader. We went because we were 'misbehaving' in public, and smoking dope and drinking. When I came back from juvie that time, I went to a different school to finish junior high to see if I could sort out my life a little bit. I quit the drinking and dope, but I struggled to give up guys."

"Oh." *If he's gonna talk, he might as well answer my damn question.* "You still haven't answered my question, Vin. Why are you sorry now?"

He held up his hand in a gesture of 'I'm getting to that.' "In 8th grade, I met this guy, a 9th grader that hung out with other kids at my school sometimes. He was wicked good-looking, funny, kind, generous, athletic—in many ways reminded me of you, to be honest. We went fishing, committed a little petty theft, even came out here to the fort once or twice to camp out... it was almost like being with you and Blake again. Felt like my life was starting to get back on track."

"Then one day, he invites me to his place, says he's wanted to have me over for the longest time and now his parents will finally be away for a few days, so we can have the place to ourselves. He and I take the bus to his house after school. After getting a snack, we go to his room. It's great! King-sized bed, private bathroom. He invites me to put my stuff in the corner of the room and to share a shower. Naturally, I'm stoked. While I'm getting ready, he hands me a mixed drink, promising me we'll go 'light' on those. I accept it, suck it down, and by the time the shower starts, I'm passed out cold 'cuz he's drugged me."

"I wake up a few hours later and I'm in a lot of pain. I'm sorry, I know this is graphic, Jack, but it's what happened. My host comes into the room and asks, 'How does it feel to be messed up, you little pervert? Get dressed and get out of my house!' It turned out that the guy I'd fooled around with in sixth grade was his cousin, and *that* kid had tried to kill himself. He failed but caused himself permanent injury. That 9th grader had used my desires to get revenge on me, Jack!"

"It showed me the consequences of uninvited and unwanted personal contact. Eventually, when I'd begun to recover from being assaulted while unconscious, I was able to process what *you* must've felt, and *that,* Jack, is why I'm so sorry for what I've put you through. Please accept my apology."

I ran my fingers through my hair, sighing as I did so. "Holy shit, Vinnie, that happened to you, for real? And that's where you've been the last two years, plus?" *Don't get me wrong. It's horrible that these things happened to him, but I feel a little vindicated that karma hit him a little for the crap he pulled on me. I can show a tiny bit of sympathy now.*

"My life's been all the hell over the place, Jack. A complete train wreck. Just started to recover recently."

"What's making the difference, if you don't mind me asking?"

"Religion."

"No shit. Really? Jesus and all that?"

"No, not that at all. I've been learning about accepting myself for who I am. The way fundamentalist Christians like Andy twist the Bible to make it say that homosexuality is wrong isn't what the Bible means. For example, you know how they use the 'Sodom and Gomorrah' story to say God rained down sulfur on those cities because all the men were gay? Not true! The men of those cities weren't gay at all. They weren't nice to those angels, but it wasn't that they were gay. That's just bad interpretation.

"And Jesus never mentions homosexuality in anything he says, so they need to back off their condemnation! I mean, Jesus was a good man and we should follow his example to be kind to each other, but all that nonsense about miracles and the virgin birth and stuff? No way, man. That's just stuff his followers made up to make him seem extra special. *No way* that stuff is true."

"Anyway, self-acceptance and self-reliance are key. Self-acknowledgement of your own values can lead you to knowing your way is best for you. If you stay true to you, then you're not going to violate others' rights. You know what I mean? It has really helped me see that what I feel is okay for me to feel, but I shouldn't pressure others to agree with me. If someone else wants to share in my feelings, attractions, or desires, they'll let me know, and we can be part of our oneness journey together, without violence or mistrust. It has really helped me calm down and get my priorities straight, and that's how I knew that I needed to apologize to you and clear the air with you. Our friendship is too important to leave the poisoned arrow in place, slowly killing us over this awful incident."

I had to agree that the 'awful incident' was like a poisoned arrow that was slowly killing me, but that was about as far as I could comprehend what Vinnie was saying. His talk about staying true to himself as the standard for right and wrong made about as much sense to me as rubbing yourself in manure and declaring that you were scent-free.

But Vince had finally comprehended what his horrific actions had done to me psychologically and had apologized, so I decided to accept his apology. It seemed likelier to me that I'd overcome this issue in my life if I handled it this way than if I refused and let it fester more. "Vince, I accept your apology."

He shrugged. "Thanks, Jack. It's been tough, but now that I know that I can accept me for who I am, I'll be fine. Like I said earlier, I've been fighting my sexual desires for a long time, and I've finally learned that fighting is unnatural. I never should have been so violent over something like this! I listened to the culture around me that said it was wrong for me to love a boy instead of a girl, but now I know I should listen to myself, to my own needs. Fighting inside me made me angry on the outside and led me to assault you and Blake and others. I was sick, Jack. Now, I'm healthy, because I embrace the love I have and can give to others. If a boy says no, I accept his answer and move on. When you accepted my apology just now, you've helped me heal a little more from the hurt and damage I caused in the past. Thank you."

Vince got up from his seat in the old fort. "I know we probably can't be friends again, Jack, because I destroyed our trust, but if you ever need someone to talk to, I'm here."

I stood up, too. I had one more comment for my former friend. "All right, Vince. I think it's best if the friendship ends. It was good for a while there, but we're very different people. While I accept your apology, it's going to be a long time before I forget that you assaulted me, and I don't think that I can be friends with my attacker. Good-bye."

And with that, he was gone. *Well, God, I certainly don't trust Vinnie! What a whack job! You're not doing real well at convincing me you know what you're doing, God. In fact, you're still batting .000, according to my scorecard.*

36: Shock and Awful

Content Warning

There was no warning that I could see. I hadn't been to the Madison farm in several months, so I didn't know what was happening there, but the phone call seemed to come out of nowhere. Once again, God threw my life into a tailspin.

Ring *Ring* *Ring*

"Hello, this is Stephanie. May I ask who's calling, please?"

"H-hi, Mrs. B-baannis-ster, t-this i-is A-andy M-madison."

"Andy! What's wrong??"

"M-M-om d–d-died."

Obituary

"Sarah Madison, age 46, beloved wife of Peter Madison, adored mother, friend, confidant, teacher, and sister in the Lord to countless in our community, finished her journey on this earth today as the cancer that had sapped her strength and vitality for the last ten months claimed its final toll. Sarah was a birth mother to some children but an adoptive and spiritual mother, too. Indeed, it was the love of God in Sarah that led her to be mothering to boys and girls who knew love, discipline, listening ears, advice, prayers, hugs, and even the occasional smack on the back of the head or swat on the behind with a wooden spoon.

"We rightfully lament our loss, for we loved Sarah deeply, and we will grieve her absence from our lives for a long time. However, this dear woman did not belong to us. She belonged to Jesus Christ, her Savior and Lord, whom she loved more dearly than she loved her husband or children or anyone else. Sarah has achieved what she longed for most in life: She sees with her eyes what she believed by faith. Her suffering is over. Her worries are done. We are no longer her concern. Her heart is full of God's glory. Our sadness is temporary because she is in heaven, and we will join her there someday.

"Pray for us. Pray that we will not forget the promise of God's hope while we suffer this loss. We want to share God's love with others, even as we grieve.

To God be the glory, great things he hath done! So loved he the world that he gave us his Son, who yielded his life an atonement for sin, and opened the life gate that we may go in.

O perfect redemption, the purchase of blood! To every believer, the promise of God; the vilest offender who truly believes, that moment from Jesus forgiveness receives.

Great things he hath taught us, great things he hath done, and great our rejoicing through Jesus the Son; but purer and higher and greater will be our wonder, our transport when Jesus we see!

Praise the Lord; praise the Lord; let the earth hear his voice! Praise the Lord; praise the Lord; let the people rejoice! O come to the Father through Jesus the Son, and give him the glory, great things he hath done!

"Finally, thank you for your love, prayers, and kindness to us during this time. God is sustaining us. As her favorite hymn says, 'To him be the glory.'"

Early in the school year, our conversation was weird when I called Andy and Blake to invite them to my soccer game. I missed a significant clue because I was so wrapped up in my drama. Mom Madison had sounded so tired that day, but as soon as she knew who I was, she tried to sound okay. I remember thinking how unusual she sounded. Andy was also at a loss for words, which was weird. He finally said, "God was meeting [their] needs," or something like that. I never followed up to find out what was going on. Yeah. Cancer. And now Blake and Andy know what it's like to lose their mom, like I know it. And I loved Mrs. Madison, too. This sucks.

I never saw it coming. I never had the chance to tell her how much she means to me, how her love changed my life and kept me from doing stupid crap all.the.time. They never told me she was sick! They never told me she was dying! *I never saw it coming.* I melted into a puddle of tears on my bed. Fifteen years old and I was sobbing like a baby.

Content Warning

Once or twice, when I was in sixth grade and visiting Andy, I went to church with his family. There were usually several empty seats, even though the church had good membership numbers. On the day of the memorial service, it was absolutely packed. Dad said that if the fire marshal stopped by, he'd probably close the building down because the aisles were full, and the place was standing room only. Then Dad and I had a little chuckle about that, 'cuz the fire marshal *was* there, as part of the congregation.

I will admit that that church knows how to *sing*. I got *chills* when they sang during the service. They began with the song from the obituary, "To God Be the Glory." *Wow.* Even *I* had to admit that if God was paying attention, he was being glorified by the congregation singing it.

Later, when they sang, "It Is Well with My Soul," I *cried.* It was impossible not to! I mean, look at the words:

'When peace like a river attendeth my way, when sorrows like sea billows roll, whatever my lot, thou hast taught me to say, "It is well, it is well with my soul."

Though Satan should buffet, though trials should come, let this blest assurance control, that Christ has regarded my helpless estate, and has shed his own blood for my soul!

My sin—O the bliss of this glorious thought!—my sin, not in part, but the whole, is nailed to the cross and I bear it no more, praise the Lord, praise the Lord, O my soul!

O Lord, haste the day when the faith shall be sight, the clouds be rolled back as a scroll, the trump shall resound and the Lord shall descend, "Even so"—it is well with my soul!'

They sang that last verse *a capella*; something like four hundred voices, no instruments, singing. It was moving, and I wasn't the only one crying. I could tell they believed what they were singing.

It must be nice to believe something so fervently, but how can you? How can you sing like this when your God has just taken your loved one away from you? My tears dried up as I considered what they were ignoring. No, I couldn't be part of this sham. My heart was breaking for my friends, but to make it worse by suggesting that God cared when he hadn't cured Mom Madison was too much for me.

But the sham would only worsen, and I couldn't leave my seat. There was no way to get out, but I had to stay to hear what he would say. Who? Blake. Blake Harris Madison was going to speak. Oh, God, how? He stood up at the pulpit and looked at everyone. At first, he was a little nervous, but once he found his voice, the words spilled clearly and powerfully.

"Hi, everybody. Th-thanks for coming today. A lot of you don't know me. I'm Blake, the adopted son of the Madison family."

There were a few murmurs of understanding that passed through the congregation.

"I've only been in this family for a couple of years, but I'm here today to tell you how God has worked his mighty grace and mercy through them for a very long time. Honestly, standing here and looking at all of you, I probably don't need to say what I prepared. You wouldn't be here if you didn't know how much the Madison family, and Mom Madison, in particular, love others because of what God has done in them." Heads nodded, and a few 'Amen!' comments were heard.

"So, instead of what I wrote," Blake said, *"I'm going to tell you how I became a Madison."* He smiled. *"Don't worry. I'll give you the short version."* A light chuckle rippled through the crowd.

"I was raised in an abusive, loveless home. I became a manipulative, selfish bully and thief. When my home life became unbearable, I was ready to make a desperate choice. I had a plan to take my own life to avoid returning to my house. Then, I remembered that one of my friends knew one of my bully victims, a boy who knew Jesus. On a whim, I ordered my friend to bring that kid to me the next day so I could find out if that Jesus character was worth knowing."

I looked at Blake, and then I glanced around the room. His speech riveted everyone. He cleared his throat to continue.

*"Andy Madison arrived the next day. Somehow, I felt prompted to apologize to him for being his bully. To my shock, he forgave me, telling me that because God has forgiven him much, he must forgive me. Dear friends, **that** is when God took hold of my heart, and he hasn't let go since. By the end of that day, I was in Christ's family. With **love** in*

my life for the first time, I faced my challenges without the desperation I'd had before. Mom and Dad Madison opened their hearts and home to me that night. A Christian judge—I see him here today!—provided the authority required to allow me to be in their guardianship and ultimately to become their adopted son."

"My life was upside down when I met the Madisons. Through them, God has turned my life right side up. I've had two amazing years as the third son of Mom Madison, and I wouldn't exchange them for anything in the world. I'm going to miss her so terribly much. My natural mother never loved me, yet Mom Madison more than made up for that, and I can never thank God enough for her! This really, really hurts, and I don't know how I'm keeping it together up here."

*"Let me close with a few more comments, friends. Would we have preferred to have Mom healed and staying here with us? Absolutely! But Mom is with Jesus, and if we overcome our doubts and fears, and cling to Jesus in faith, we'll be with him in heaven when we die. Losing our beloved Mom is so hard, but God **is taking care of us.** He has given us comfort and peace by his Holy Spirit that we never knew we could have.*

'My sweet sisters, thank you for being here for me. To David and Andy, you're greater brothers than I ever imagined having. Dad Madison, I love you so much! I'm so sorry you've lost your b-best f-friend. I...I..."

And that's as far as my brave friend lasted. His emotions overflowed, and his dad met him with open arms, joined quickly by his brothers, sisters, and brother-in-law. The impromptu family hug lasted several minutes.

While the family was tending to their own, the pastor stood and invited the congregation to stand to sing a hymn. He chose "Amazing Grace." We sang without accompaniment. It gave the Madisons time to recover from the family hug and return to their seats. While the final two verses were being sung, Peter Madison waved the pastor over, and I watched them converse briefly. The congregation was seated after the song, and the pastor stood to speak.

"Folks, Peter Madison was scheduled to speak next, but the family has decided that they want Blake's message to speak for all of them. Each of them has something to say, but they will choose another time and place to say it. I am going to add that Blake has given the foundation of my message to you: for the Christian, death is not the end, nor is it natural. It is not the intended part of God's creation. It is a result of sin entering the world by man's disobedience to God's commands. Following sin's entrance to the world, all pain, suffering, trials, agonies, wars, and troubles have brought to us the ultimate negative end that we reach: death.

"To die without surrendering yourself in repentance and faith to Jesus for the forgiveness of sins, death means entrance to eternal judgment, no matter how much people try to claim that it doesn't happen. However, to die after giving yourself to Jesus, death is the entrance into his presence for eternity, leaving behind the misery of this world.

"Is there anyone that wants to be judged by God? I doubt it, but too many people see God's commands to obey his Word as restrictive tethers and not as the loving response of forgiven sinners. Our pride rejects the idea that God must save us, so we try to justify ourselves, instead.

"This is a theme that Sarah Madison discussed often, and by God's mercy and grace, she answered when God knocked on her heart, and she lived her life following him. Everyone she met was invited by her to meet Jesus, to submit their lives to him in repentance and faith, to answer that knock on their hearts.

"Today, if the Lord is calling you to repentance and faith, believe! Do not let another day pass without trusting in Christ for salvation from your sins! That was the desire of Mrs. Madison. It is our desire that you be able to follow her into heaven, too."

It wasn't the best sermon I'd ever heard, but after Blake spoke, no one was going to sound good, to be honest.

Following the service, I finally had my chance to see the Madison brothers and Mr. Madison. I hugged each one, telling them I was sorry for their loss. I felt like a fish out of water. Andy sobbed and wouldn't let go. "Now I know how you felt, Jack. I'm so sorry."

He was sorry for how I felt?

"Oh, Andy, it's your turn to grieve. Just let it out, bud." I let him cry for as long as he needed, which turned out to be several minutes. Have you ever stood in a hug with someone who was sobbing for more than two minutes? Honestly, it feels like an eternity, and our embrace lasted at least 7 minutes. Still, I figured the longer it lasted, the better off Andy would be in the long run. I knew from experience how bad it was to bottle up emotion.

When Andy was done crying, he looked embarrassed. I spoke to settle his nerves. "Don't be ashamed, Andy. Crying is good for you, bud." And I shocked both of us by giving him a little kiss on the cheek. "That's just a friendship thing, okay? You need a little love from your friends today."

He nodded and cracked a small smile. "Thanks, Jack. I'm glad you're here. I've missed hanging out with you." He grew silent and contemplative. "Jack? I'm sorry we didn't tell you what was going on with her. She was really sick last fall, but then she got better, and it looked like she was going to be okay, so we didn't tell our friends about it. The end came wicked quickly."

"How quickly, Andy?"

"A week."

"A week?" My breath caught.

My friend's head bobbed again. "David and the twins barely had time to get home from college to see her before she died. They arrived about ten hours before the end. Somehow, she was alert for long enough to recognize them, but not long enough for much conversation. This is so hard for all of us. Dad's devastated. Blake's hurting. I'm...I'm okay for now. Thanks for letting me cry. I *really* needed that."

"You bet, Ands," I said, using Cody's nickname for him. "You've been one of my best friends for years, Ands. I miss the times you and I had, just the two of us. Don't get me wrong, okay? I love our other friends, too, but you and I? The Jack and Andy Show? We had good times. I've missed that. I'll admit it; I've been lonely, Andy. I need to reconnect with you, and with you and Blake."

"I'd like that, Jack. C'mere, give me another hug. Your dad's waving for you to go."

We hugged again. I whispered into his ear, "I'm really sorry about your mom, Andy. She loved you, and she loved me, too, and I'll never forget her."

I released him from the hug and walked away quickly so he wouldn't see my tears or hear my sniffles.

37: Sarah's Love and Trust

"Coach Williams? Can I talk with you, please?" Blake Madison jogged down the hall of Newtowne High School to catch up with his therapist, even though he knew it was against the rules to run there. He wanted to ensure the man didn't leave before Blake could talk with him.

"Sure, Blake, what is it?" TJ Williams turned and smiled at the 16-year-old. "Let's step into my office for privacy."

Blake followed him inside and sat opposite the coach. "Thanks, Coach. By the way, thank you for coming to Mom's memorial service. It meant so much to have you there."

TJ's smile dampened with a bit of sadness, but he said softly, "You're welcome, Blake. Your mom's love for God deeply affected so many of us, including me. It was my honor to be there. Now, what can I do for you today?"

"Actually, it has something to do with that." Blake was looking at his hands, which were twisting and intertwining with each other nervously. Then he looked up at TJ. "You see, a -a few d-days before M-mom died..." he paused for courage, "she had Dad send me in to talk with her, alone."

TJ said nothing, knowing Blake would say more if his counselor waited until the boy was ready to speak again. They sat there, looking at each other, at the floor, the table, the window. Coach finally gestured for Blake to go on.

"Okay, yeah, sorry. Aside from all the other things we talked about, she had one thing she wanted me to do when she was gone, and I'm kinda scared about it because it's such a big responsibility. I know I can do it, but I just needed to talk to you about it, if you don't mind."

"I don't mind, Blake." *I don't mind at all!!* "What is it?"

"She wants me to keep an eye on Andy and make sure he's okay."

"Mmm. I see. Yes, that's a big responsibility. Was that all of it?"

"No." His voice trembled a little.

"Okay. What else is there?"

"She wants me to keep an eye on David, too."

"Wow, she really trusts you!"

"Is that what it is? That's why she asked me to do these things?"

"Yes, Blake. She *knows* you so well that she *trusts* you to be concerned about your older and younger brothers and to help take care of them in her place. **That** is big-time trust right there, young man."

With his eyes brimming with tears, Blake said, "Then what does it mean when she asked me to keep an eye on Dad, too?"

Coach Williams fought back his own emotions as he said, "That? That's *true love*, Blake. Your mom truly loved you. She knew you could help your dad fight his way

312

through his heartbreak because you've known heartbreak like no one else in your family has. You are Sarah's *special son* because she got to *choose* you. I'm sorry, Blake. I can't..." With that, TJ Williams lost *his* composure and wept openly for his client's loss.

A couple of minutes later, when he'd pulled himself together, he apologized to Blake, who cut him off. "Coach! TJ, please don't apologize. I love you for showing your humanity so openly!"

"Thanks, Blake. It's unprofessional of me to become so emotionally involved."

"I don't care about that, TJ. Calling you 'TJ' is unprofessional, too, but you let us do that!"

Coach chuckled. "Yeah, I suppose you're right. I recall how Sarah and Peter described the Lord opening their hearts to take you into their lives and home as they prayed for Andy's time with you that Sunday afternoon. I don't know if they ever told you this, but within moments of David and Andy leaving their house that day, Sarah turned to her husband and said, "Peter, the Spirit is impressing on my heart that our boys are coming home with another kid for us tonight, and whoever it is, we're going to love him like one of our own."

"She said that?? I never heard that before. Wow!" Blake cried happy tears. "I knew my Mom was special, but wow! How am I gonna live up to my promise to her, TJ?"

"By God's grace, for starters, Blake. And with the help of others." The clinician glanced at the clock on the wall and realized he had to wrap up their session, so he changed course. "We're out of time for this week, Blake, so I'm going to give you some homework by way of a question:

313

What do you think Sarah meant when she asked you to look out for others in your family for her? Go ahead and think about that, and we'll talk again soon, all right?"

"Okay, Coach. Thank you. See you soon." Blake was surprised to see his younger brother coming toward him as he was leaving TJ's office. "What's going on, Andy?"

"It's my turn, Blake. Dad signed me up to meet with Dr. Williams, starting today."

"Oh! You'll like him, Andy. He's good. I'll see you later, slightly younger bro."

"Thanks, my slightly older bro." Andy gave him a slight smile, as he reached the clinician's door and knocked.

Content Warning

"Come in!" TJ called out. As the teen entered, Doc said, "Hi, Andy. How are you doing? I'm glad to see you. Sit wherever you like."

"Thanks, Dr. Williams. Dad wanted me to talk to you. He's worried about me, I think."

"What makes you say that?"

"Well, I've been upset a lot this school year, and now, with Mom... I think Dad's been planning to have me come see you for a while but decided now's the time to get it started."

"I see. Do you agree with him?"

"Actually? Yes, I do. Dr. Williams, I've been dealing with a lot of shi– er– crap in my life, and I don't like what's happening in my thoughts. I've loved the Lord for so long, yet I haven't felt far away from him before. I know the words to say to make it sound like he and I are like this," he crossed his index and middle fingers in the well-known symbol of intimacy, "but I couldn't feel further from him.

My prayers seem to fall on deaf ears. Reading my Bible is a chore. Going to church is painful. Nothing I used to enjoy about my relationship with God has life in it anymore."

"When did this start, Andy?"

"I dunno. I guess it began last year sometime."

"Last school year or last calendar year?"

"Both."

"Okay. Now, I'd like you to think about situations or events happening in your life at that point. Did something take place that triggered this for you?"

"No, I don't think s–...wait. Yes. Yes, something happened at school at this time last year. I didn't realize it had affected me that much, but maybe it did."

"What was it?"

"Well, there were some half-brothers at our school, and they were talking about some inappropriate behavior they said they'd done with...each other. And then they invited me to stay at their house to do that with them."

"I see. And did you go?"

Andy turned a shade of deep purple before whispering, "No, but I wanted to."

"So why didn't you?" Doc knew his client needed to acknowledge this to overcome what was plaguing him. "Andy, why didn't you go?"

"I was afraid my parents would find out."

"Why were you afraid of your parents finding out?"

"Because behavior like that is sinful!"

"So, 'because that behavior is sinful,' as you just said, you didn't want your parents to find out that you were attracted to that behavior? Do I understand you correctly?"

Andy only nodded his head.

"Are you still attracted to that, Andy?"

Again, he nodded.

"Is that what's been bothering you for the past year?"

He nodded so hard it looked like his head might fall off.

"I've b-been doing extra B-Bible studies with B-Blake about it, and p-praying and asking God to help me, b-but nothing seems to help! I'm f-fifteen years old, Doc! I know the difference b-between right and wrong, and what I'm attracted to is wrong!" Andy was shouting by the time he finished. He realized he'd raised his voice and was immediately cowed. "Sorry," he mumbled. "Get carried away sometimes."

Dr. Williams just nodded his head almost absentmindedly. When he spoke, his voice was gentle and quiet. "Andy? Do you want me to talk to you as a secular therapist or as a Christian counselor?"

Andy looked at him in surprise. "I have a choice?"

"Yes, you do. Not all of my clients are from Christian homes or backgrounds, so I'm prepared to approach your concerns with advice or ask questions that don't involve your faith to help you work through this. Or I can do some of those things while addressing spiritual and Biblical approaches to you directly. Think about it for a few minutes and let me know."

His client stared at him. "How do you do that?"

"Do what?" Doc said.

"How did you know that I might want some of both?"

Doc Williams smiled. "I didn't know, Andy. It comes from experience, and I guessed you might want a balance of treatment approaches."

"Huh. You guessed right. So, where do we begin?"

"Let's begin with the foundation you've always based your life on, Andy: The promises of God. Do you think God tracks how often you commit the same sin?"

Andy sat there, not answering, so his therapist asked again. "Andy? Does God keep track of how many times you commit the same sin?"

Still, the teen sat in his chair, looking at the floor, but he began to fidget and kick at the carpet. The clinician spoke more firmly. "Andy, look at me!" The boy looked up. "Does God keep a list of the number of times and dates when you lust in your heart? Does he go back to the list each time that you ask him to forgive you and say to himself, 'You're piling up the same requests there, Andy. I don't know how many more times I can forgive you for this!' Is that what God does?"

"No."

"I'm sorry, I couldn't quite hear you over the carpet lying there."

"NO."

"What? Can you speak up please, Andy?"

"NO!! NO!! THAT'S NOT WHAT GOD DOES!!"

"You mean, God *doesn't* keep a record of our wrongs?"

"No."

"I bet a Bible scholar like you knows *exactly* what God does when he forgives us of our sins, don't you?"

"Yes."

"Well?" Doc pressed Andy for answers.

The young man replied, "In Psalm 103, verse 12, it says, *"as far as the east is from the west, so far has he removed our transgressions from us."*

"As far as east is from the west? That's infinity! But does he remember them, Andy? What does the Bible say about that?"

"In Isaiah 43:25, God says, *'I, even I, am he who blots out your transgressions, for my own sake, and remembers your sins no more.'"*

"He remembers your sins no more? Can that be true?"

"Dr. Williams?"

"Yes, Andy?"

"Are you *mocking* me?"

"No, Andy, I'm not mocking you. I'm asking you extremely serious questions that you've apparently forgotten the answers to."

"I have *not* forgotten the answers to these questions! How can you say that?" The boy was defensive.

"Are you *sure* you haven't forgotten, Andy?" The doctor pushed his new client to consider his situation more carefully. "If you *haven't* forgotten, then *why* are you looking at yourself, instead of looking at your Savior?"

"Wait...what?"

"Let's run through it one more time, Andy. Does God keep track of your sins?"

"No!"

"Does he forgive you when you ask for it in repentance and faith?"

"Yes!"

"So why do *you* cling to your sin in disobedience and unbelief? Why do *you* nurture your sin, dwell on it, pet it, feed it, and keep it alive in your thoughts, feelings, and actions? What does the Apostle Paul tell us to do with sin?"

"He says to put them to death, Doc."

"Okay, Andy, and if we're putting our sins to death, doesn't that mean we should stop thinking about them? If *God doesn't remember* them, why do *you* remember them? If you are saying that you've repented of sexual impurity but you keep thinking about that impurity, you haven't killed it. You're resurrecting it every time you rerun it in your mind, Andy. It's like rewinding a VHS tape to watch your favorite movie scene. You want to get that thrill again and again. And if that's what you're doing, then you're fooling yourself by saying religious words while you play with hellfire a little longer." Doc stopped and looked at his client.

Andy sat still, unblinking and silent.

"Am I offending you, Mr. Madison? I hope so. In this practice, I don't sugarcoat the truth. You are playing with sin, and your heart is becoming as solid as concrete to the gospel that used to reign freely there. For as long as you have desired to gratify your sexual desires in ways dishonoring to God, you've been building defenses to justify your sin. If you truly belong to Jesus, he will break you of this, and it will hurt. But if you've only been a pretend believer, you may die in your unbelief. You must truly repent and leave this sin behind to find true peace, young man, because what does the Bible say about Christians that do not burn with the holiness of Christ in their hearts?"

"That we're lukewarm, and Jesus will 'spit us out of his mouth.'" Andy was looking more defeated than when he'd arrived in the doctor's office. "How...did... How did you know?"

"How did I know what? That that's how you've been living your life?"

"Yeah."

"You told me."

"I-I did??"

"Don't you remember what you said when you arrived today? 'Nothing you used to enjoy about your relationship with God had any life to it anymore,' or something close to that, because you'd fallen into a pattern of sin. Andy, sexuality is a gift from God, and it is to be enjoyed, but only in the way he intended. He gave us that gift to express our love to our spouse, as man and wife, as a reflection of the intimacy that our Triune God enjoys in himself. He's given us this gift to express in the bonds of marriage. Sin twisted everything good God made, including this gift. We find ourselves at odds with God every time we try to enjoy his gifts apart from his intended uses."

"Therefore, when you feed your desires apart from God's design, you create barriers between you and God. You say you repent, right? But did you truly repent if you immediately consider or daydream about those sinful desires again? Words are cheap, Andy. Actions speak louder. What do you need to be doing to protect yourself from sinful desires?" Doc stopped to let his client respond.

The teen sat before him in thoughtful silence for several minutes. Dr. Williams was about to prompt him again when Andy finally spoke. "I need to replace those thoughts with Scripture about the beauty of God and his plans for my life and ask him to help me kill the sin in my heart?" He began tentatively but then picked up steam. "Don't place myself where I'll be tempted. Ask a trusted friend to help me. Memorize Scripture to recite when I'm being tempted and call on the Holy Spirit to strengthen my resolve when I'm at my weakest."

"Those are healthy choices, but even more importantly than those, Andy, *don't* keep a record of your own wrongs! Don't replay your sinful thoughts and actions when God forgives you. He forgets it, so *you* must forget it! Repenting means turning away from something and leaving it behind. You hafta walk away from this crap in your life, to be blunt about it."

Andy sat quietly for a few moments. Then he said, "Honestly, Doc, no one's ever said it this way before. That makes sense. It's like I've had it cassette and keep rewinding it to listen again, but I need to tape over it with God's promises of forgiveness! Thanks, Dr. Williams!" He wiped his leaking eyes. "What's next?"

His psychologist looked at him. "I want you to start keeping a journal. Each day, when you read your Bible, write down the reference and your thoughts on the passage. If you find that you're tempted to lust or pursue impure thoughts, note in the journal the situation, including the time of day, the circumstances, and how you respond. Bring the journal with you for our next visit, and we'll see if triggers or other events are happening that can identify a pattern, a warning system, or different understandings to help you."

"Okay, Doc. See you next time."

Andy left, and TJ Williams wrote up his notes. Before he filed them away, he bowed his head. *Oh, Lord, have mercy on us all. Give me wisdom for these kids. Please teach me how to help them. Guide us through these difficult times. And Lord? Bring Jack Bannister through the darkness in his heart and deliver him home to your family. I pray in your Name, Amen.*

38: Jack Reveals His Secret

"Welcome back, Jack. It's been longer than either of us expected since our last meeting. We had a plan for today, but is there anything else you want to discuss before we get to that?" Doc Williams greeted me when I arrived for my next appointment.

"Like what?" I was in a sullen mood, "Like God taking my best friend's mom away?"

"Is that how you see it?" TJ prompted me.

"Of course! How else could anyone see it? Andy's mom was the most wonderful Christian woman on the face of the earth! She loved everyone, she cared about everybody, she was a kind person—she was the one adult I knew I could trust—so naturally, God killed her. He didn't want me to have her as my trustworthy adult, so he took her away, which means my friends don't have their mom anymore, and *they* have to suffer, too." My bitterness splashed all over Doc's office.

"I see." The psychologist tried a different tack. "Did you do your homework?" Coach Williams looked at me keenly, expecting me to say "No."

"I worked on it." I did. I tried to figure out who I could trust to be that person I could talk to about what was happening in my head. I didn't have a final answer, though.

"What does that mean, that you 'worked on it'?"

"It means that I tried to figure out who I could trust, Doc, but I didn't decide yet, okay?" I said it with more sarcasm than I meant to, but I wasn't sorry.

"Did you learn anything important in the process?"

Goddamnit! How the hell can he stay so calm??

"What's frustrating you, Jack?"

I caught myself this time. "What makes you think I'm frustrated?"

"Ah, you caught yourself this time, Jack, but the first time, a wave of anger swept across your face. You know, when I didn't get angry with you for being sarcastic with me?"

I *didn't* catch myself *this* time. I half rose out of my chair, saying, "How do you do that?!"

He put his hands in front of him, palms down, suggesting calm. I sat down. He gestured for me to proceed.

Content Warning

"What?" I couldn't remember the question. He waited and made me think. *"Did you learn anything important?"* Boy, did I! And just like that, everything was awkward again. I shifted in my chair, my frustration with Coach gone, replaced by neediness.

Dr. Williams noticed the difference. *Jack came in here testy and sarcastic, but suddenly, he's back to needy and vulnerable. Whatever happened since our last appointment must have cut away some of the wall he has used to block out pain. This could be a tough session, especially how we started.* "Whenever you're ready, Jack," he prompted gently.

"Doc? This is hard to tell you." And with that, I fell silent.

We sat in silence for several minutes. Psychologist and patient. Soccer coach and player. When Doc didn't say anything, I took a deep breath and began to speak.

"When I left here last time, I went home. I was upset about a lot of things. Talking to you had helped a little because I'd never told anyone other than Blake what Vince had done to me. I've kept that secret bottled up inside me. It's made me feel broken, used, dirty, betrayed. It's different from what Phil and Kevin tried to do at Cody's house, because I wasn't friends with them. Vince was one of my closest buddies, and he took horrible advantage of me."

"When I got home, I was so wound up that I went to our old fort. It's all broken down now, but I went to yell at God again. He's taken so much from me—so many people that I love or from people I love. While I was doing that, Vince showed up. When I confronted him about what he'd done, he said he was sorry, but I found out something else, something much more horrible he'd done while I was knocked out."

"That time he attacked me, I was unconscious longer than I realized because Vince said he unzipped my jeans and put..." I dry heaved, regained control, and said, "He said he gave me..." I stopped. "Oh God, I'm gonna be sick!"

Doc Williams rushed a trash can in front of me just in time for whatever I had eaten in the last twelve hours to arrive in technicolor from my mouth. He provided tissues and a paper cup of water while I kept heaving. Then he swiftly removed the sick-filled liner for a clean one, tied off the full one, and set it in the hallway. "Are you okay, Jack?"

"Yeah, yeah. I'll be all right." I sighed. "I'm sorry, Doc. I couldn't believe that he admitted that to me! *We were 12, for God's sake!* He said I must've liked it because my body responded to it, but that's bullshit! I can't control what my body's doing when I'm not awake!"

"What did you do when he told you that?"

"I didn't hit him if that's what you mean. I just asked him why he's sorry now. He gave me his sob story. He's talked about multiple partners, getting caught and sent to juvie twice, getting assaulted by an older kid that was related to one of his younger partners—the guy's a mess, Doc. I accepted his apology and I told him our friendship's over. I don't want him in my life. He said he's accepted liking guys because his religion lets him. That's not my problem, but I can't be friends anymore, and he knows it."

"How do you feel about Vince now when you see him at school?"

"Nothing. He's just a body passing by."

"Are you okay with that, Jack?"

"Yes, I am. But Doc?"

"Yes, Jack?"

"I haven't figured out who I can trust yet."

"That's okay, Jack. You can keep working on that this coming week. Is there anything else you want to talk about today?"

"Well.." I hesitated but realized Doc couldn't help me if I didn't reveal all of it. I inhaled fully and exhaled sharply. "Andy and I were at Cody James' house one time. In fact, it was after our final game of the season, and after

Andy went to bed, Cody and I were talking about stuff, when I had some kind of 'episode.' It freaked me out to the point that I couldn't sleep alone."

"Interesting. Can you describe the 'episode,' as you called it?"

"I'll try, Doc. We'd gone upstairs to get ready for bed, when I suddenly started mumbling something about 'no, no, that's not it,' and then I raised my voice and it became 'what are you doing? Stop!' and my voice got really weird and shi—I mean, stuff. I couldn't believe it was my own voice."

"Hmm. What happened next?"

"Um, well, uh," I stopped and my face tinted pink. "Please don't think I'm weird, Doc, but Cody and I shared his bed because I was scared to be alone. It'sakingsizedbedsoweweren'tanywhereclosetoeachother, okay?" My words rushed out in my desire to clarify that we weren't sleeping together like *lovers*.

Doc Williams looked puzzled. "I'm sorry, Jack. Could you say that last part more slowly?"

My shoulders sagged. "It's a king-sized bed, so we weren't anywhere close to each other, okay?"

"Oh! Got it. Naturally, you just shared the space to avoid being alone after a disturbing event. That makes sense. Was that the only time you experienced such an 'episode'?"

I shook my head. "It happened again the day I quit CCS, but this time it happened at my house, and Dad saw it with Cody present. I'm pretty sure Cody told Dad about the first one that day, too."

326

"And what do you think these episodes are connected to?" Doc asked me, though I think he knew the answer before I said it.

My feelings and my voice felt very small as I expressed what I'd hidden for so long. "I think they're connected to being assaulted by my close friend, not telling anyone about it, and my body responding to stress."

My soccer coach and psychologist looked at me tenderly. "I think you're right, Jack. That is an impressive conclusion to reach at your age."

I shook my head. "I can't claim it as my own, Doc. I read it in a library book while trying to find something for a class report last week. It seemed to fit my situation."

He nodded. "Well done, Jack. These issues are connected, and the sooner you can find that trustworthy adult and begin sharing this part of your life with him or her, the sooner you'll find greater healing for this area of your life." He rubbed his hands together. "Is there anything else you want to review for this week?"

"Thanks, Doc. No, that was it. See you next time."

"You got it, Jack."

39: Cody's Party

Cody said he'd made all the arrangements, and all I had to do was show up. Unlike other parties at his house, he couldn't pick me up, so I had to ask Dad to give me a ride. When we arrived, I saw the Madisons' car was already in the driveway. I was going to hop out and let Dad leave, but he shut the car off and got out.

"What are you doing, Dad?" I wasn't disrespectful, just surprised.

"Cody asked me to come in when we got here." He said it as if I should have known that.

"Oh. Okay. Well, the door is this way." I led him to the house, where I knocked and entered without waiting for Cody to open the door.

"Jack, where are your manners?" Dad was shocked by my comfort in walking in so nonchalantly.

I rolled my eyes. "Da-ad. Come *on*. I practically *lived* here most of this year!"

He shook his head at me while we wound our way to the living room. "Jack! Joe! Good to see you!" Cody came over and shook hands with both of us. "The Madisons are changing to get into the pool. Why don't you?"

"Sounds great to me, Cody! Point me in the right direction." Dad grinned.

Did I miss something? After Cody showed Dad where to change, I pulled my friend aside. "Codes? Did I miss something? I didn't realize my Dad was going to be here?"

Cody laughed. "Loosen up, Jax! You and your dad need to spend more quality time together; this is a good place to do that. Your closest friends are here, too. You have friend time. Your dad and Peter can have friend time, and it's a good thing for all of us." He laughed at me again. I punched him in the arm and went to change for swimming.

When I got to the pool, Cody was there, too, along with Dad and the four Madison men.

"HI, Jack!" They all hollered.

"HI, everybody!" I hollered back. I jumped in. Cody wasn't in the water yet, so I turned to see why.

"Can I have your attention, please?" Our host yelled louder than I was used to hearing him, but it did the trick. All chatter stopped.

"Thanks for coming today, guys. This is important for us. We need time together. We are friends, and in various ways, we are family. Before we get too far into our stuff, let's pray." *'Heavenly Father, thank you for this day of fellowship. Bind our hearts in you and in your love. In Jesus' Name, Amen.'* Let the fun begin!"

We swam around for a while, and eventually, it turned into some form of keep-away game. Aside from the obvious physical size differences between the adults and us teens, we were so relaxed that we just had *fun.* I don't think I'd enjoyed myself so completely around my dad since, well, since the camping trip he and I took with Andy a few years ago.

It lifted my spirits to see Mr. Madison enjoying time with his sons. I was so young when Mom died, yet I could still remember that aching emptiness when she suddenly wasn't in my life anymore, so I *could* imagine how they felt. However, for an hour or two today, they were here, splashing around with friends and family, and forgetting their pain. It was good and healthy.

I didn't know all of Cody's plans for today, but given that he had surprised me already, it made me wonder what other tricks he might have planned. I tried to corner him to ask, but he was in rare form, and he clammed up every time I pumped him for information. All he'd give me was a smile and a 'wouldn't you like to know' to which I'd say, 'yes,' and he'd just laugh at me.

When I got out of the pool, toweled off, and dressed, I offered to help my host get lunch ready. As we worked, I asked him how he was doing. "I'm doing well, Jack, thanks. The school administration has been great to work with as I transition to my part-time role for next fall. They have been very understanding of my particular situation. To be honest, Jack, they've put CCS to shame! NHS treats me more lovingly and more Christianly than the Christian school did."

Then he shook his head. "I'm trying not to be bitter because that would only hurt me and I like NHS so much better, anyway, but by acting so judgmentally toward their students, the administration at CCS is ruining the reputation they try so hard to create!"

I shook my head, too. "I have to admit that I was very proud of my stepmom for quitting when she found out about Stephens' threatening her job when I praised you to that reporter."

Cody looked startled. "What did you say??"

"What?"

"What was that about praising me to a reporter?"

"Oh, she didn't say anything about you. I was starting to tell her that you deserved to be a starter, and that's when Stephens interrupted and threatened my stepmom's job."

Cody looked like he'd swallowed an ice cube wrong. *"That's why he issued his threat?* Because you were speaking well of *me? That bastard!"* His face tinted pink. "Sorry for the language," he mumbled.

"Don't apologize on my account, Codes! Hey, hey...what's wrong, Cody?" My friend had stopped working, and tears were trickling down his cheeks. I walked over to him and side-hugged him. "Dude, you're my *friend, and* Mom doesn't regret leaving that crappy place. *You* were worth it!" I pulled out of the hug and looked my friend in the eye. "Principal Stephens isn't worth the grudge."

Dad spoke from behind me. "He's right, Cody. That man and that place are not worth another thought. They failed you. They failed us. They failed the Madison family, too. Don't fall into bitterness. Just recognize what they are and move on." I was surprised to see Dad but comforted to hear him affirming us. "Let's get lunch finished, boys. Everyone is hungry!" He smiled at us as he took over the grill.

When did Dad become so good at grilling...oh yeah...camping! I laughed, and to cover for it I told Cody to help me take the chips, drinks, potato salad, and plates to the dining room. Within 20 minutes, lunch was on the table, grace was said, and the seven of us were digging into burgers and chicken. After lunch, we all pitched in to clean up.

"Thanks for getting everything cleaned up, guys," Cody said. "I'd say we've had a good day so far, right?" Heads bobbed up and down in agreement. "Glad to see that, and while fun and games are healthy for us, we have some other things we need to do, too." He reached into a basket and pulled out several envelopes as he talked. "Our next exercise is about communication, and *everyone* is involved."

As he emphasized the word *everyone*, I noticed that he looked directly at me. "What? I get it. I'm involved." *Why was I suddenly feeling defensive?*

Cody handed out envelopes to everyone and said, "Each of you has been assigned someone to talk to and listen to. For the next thirty minutes, you and the person identified in your envelope need to find some place to talk about whatever is weighing heaviest on your mind. The notes in the envelopes specify who listens and who speaks. When the 30 minutes are up, then you will return here to get new envelopes. This will continue until everyone has had a turn as speaker and a listener." He gestured and we ripped open our envelopes. Suddenly, I wanted to be anywhere but Cody's house.

40: Enveloped

Content Warning

POV: JACK with JOE

I ripped open my envelope, eager to see my first assignment. My face fell immediately, my stomach twisted into knots, and I grabbed Cody by the arm, pulling him aside. "What is the meaning of this!" I hissed.

He smiled, pulled my hand off his arm, and replied, "Do it, Jax. You need to do so much more than you realize." His smile faded. "Now, Jack," he ordered.

I walked off to find my partner. He was waiting in the next room with an expectant look. "What do you need to tell me, son?" Dad's tone reminded me of when I confessed to breaking his fishing pole. He couldn't have been gentler or more supportive. I sat down next to him on the couch.

333

"This isn't something I've ever expected to tell you, Dad. I'm sorry that it's taken me so long, but I thought if I shoved it down far enough, I could ignore it forever. But I can't." My voice caught a little, surprising me. I swallowed to regain my composure, moved closer to Dad, and continued.

"I don't know how much you remember about the night that Blake's pop got arrested, but Vince Jackson assaulted me that evening."

Dad nodded. "That's when you and your friends were out at your fort, right? And Vince hit you? I recall Blake saying something about that at the time. Wait, is there something more to the story, Jack? Son? What happened?"

Dad moved next to me and put his arms around me. "Oh, my boy! Please tell me!" He released me from the full embrace but kept a hand on my back, rubbing me gently as I told him the story.

When I was done, he pulled me close to his side in a shoulder hug, kissed my head as he buried his face in my hair, and wept with me. "I am so sorry you have dealt with this alone for so long, my dear son."

"Thanks, Dad." I hugged him back. "Um...there's more."

He nodded. "Go ahead, Jack."

He nodded? How in the world? Ohhhh...Cody....

"How much do you know, Dad?"

"Only that you have two important things to tell me."

"Oh. Okay." At least I'm not telling my side of a story he's already heard. "On my first visit here to Cody's house, I got drunk and high, and a friend of one of my teammates tried to assault me. Cody stopped him before he did anything to me, and both ended up with felony charges against them eventually. Cody was given community service for furnishing alcohol to minors." My words came out in a rush.

I saw Dad flinch when I said certain words, predictably, but I had to finish before I lost my nerve. He drew a deep breath and let it out slowly through his teeth.

"That was the beginning of this school year, wasn't it?" He noted. "I'm going to talk with Cody about some of this."

"Dad, please...."

"Jack," he began in one voice, then caught himself before continuing more softly, "I want to thank him for protecting my boy. I love you, Jack. Thank you for telling me these secrets. May I share them with Stephanie? She loves you like her own, you know."

Surprising myself, I said without hesitation, "Yes, Dad. You can share this with Mom." We stood up, hugged again, and headed to get our next envelopes.

Cody was there alone. He saw the looks on our faces and smiled slightly. Dad and I reached out and pulled him into a group hug. *"Thank you, Cody,"* we both whispered hoarsely. We stepped back and held out our hands for our following assignments.

POV: PETER with ANDY

When Cody James contacted me about this gathering, I wasn't sure I wanted to be part of it. It sounded like a great idea for Andy and Blake, but why was I part of the invitation? The young man was insistent, however, that David and I come along and participate fully, whatever that meant, so I said we would. Now, I was glad we'd done so, though this 'envelopes' exercise puzzled me a bit. What did he expect me to gain from it?

My first envelope had a note that said Andy needed to open up to me about some struggles in his life, and I immediately understood a purpose for this project. I had suspected that Andy was experiencing questions about his standing with God for some reason, but with Sarah's illness and death, I've been too distracted to talk with him. Now is my chance to find out what's going on.

We walked into the spare bedroom he'd stayed in the night after the soccer game last fall and sat on the made bed. My youngest boy got right to the point.

"Dad?"

"Yes, Andy?"

"I'm dealing with same-sex attraction, and I have been for a couple of years now. I haven't acted on it, though sometimes I desperately want to. I've already told my closest friends; they've been helping me resist it, especially Blake, but it's not fair for them to have to help me all the time, nor for you not to know. I want to be faithful to God, Dad. Sometimes, my attractions are just so strong that I struggle to fight them off. It's something I've been talking to Doc Williams about."

I didn't expect this to be why Andy was struggling with his faith. Not at all! But at the same time, sin is sin, and this is, apparently, the sin that will plague my youngest. *Okay, Lord. You can handle this.* I reached out and hugged Andy. "Thank you for telling me, Andy. I will pray for you and do all I can to help you." A thought struck me. "Did your mother know?"

He pulled back from me in tears and nodded. "I-I t-told her the w-week she d-died. She t-told m-me she loved m-me anyway." My son broke into deep sobs as he leaned into my arms, and I embraced him as I pictured our Heavenly Father loving us.

"Andy? What brings on the temptation for you?" My son looked puzzled for a few moments.

"Well, I've noticed that when a lot is happening at once, and I feel overwhelmed, I feel like I want to escape, so I try to find a TV show or a book that has characters that will feed my imagination, or when kids at school act out, even if they're straight, you know?"

"I see. Can you think of something I can do to help you when you feel tempted or overwhelmed?"

"Honestly, Dad? I need you to be available for hugs. Momma was always ready with a hug. She didn't have to say anything, and I don't need you to say a lot, but I need hugs, especially from you."

"I'll do my best, Andy. Let's pray before we run out of time." After praying together, I hugged Andy again, and we went to get our next envelope assignments.

POV: DAVID & BLAKE
David

I was thrilled that Cody was planning this party for us. The Bannisters were good friends who had experienced a similar loss, and we "Mad" men needed bonding time. Still, I was concerned that he was on the outside of all this because he figured into the mixture of our lives more than most of us realized. However, it was his party, and he could run it his way.

Blake was paired with me in the first round. The note in my envelope told me that he had a 'precious task' given to him recently and that he could use my help to achieve it. When I read it, I was in the same room where we'd all been when this started. I glanced up, and Blake was looking for a place to hide.

"Hey, little brother! Don't hide! Come over here. Let's sit at the table and talk. Everyone else has gone to other rooms, so we might as well use this one." I grabbed him for a hug as soon as I could reach him. "Tell your big brother what's weighing you down, Blake. What did Mom ask you to do?"

Blake

When David called me to join him, I dreaded telling him about the topic on my note. It had read, "Share your mother's burden with David." Then he said directly, "What did Mom ask you to do?"

"How? What? David, what are you talking about?" I was flabbergasted.

"She asked you to keep an eye on Andy and Dad, I'll bet. Oh, and me??"

"How do you know that, David??"

"She asked me to do that for our sisters."

"Oh."

"Oh is right, little bro. That's a lot of responsibility! How about you and I help each other? I mean, I need to keep an eye on you, too. You're my little bro that's been through a ton of life-pain; I gotta do for you!"

"Thanks, David! You're an awesome big brother, y'know that?" I wrapped him up in a giant hug. He laughed and messed up my hair.

About that time, everyone else returned for their second envelopes. Once again, Cody distributed the assignments. "This time," he said, "return here for a group exercise when you finish. Off you go!"

It wasn't a surprise to see the two dads paired off. As Dad and Peter walked to the den, we "kids" sorted out our partners. There was a surprise for us, but we got to work on the respective assignments, and the project continued.

POV: JOE & PETER

Peter spoke first as he and Joe sat down in the den. "Joe, I'm at sixes and sevens trying to figure out each day without Sarah. How did you manage when your first wife died?"

Joe looked at his friend and spiritual mentor with compassion. "It was chaotic for a while, Pete. I took whatever help I could get. You should, too. You have a great church family who want to serve by helping you. Let them. It's how they'll obey God and participate in your grief."

Peter nodded, thinking about his friend's words. "It's so...lonely. Everywhere I turn, I think she's there. When I lie down to sleep, her side of the bed is always cold. I... I can't remember the last time she and I, you know...it was at least a year before she died. She was so sick she never had the energy or the interest."

Joe listened but said nothing. There were no words for his friend. It was enough to be there.

"Joe?"

339

His friend startled him from his thoughts. "Yeah, Pete?"

"Sarah and I were married to each other for 28 years. Our vows to each other were till death parted us. Our vows were fulfilled, Joe. We were faithful to one another."

Joe sensed something else coming. "That's commendable, Peter."

"Thanks, Joe. I'm 48 years old, and I'm a widower. I'm not dead as a man. I need your guidance because I don't want to wait long before marrying again. Three teenage boys need a good mom figure and I need a wife."

Joe understood. "From what I know of you, Peter, you're looking for a godly woman who loves kids. Pray for God to bless you in this way, and let the word be known in your denomination for a woman willing to move to this part of Maine."

"Wow, Joe. That's fantastic advice! Thanks!" Peter slapped Joe on the back in gratitude. "Oh, hey, there's something else I should mention, Joe. My boys will be transferred to NHS shortly. We can't afford the tuition at County Christian anymore, and the high school is failing, anyway. If we can arrange carpooling with you guys some mornings, that'd be great."

POV: We Three Teens

In a twist we didn't see coming, we three 15/16-year-olds were grouped for the second round. According to the note in my envelope, I asked Andy and Blake to speak to me.

Andy took the lead. "We're leaving County Christian when we resume school, Jack. We can't afford tuition."

Blake interjected, "That means we're coming to NHS, Jack! Uh, sorry, Andy."

His slightly younger brother smiled patiently. "I forgive you, Blake. CCHS won't continue next fall because it's too small. We're switching schools sooner than expected."

We changed the subject after that and asked each other what we revealed in our first session. I shared how I'd finally told my dad about the sexual assault attempts by Vince and Kevin, and how loving Dad had been.

Andy told us he'd finally told his dad about being physically attracted to guys. He said it shocked his dad, but not to the point of rejection or criticism. Instead, his father told Andy he loved him and would support him.

We were called back for the group activity just as it got to Blake's turn.

41: Cody's Big Move

We gathered in the dining room, where Cody and David had laid out fresh fruit, drinks, and cookies. Another guest had arrived. I connected a few dots on the activities we had been doing, and they led to him, Dr. TJ 'Coach' Williams, clinical psychologist, and varsity soccer coach at Newtowne High.

He spoke before we could ask questions. "Good afternoon, Gentlemen. It's good to see you all today. I hope you're having a good time. I trust that Cody has been a great host?" He smiled warmly. "Before you ask, No, I didn't plan any of this. This is all Cody's idea. I guided him a bit, but he had the ideas, and I am immensely proud of him. However, he asked me to come for this last part, which is also good planning. Cody?"

Our host stepped forward. "Doc is correct. He guided me just a little, but I planned this because I love every one of you. Each of you has made a deep impression on my life in one way or another, and we all have suffered. Our suffering intensified recently when the Lord decided it was Sarah Madison's time to enter glory, leaving us behind for now."

Cody looked from man to man as he spoke. "Peter, you lost your wife, helpmeet, dearest friend."

"David and Andy, you lost your Mom of many years."

"Blake, you had finally found a Mom that truly loved you, and she's gone already."

"Jack, you've lost a confidant, a 'second mom,' a woman who did her best to keep you on the straight and narrow and who clearly cared for you."

"Joe, Sarah supported your wife, and Peter counseled and mentored you. Now you can return the favor."

"Each of you has needed to talk, and each has needed to listen. There is still more to be done. I've been working on an idea, and I recently talked to Doc about it. We will present it to you now, and we want your feedback on it. Doc?"

"Thanks, Cody. Gents, we would like to open an independent counseling office in Newtowne, not housed on the school campus, so that the gospel can be freely integrated in the treatment. We've been looking at a few locations that are available and accessible, but we want input from you as we consider how to move forward."

Peter spoke first. "Another element is also involved in pushing this off campus."

"Yes. A 10-month intern is joining my practice, and since he isn't a school employee, he can't work on campus."

Doc was interrupted by groans and complaints from Andy, Blake, and me. He held up his hands, laughing. "Apparently, you don't know who the intern is!"

"Who is it??" I demanded.

"*It's me.*" Our heads swung around as our mouths went slack. David was looking at us with a goofy grin on his face. "It's part of my college requirements."

Doc spoke again. "So, what do you think?"

The consensus was that the idea was a great one. We all knew a clinic like that was needed, and with David coming on as an intern, Doc would have to move out of his school office very soon. Also, during the few months he'd been working at NHS in dual roles, it had become evident that keeping his clinical work physically separated from coaching would be infinitely preferable.

What *wasn't* agreed on was where to locate the new practice. Rumors were flying that a new high school facility would be built soon. Still, until its location was known, Doc didn't want to settle his practice anywhere too permanently because he wanted to remain easily accessible to his students. On the other hand, changing locations frequently wasn't good for business, and he tried to avoid that common pitfall of entrepreneurship. Ultimately, they agreed to commit the matter to prayer and to wait for God to show them the best path forward.

They began praying right away, and I say "they" because while I was with them, I wasn't praying. Don't get me wrong! I hoped for a good result for them, but I still wasn't convinced God cared about details like this. Almost everyone took a turn praying out loud, with two or three exceptions. Just about the time Cody finished the prayer, they all said, "Amen," the phone rang. He excused himself to answer it.

We waited patiently, chatting socially about the day's fun and Cody's project. Then we heard him exclaim, "Really? ARE YOU SERIOUS?"

He sounded excited but not angry. David was the first to react by running to the kitchen to stand with Cody. Then Doc followed David, and the rest of us got up. Soon, we were all crowding into the room with him, straining to hear whose voice was speaking to him and to determine why he'd replied so excitedly. For his part, Cody gestured for calm, tried to remain himself, and beamed with happiness.

"Wow, Dad. Are you sure about this? Okay, okay, I'll stop asking. Is there paperwork I have to sign? When? And Mom's okay with this, too? It was? You are?? I...No. No, Dad. I-I..." Our friend's face crumpled into tears for a moment. "I'm so glad to hear you say that, Daddy. Huh. Hahaha. Didn't even realize it. Oh, Dad, thank you so much! Praise God! I love you, too! Give my love to Mom. See you soon. Bye."

While his phone call ended, Peter and Dad were herding us back to the other room. "Give him a moment, everyone. He'll tell us what he wants us to know." When Cody returned, he went first to Doc, who opened his arms

344

and hugged the young man. As they embraced, Cody whispered something to Doc, making TJ's eyes open wide with surprise. Then Cody hugged Joe and Peter, quietly thanking them for their presence of mind in emptying the kitchen while he ended his phone call. Finally, he turned to talk to all of us.

"As you just witnessed, I've had a phone call from my Dad. Honestly, I don't remember the last time he c-called." Our friend's voice filled with emotion as he said that, but he controlled himself. "I rarely see my parents anymore. It's been years since they lived here—almost five years now that they've been gone most of the time, and during that time, they've been on the run—from God. Before that, they were deeply involved in church, and so was I. When some sinful stuff went down at our church, directly affecting us, we all ran from God. I was too young to run off physically, so they left me at the house with money, and I did whatever I wanted to. They took off, stopping by to check on me twice a month, and then once a month, then less and less often."

Cody took a drink of soda and continued. "They stayed with each other, but their love grew cooler by the month. I was sure they were headed for a divorce after their last visit here, but when Dad called just now, I learned a few things that renewed my hope for them. First, they have repented of their sin before God and each other, and they will return to live here in Maine at this house. Second, they are kicking me out of this house."

The uproar at this point drowned out his attempts to keep speaking until we realized he was grinning like a fool. "What's the big idea, Codes?" I demanded.

"*They* are going to live here. *I* will have my own place, which they will pay for. They realize that I've been independent for so long that it would be extremely awkward to live under their authority again, so they've made an offer on a place in *Newtowne* that is halfway between our high school and one of the primary places discussed for the new high school. Dad was describing the place to me, and guess what?"

"What?" we all shouted.

"It's a house with a small, detached office building on the property because the previous owner was an insurance salesman or something. At any rate, the lot is already zoned for mixed purposes, and the separate building may be large enough for what Doc and David need for the counseling clinic!" Cody's face glowed with delight. "We *prayed*. God *answered*. *To God be the glory! Amen!*"

"AMEN!" My father and friends shouted. I whispered it, because even I couldn't deny the timing of *that* provision.

"Can I ask you something, Codes?"

"Sure, Jack, what is it?"

"You said something to your dad about your mom 'being okay with it.' What was that about?"

"Mom was the one most directly hurt by the sin that was going on at our old church, so coming back to live here is more painful for her, and I wanted to know if she's okay with doing that. Dad said it was her idea! They've returned to God, Jack. That's what repenting is—you know that. They've turned away from their years of not believing in his love, not trusting that he cares about them."

346

Suddenly, Cody directed his comments at me. "When are *you* going to do that, Jack? When will you let go of your fear, anger, and sin? Every.single.one.of.us. has been faced with that crap in our lives, Jack. You're not the only one!"

"I chased lusts of my heart and body with girls and boys, Jack. David craved success in school and on the baseball diamond. Andy worshiped the praise of others for his moral behavior and Bible knowledge, even as he found gratification in thinking about being intimate with other boys. Blake bowed down to power, manipulation, theft, and sex, both before becoming a Christian and since, having to fight against the devil's schemes repeatedly—as we all do. Your dad, Joe, has dealt with anger issues and wanting control over others. Peter is full of pride and plagued by an unwillingness to ask for help—a lack of humility."

"My parents lost their way, Jack, for many years. It nearly cost them their marriage. It almost cost them their *son*. I'm crying happy tears today because Dad called to say they *love me*. Jack, I haven't heard those words come out of his mouth before. NEVER! Today was the first time *he* ever said that. Mom was always the one to say it, but to know that my *father* loves me..." Cody's composure crumpled again into tears of joy and contentment.

A few minutes or an hour later, Dad touched my shoulder. "It's time, son."

"Wha-what?"

"It's time to go, Jack. Are you okay?" Dad peered at me closely.

"Uh, y-yeah. Just a bit tired, I think. Long day." I couldn't get Cody's words out of my head. *"When will you release your fear, anger, and sin? We've all faced that crap, Jack. My Dad called to tell me they loved me. To know that my father loves me... ."* Cody sure pulled a big move with that one.

42: To Know My Father Loves Me

Those words kept rattling around in my head. *"To know that my father loves me."*

I spent a lot of time thinking about those words for the next week. They triggered many other thoughts, and a week after the party at Cody's, my streams of consciousness—what Cody had once jokingly called a river—flowed together into connections that began to make sense.

When Mom went out that afternoon to visit the old, sick lady, which one of us knew she'd die coming home? None of us. Exactly. Had she known that ahead of time, would she have stayed home? Nope. She might have hugged me a little tighter before leaving or told me to "trust God anyway," but Mom knew that old lady needed her that day because that's what God put on Mom's heart to do. Mom trusted God, and he took care of her right to the very end. For Mom, it indeed was "to know that my Father loves me."

I was 8 years old. All I knew at that point was Mom was gone, God hadn't brought her home to me, and my world was shattered. Dad was broken, too. He had loved Mom and me, but when she died, he couldn't even love me anymore, not for a long time. I don't know how he found Stephanie, but they met and married. Looking back, I realize that my "Dragon" is probably the one to thank for Dad realizing he still loved me. It took a few years. Stephanie helped, and so did Peter and Sarah Madison, but Dad came around, and I learned "that my father loves me." I had reached that point before going to Cody's get-together last week.

When Cody spoke very candidly about his sin and everyone else's, I was shocked by how openly he shared what he saw in everyone else. Naturally, I had no idea that they had given him that knowledge ahead of time so that he could use it, if needed, to get my attention. When I found that out later, I agreed it had been a shrewd move on their part because it worked as planned.

Honestly, I'd never expected any of my friends, especially Cody, to be so blunt about my refusal to believe that God is trustworthy. When Blake was converted to Christianity, I revealed my concerns about God's reliability. Again, in Cody's case, I brought up my fears that God couldn't be trusted long-term. Neither of my friends had listened to me. Then, when Andy's mother died, I thought for sure one of them or more would see my point, but no. They all insisted that God still loved them and would comfort them in their pain.

Who wants comfort in pain? How about not having the pain to begin with? Isn't it within God's power to do it that way? These were the questions plaguing me, but when I raised them, the answers included points such as, "Because of sin in the world, suffering will be present, too, so the question isn't how to avoid it but how to deal with it as best as possible. And the best way to deal with suffering is with the comfort of God through his Holy Spirit."

Codes was so happy to hear his father say, "I love you." I used to squirm when Dad said it, but now, when I hear him say it to my little brother Matthew, it fills me with joy to see Matt's face light up. I loved my mom so much, and it still hurts that she's gone, but the pain isn't as much now as it was the first two or three years. Knowing that Dad and I get along again has helped *so* much.

*What changed for Dad and me? C'mon, Jax, be honest; it was admitting I'd been sneaky, deceitful, dishonest...coming clean to Dad, and he didn't yell at me. He forgave me. He still loved me. Oh, God, is **this** Cody's point?*

I got up from my bed and left my Walkman and headphones on my pillow, whatever music I'd been listening to utterly forgotten as I went through the house looking for Dad and Steph. I heard them in the kitchen, their usual landing spot. "Dad? Mom? Can I talk to you?"

"We're in here, honey," Steph spoke to me. She reached out to hug me as I entered the kitchen. I no longer viewed her as the 'Dragon,' and usually called her 'Mom,' as I had been for over a year. Sometimes, I'd still use her first name for emphasis, but it was rare. "What's on your mind, Jack?"

"I keep thinking about the party at Cody's house last week. He said something near the end that's been running around in my head ever since, and I want to talk to you about it." From the look on my face, they knew it was serious.

"Let's sit at the table for this, son," Dad said. He poured a cup of coffee for himself and offered me some. I declined, but Mom took some. "What's been running around in your head, Jack?" His tone was inquisitive yet tender.

"Dad, do you remember what he was saying about his father telling Cody that he loved him, and that it was the first time he'd ever said that to Codes?" Dad's head bobbed up and down. "Then Cody said that what touched him was "to know that my father loves me." He kinda left it there that day. Or maybe he didn't. I don't remember what he said after that because that's what's been running around my brain for the past week."

"Have you reached any conclusions or ideas you want to share?" Steph asked.

"Actually, yeah. My ideas are scattered, but here they are. When I was a very little kid, I knew that you loved me, Dad, because you used to tell me. Then Mom died in that accident, and I didn't hear it from you until Steph helped you learn to say it again." I reached over and squeezed her hand in thanks. "I didn't hear it often, though. I was a difficult child, but when I came clean—repented, as Cody would say—about being deceitful, sneaky, dishonest, and stuff, you forgave me instead of yelling at me, and you started telling me more often that you love me. You said Steph and the Madisons were helping you learn about God's grace."

"Mmmm, I remember that. Thank God for them." Dad's voice was quiet but full of emotion.

"Dad?"

"Yes, son?"

"You modeled God for me." My eyes filled with tears, and my voice cracked.

"I did?"

351

My stepmom was silent. I think she was praying, even though her eyes were open. The love and respect in them for her husband were unmistakable.

I cleared my throat and continued. "I was sinning against you and Mom—Stephanie—and when I repented, you *forgave me*. You *loved* me. I got *to know my father's love for me*. That's modeling God for me, right? And my first Mom, she loved God; he loved her, and she got to know his love for her. I was thinking about this, too. If she'd known before she went to that lady's house that day that she was going to die in an accident, I bet she would've gone anyway, because Momma loved helping others. Maybe she would've told me to trust God no matter what, but she still would've obeyed God, right?"

My dad's eyes were leaking tears at this point, too, and all he could do was nod in agreement.

"Dad? I'm ready to do what Cody's parents have done. I'm ready to stop running from God. I don't want to resist him anymore. When all of you shouted 'AMEN' last week to the news that the clinic might have a home, I didn't shout, but I had to at least whisper 'amen,' because even I had to admit that God had provided. And if God can provide for something like that, and if God can change the hearts of Mr. and Mrs. James and the hearts and attitudes of Cody, David, Andy, Peter, Blake, and you, then I *have to believe* that he can change my heart, too."

"Dad and Mom, will you pray with me to ask Jesus to come into my life and to show me how He is the Way to God?"

"Sure, son. Let's pray."

352

John 14:6:

"Jesus answered, "I am the Way and the Truth and the Life. No one comes to the Father except through me."

Luke 15:10:

"In the same way, I tell you, there is rejoicing in the presence of the angels of God over one sinner who repents."

John 6:37:

"All those the Father gives me will come to me, and whoever comes to me I will never drive away."

Epilogue by Mack D. Ames

I've always been told, "Write what you know," so I did. I took something familiar from my childhood and spun it into something familiar to my present life. Since 2011, I have worked with youth and men detained and/or incarcerated who have experienced the kinds of situations described in this story (and worse), and I have heard countless tales of healing, growth, pain, despair, hope, longing, yearning—you name it, and I've heard it.

Some turn to philosophy, others to Islam, Judaism, Buddhism, Nihilism, humanism, atheism, agnosticism, or some other 'ism' to give them peace of mind for the trauma and turmoil in their lives. Occasionally, they'll turn to the God of the Bible for help. Sometimes, their trauma has come at the hands of so-called Christians, and that turns them off to Christianity. In my interactions with them, I seek to build relationships that develop mutual respect and trust. When they reach out with questions, I offer what I know and what I believe without coercion.

The story of Jack Bannister is not my story, though elements of it could be. I was touched inappropriately against my will by a trusted childhood friend when we were about eleven years old. He laughed at my reaction of insecurity and fear while pointing out that my body seemed to like it, so I must have liked it, too. While his actions triggered problems for me for years to come, I highly doubt he even remembers the situation. *Write what you know.*

This is my first time writing anything this lengthy. I do not doubt that there are plot holes, inconsistencies, dialog issues, and other errors, but overall, I hope you've found it readable and understandable. One high school friend who read and reviewed it commented, "Your book doesn't fit into any genre I know. I suggest a new one: Gritty Inspirational."

From the readers I've talked to, including Christians and non-Christians, "gritty inspirational" seems to fit. Some have loved the book, and others have said that while they liked my writing style they didn't like the content. Some don't want their lives of innocence spoiled, and others' personal philosophy is too contrary to the one in the story to read it. I wrote this to tell a story. To each his or her own.

If you have read it, I'd appreciate an honest review on Amazon.com. Thank you!

Find and follow the One, True Way to God, Jesus Christ.

Bill "Mack D. Ames" MacDonald
Orrington, Maine
December 31, 2024

Acknowledgments

My wife, Laurel, is the godliest woman I know. We became friends on the mission field in Japan in 1993, and she has been one of God's greatest gifts to me ever since. Together and in God's grace, we are raising two boys brought to us through foster and adoptive care. It's a little shocking to believe that they're both nearing the end of high school now, and as challenging as parenting can be, they delight us regularly with the young men in Christ they are becoming. I cannot thank God enough for my wife and sons.

Thanks to God for my late parents, Paul and Sally MacDonald, who taught me that Jesus is the Way, the Truth, and the Life. Admiration and appreciation for my father-in-law, Bob Boettger, whose love for the Lord shines as an example to all, and deep gratitude for my late mother-in-law, Karen Boettger, who loved me like a son and filled in some gaps in my learnin' that Mum never had the chance to teach me.

I have a lifelong thankfulness for my brother Dan (Sue) and sisters Priscilla (Len), Judi (Paul), and Mary (Logan), all of whom walk with the Lord, married in the Lord, and parent in the Lord. They demonstrate to me the joy of Christian love for one another.

Thank you to my wife's sister Nancy (David), brother Karl (Kelly), Aunt Sue B, my stepmother Jo M, and my 'adoptive' sisters Susan (Brian) and Martha (Stephen), all of whom are members of the Family by the grace and mercy of God.

Blest be the tie that binds our hearts in Christian love!

Early in writing this story, my wife provided vital critiques on writing age-appropriate character dialogue. Laurel has been my best friend for more than 30 years, and she has a fantastic sense of how to develop stories, dialogue, and plot lines for every age group. Many years ago, she helped me learn how to teach creative writing more effectively than I did without her help, and whenever I'm smart enough to listen to her in writing and life, it all works out better.

The youngest of my three sisters was the first to read my completed story. She called it a "gritty, compelling, redemptive" read. I especially value her input as a freelance editor and avid reader. I'm immensely grateful to her for the hours she spent combing through the manuscript, suggesting changes and corrections, and cheering me on as a writer and a brother. To honor her wishes, I do not identify her by name here.

Everyone in my life (family, teachers, church, colleagues, friends, neighbors, acquaintances, and students) has contributed in one way or another in shaping me, for good or ill. The residents where I work have given much encouragement to my writing, and I am grateful to them. Their contributions are too numerous to list. However, one young man offered to be my publicist for free with the following idea.

He suggested a promotional video campaign where I would assault one of Maine's most famous authors while holding a copy of *Lost My Way in the Darkness.* When I protested that I'd be jailed for that, he replied, "Sure, but just think of all the publicity you'll get! Your book will become a best-seller overnight! And when you get out of prison, you won't have to worry about teaching no more." Then he added, "You need a middle name, Mack. I know! 'Daddy.' From now on, I'm calling you 'Mack Daddy Ames!' I'm your publicist, Mack Daddy, for real, for real. Hey, everybody, listen up. Give it up for my man, Mack Daddy Ames!" Jonathan A was quite the character to have around. Residents J LaPorte, Tom H, and Tyler T provided key input in the final drafts. Ethan Y. and Hunter S., one a teammate of my younger son and the other a current adult ed student, offered some timely insight and input to keep the project going down the homestretch.

In my last several years 'on the hill,' I have been blessed to work with Gary G, N Knight, Matt D, Kathy J, Martin F, and many others who have collaborated to make my teaching experience as positive as possible. Their professional and personal input has made me a better person, teacher, and writer. Shelley Burbank, author and reviewer, has provided me with amazing guidance, and I'm forever grateful to her for that. Visit her website and read her books! www.shelleyburbank.com.

Peter S and Luke L, thank you for praying with me over the years and tossing hay bales with me eons ago when I struggled to do that alone. Luke H., Dan K., John T., Mike L, Becky (R) M., Allison B., Kristi S., Charlie R., JB S., James M., Amy M., the late Jay M., Peter B, Cousins Jon, Julia, David, Andrew, Sam & Sarah, and so many other childhood friends, none of this would have been possible without knowing you. Pastor Russell H, Sy S, and countless other men & women at Pilgrim Church have influenced my life in recent years. Russell and Sy, I particularly thank you for the time and prayers you poured into my life in 2023. Dr Allen Curry, your encouragement has meant so much to me when doubts swirled all around, both for this book and in life; thank you for your input and faithful preaching of the Word of God. Rosaria Butterfield provided tremendous inspiration and perspective, as well. Pastor Danny P of Second Parish OPC, thank you for your prayers and encouragement in this journey.

Lastly, Ben & Leah W. are the happiest couple I know. You two (and Li'l Woj) put a smile on my face whenever I think of you. Your love for God, one another, and your 'neighbors as yourselves' shine as examples of Christlike godliness. I love you.

Some of you have no idea of your impact on me, and at least one of you has already reached heaven ahead of me. I look forward to the day of our reunion because I can't wait to see our Savior face to face!

The Lord redeems every experience for His purposes. I'm so glad He rescued my life from my sin and misery. I belong to Jesus because He is faithful, not because I'm someone special in and of myself. It is <u>all God all the time</u>. <u>That's</u> what makes me say:

To God be the glory!

"Do not let your hearts be troubled. You believe in God; believe also in me. ² My Father's house has many rooms; if that were not so, would I have told you that I am going there to prepare a place for you? ³ And if I go and prepare a place for you, I will come back and take you to be with me that you also may be where I am. ⁴ You know the way to the place where I am going."
⁵ Thomas said to him, "Lord, we don't know where you are going, so how can we know the way?"
Jesus answered, "I am the way and the truth and the life. No one comes to the Father except through me."
John 14:1-6

New International Version
www.biblegateway.com

Bill "Mack D Ames" MacDonald

www.facebook.com/MackAmesBooks

Made in the USA
Monee, IL
17 March 2025

552d56f6-1c39-4244-b6a5-831b6a937e85R01